Under the editorship of

WAYNE C. MINNICK

THE FLORIDA STATE UNIVERSITY

EVIDENCE

Robert P. Newman ·

HOUGHTON MIFFLIN COMPANY · BOSTON

Dale R. Newman

THE UNIVERSITY OF PITTSBURGH

NEW YORK   ATLANTA   GENEVA, ILL.   DALLAS   PALO ALTO

TO JACK MATTHEWS

We are grateful to the following authors and publishers for permission to reprint material now in copyright.

Curtis Brown, Ltd., for Canadian distribution rights to the excerpt from George F. Kennan, *Russia, the Atom and the West*, copyright © 1957, 1958 by George F. Kennan (New York: Harper & Row, 1958), which appears on pp. 59–60.

Theodore Draper, for the excerpts from his *The Dominican Revolt* (New York: Commentary, 1968), which appear on pp. 124, 125, 131, 137, and 157.

Foreign Affairs, for the excerpts from George F. Kennan, "Disengagement Revisited" (*Foreign Affairs*, January, 1959), which appear on pp. 45 and 45–46.

Harper & Row, Publishers, Inc., for United States distribution rights to the excerpt from George F. Kennan, *Russia, the Atom and the West*, copyright © 1957, 1958 by George F. Kennan (New York: Harper & Row, 1958), which appears on pp. 59–60.

Robert A. Nisbet, for the excerpts from his "Project Camelot: An Autopsy" (*Public Interest*, Fall, 1966), which appear on pp. 189, 192, and 193.

Oxford University Press, for the excerpts from C. Wright Mills, *The Sociological Imagination* (New York: Grove Press, 1961), which appear on pp. 5, 181, and 206.

The RAND Corporation, for the excerpt from Olaf Helmer and Nicholas Rescher, *On the Epistemology of the Inexact Sciences* (Santa Monica: RAND, 1958), which appears on pp. 48–49.

Random House, Inc., for the excerpts from David Halberstam, *The Making of a Quagmire*, copyright © 1964 by David Halberstam (New York: Random House, 1965), which appear on pp. 107, 122, and 152; and for the excerpt from Richard N. Goodwin, *Triumph or Tragedy — Reflections on Vietnam*, copyright © 1966 by Richard N. Goodwin (New York: Random House, 1966), which appears on pp. 9–10.

CONTENTS

v

May 5, 1965

Dear Professor Rapoport:

I guess we are not getting anywhere. Your use of evidence and assumptions, inference and innuendo, are so foreign to my own standards that I doubt if we can gain much by pursuing our correspondence further.

McGeorge Bundy

May 14, 1965

Dear Mr. Bundy:

We agree on one point, namely, that we are not getting anywhere. I wonder, however, if some thought should not be given to our failure to establish communication. I am able to communicate with thousands of my colleagues, presumably because we have similar standards of evidence, assumptions, and inference. If by innuendo you mean the connotative use of language, then we also use "innuendo" as an aid to communication. You have not told me what your standards of evidence, assumption, inference, and innuendo are, but I am sure there are many people in responsible positions who share them. Am I to infer from your last letter that important segments of America, each a source of considerable influence (although in different spheres), can no longer talk to each other? If so, do you not find this alarming? . . .

Anatol Rapoport

(From *Teach-ins: U.S.A.*, ed. Louis Menashe and Ronald Radosh. New York: Frederick A. Praeger, 1967, p. 150.)

PREFACE

This book is designed primarily for students of exposition, discussion, persuasion, and argument who must buttress their speeches or essays with evidence. We hope it will also be useful to those who are puzzled by the contradictory assertions of public figures, those who are worried by the "credibility gap," and those issue-oriented individuals who are conscientiously trying to make sense of a tortured public policy problem.

Most of us know about the public issues of the day only what we read in newspapers, books, or magazines, or what we hear over the air. We have not been to Viet-Nam, participated in a race riot, or served in Congress. We know nothing firsthand about Asian poverty, Sino-Indian border disputes, the struggle for African nationalism, Arab-Israeli wars, Head Start programs, exorbitant drug company profits, or public opinion polls. Even in those areas where we may have had limited experience, such as education, urban congestion, medical services, or labor relations, we cannot know the whole story firsthand. Thus we depend largely on a public intelligence apparatus which feeds us "facts" over a complex communications network.

Sometimes, as Messrs. Bundy and Rapoport acknowledge, that network breaks down, largely because there are no common standards for the use of evidence, assumptions, and inference. We hope this book will help to establish acceptable common standards, and that it will focus attention on the importance of assumptions and inference as well.

The first systematic treatment of evidence was Aristotle's. Though he was absorbed with the concerns of antiquity, such as the credibility of evidence derived from oaths and tortures, Aristotle clearly considered the study of evidence to be part of rhetoric. We therefore believe ourselves to be in the rhetorical tradition, however neglectful of evidence subsequent rhetoricians have been.

Despite the fact that the term "evidence" is most commonly associated with jurisprudence, little of the material we present is derived from legal sources. The legal study of evidence is basically concerned with problems of admissibility: whether certain kinds of testimony can be admitted to consideration by a tribunal. Our concern here is with evaluation in a "court" where no evidence is excluded: we discuss the probable truth or falsehood of evidence, a decision which in law is left to the untutored judgment of jurors. Hence we derive most of our methodology from historiography and social psychology, the only disciplines to consider systematically the credibility of evidence. The principles used by historians and social psychologists in deciding whether a witness is to be believed or not are the same as those used to determine whether a Secretary of State, a prominent columnist, or a noted professor is telling the truth.

We take our usage of the term *credible* from historiography. Rhetoric and journalism tend to use credibility and acceptability synonymously: a credible statement is one likely to be believed. The historiographical meaning of *credible*, however, is "worthy of belief," hence probably true, with no concern as to whether any specific audience or reader will in fact believe it. Senator Fulbright's prediction that United States cover would not hold during the Bay of Pigs invasion was highly credible, even though the President, Secretaries of State and Defense, and assorted intelligence officers did not believe him. In the historiographical sense, his opinion was *worthy* of belief.

We also share with most historians a common-sense and nonphilosophical definition of truth: truth is what the evidence, correctly interpreted, obliges us to believe. We hold that there is such a thing as truth, and that it can sometimes be identified. Even in the chaotic war in Viet-Nam, there are ascertainable truths and falsehoods. There was a battle at Ap Bac, and it either had or did not have certain consequences. Secretary McNamara did predict that bombing North Viet-Nam would halt the movement of troops and supplies to the South, and he was either right or wrong. Hanoi either did or did not make peace overtures in 1964, and the Johnson Administration accepted or rejected them. We do not deal in ultimate Truths or truths-in-general, but in specific, limited, historical truths.

Any discussion of the credibility of public evidence demands illustration. Identifying and evaluating specific purveyors of intelligence has involved us in live policy issues, a matter which caused some concern to one of the readers of our manuscript. We share his concern with future readers, if only to acknowledge that we are aware of the dangers:

> On the third reading, it suddenly occurred to me that there may be a very good reason why writers about logic and such use examples like Socrates' mortality and who-gets-the-shade: these issues are either incontestable or else so trivial that nobody is likely to get so involved in the issue as to overlook the principle being illustrated. In each of your examples, some well-defined group of readers will get so involved with the fuss that they will overlook the analytical point.

Should this turn out to be the case, we plead guilty in advance. We prefer the risk of over-involvement to the dangers of triviality and irrelevance. The question "Who is telling the truth, and how do you know?" is ultimately inseparable from the question "What is the truth on this issue?"

We acknowledge at the outset a left-liberal bias. Consequently we have been particularly careful to compensate by subjecting those whose opinions agree with ours to intensive scrutiny. All men have biases, and the only hope of being relatively objective lies in recognizing one's own and trying to prevent them from distorting perception. For example, in dealing with the Dominican crisis of 1965, we try harder to find distortions in Draper, with whom we agree, than in the *National Review*, with which we disagree.

Our acknowledgments of help are as inevitably incomplete as they are genuine. First and foremost, they go to the Charles E. Merrill Foundation for a Faculty Fellowship in the Humanities (1963) which enabled us to spend Trinity, the most delightful of all terms, at Oxford; to Jack Matthews, Chairman of the Department of Speech, University of Pittsburgh, for granting time off from normal duties; and to Bower Aly, formerly of the University of Hawaii, for enabling us to further the task of writing in the shadow of Diamond Head.

For many indispensable suggestions we are indebted to Theodore Clevenger, Jr., Richard Gregg, L. Stanley Harms,

Roger Hufford, Steve Jenkins, Thomas Kane, Wayne Minnick, Gaylord Obern, James O'Toole, Harry Tuminello, Otis Walter, and Philip Wander. The many graduate students who have dug out obscure documents or pled with us in vain to change our erring ways deserve a special vote of thanks.

Finally, our editor at Houghton Mifflin, John W. Poindexter, deserves more than the usual credit for sticking with us through many changes in format. Had he known, in 1958, that it would be ten years before his suggestion saw the light of day, he might have looked elsewhere for his authors.

R. P. N.
D. R. N.

The Uses
of Evidence

PART ONE

1

Supporting Goals

*The trained navigator, it has been rightly said, is essential
to the conduct of a voyage, but his judgment is not superior on such matters as where it should go or whether it
should be taken at all.*

THEODORE C. SORENSEN (**206**:66)

The Place of Goals in Deliberation

This book is concerned with the use of evidence in deliberation. Deliberation is the discussion of reasons for and against a policy proposal.
Theoretically, decision makers in all types of organizations deliberate
before they act, but many decisions are influenced by irrational and
nonrational factors with which we are not concerned. To deliberate is
to offer *good* reasons for or against a proposal; this, as Karl Wallace
has rightly claimed, is the "substance of rhetoric." (**230**)

Those who deliberate about any public policy must consider three
kinds of questions. First, they must consider *directional* questions,
which have to do with the goals or ends of action: What do we want to
accomplish? What end should we seek? What are the criteria for an
effective policy? Second, they must deal with *positional* questions:
Where are we now? Are we on course toward our goal? How close to

3

our goal are we? Third, they must deal with *predictions*: Will present policy achieve our goal? Will this new policy take us where we want to go? What will be the consequences of this policy?

These different types of questions do not always arise in this order. For instance, students may be projected into serious thought about the draft by contemplating a prediction: "If I am drafted, I may be killed in the jungles of South Viet-Nam." But underneath any discussion of the draft will be the goals of military policy; conscription can be bad or wrong or unfair only in relation to a set of goals or ends. And the deeper one goes into problems of military service, the clearer it becomes that one can make no sense at all of various proposals for raising an army until one has decided what that army is for: whether to put down any insurgency anywhere, or only to defend American shores, or something in between. To evaluate our present draft policy, we must answer the directional question: What do we want this army for?

Thus, even though directional questions may not be raised first in a discussion, we deal with them first because of their importance. In order to deliberate about any policy question, one must first understand the goals which might justify action. In Sorensen's idiom, one needs to decide whether a voyage should be undertaken, and where it should go.

Some scholars believe that the policy goals of society, and the more general values underlying them, are not amenable to rational discussion or deliberation. This is a serious mistake. Even those "scholarly" enterprises which most loudly proclaim their value-free nature presuppose judgments about the worth of the information they seek, or the importance of the hypothesis they set out to test. And just as scientists can profitably discuss the merits of alternative research proposals, scholars in any field can profitably discuss the directional questions at the root of great social issues. We believe it to be a major function of a theory of evidence to illuminate the relationship of evidence to goals.

A goal is a concrete or specific objective of action. When we say, "The United States should defeat the Viet-Cong" or "The United States should support the establishment of democracy in Viet-Nam," we are stating policy goals. These specific goals are value-impregnated; they presuppose and depend on more fundamental and abstract entities usually termed values. We support specific policy goals because we believe them to be instrumentally related to higher values; we want to reach a policy goal because it will help implement some deeply held value. Values, on the other hand, are intrinsically desirable; they are not means to ends, they are ends in themselves. Even national security, a value of some abstractness, can be considered as instrumentally related to a yet higher value: the general welfare of all mankind. We do not intend to enter into the raging philosophical conflicts over values; most policy deliberation can be profitably conducted on much lower levels of abstraction. Whether peace is a higher value than justice need not concern us here. We share with C. Wright Mills a determination to bring evidence to bear upon as many specific policy goals as possible and a certain fatalism when confronted with continuing disagreement:

> But when there are values so firmly and so consistently held by genuinely conflicting interests that the conflict cannot be resolved by logical analysis and factual investigation, then the role of reason in that human affair seems at an end. We can clarify the meaning and consequences of values, we can make them consistent with one another and ascertain their actual priorities, we can surround them with fact — but in the end we may be reduced to mere assertion and counterassertion; then we can only plead or persuade. . . . In the end, if the end comes, we just have to beat those who disagree with us over the head; let us hope the end comes seldom. In the meantime, being as reasonable as we are able to be, we ought all to argue. (**155**:77)

Some goals, obviously, are more important than others, and often the goals involved in a question can be arranged in a crude hierarchy. If, for instance, one were to ask, "Why are we fighting in Viet-Nam?" our immediate answer would be, "To defeat the Viet-Cong." This answer might not be satisfying, in which case it would be followed by, "But why do we want to defeat the Viet-Cong?" Here the answer might be, "To fulfill our commitment to the Vietnamese people." And if this were still inadequate, one might progress through a whole series of goals of increasing scope: "Why should we honor this commitment?" "To preserve the balance of power in Southeast Asia." "Why should we preserve a balance of power in Southeast Asia?" "To contain Chinese expansionism." "Why should we contain Chinese expansionism?" "Because, ultimately, China is a threat to the United States." Here the dialogue will probably stop. National security is a goal of such stature and widespread acceptance that no need will be felt to go beyond it. Only philosophers would argue about whether national security was intrinsically desirable.

The interaction of means and ends can be seen clearly in this graduation of policy goals in Viet-Nam. Defeating the Viet-Cong is not only an end which may be desired in itself, but it is a means to the more significant end of fulfilling a commitment we have made, which is itself a means to the end of maintaining a balance of power in Southeast Asia, and so forth. Policy goals can be criticized or supported at any level; a rational theory of goal-criticism is possible without climbing the abstraction ladder to the "highest value."

One caution is necessary when dealing with policy goals: the language in which they are couched is often vague or ambiguous. It is necessary to understand exactly what a goal statement means to the deliberator. For the past decade, there has been much talk about a "no-win" policy on the part of the United States, and various politicians have alleged that our primary goal in Viet-Nam should be to "win." But precisely what does "win" mean? Does it mean merely to push the Viet-Cong back into the jungles and establish security in the "cleared" areas, as happened in Malaya? Does it mean to eliminate from South Viet-Nam anyone who does not support the ruling Saigon government? Does it mean to punish North Viet-Nam to the point that she will no longer support insurgency in the South? Does it mean to destroy the military capabilities of North Viet-Nam entirely? Does it mean to destroy the military capabilities of China? or Russia? One often does not know, and yet no deliberation about the goal is possible until one does know.

The process of defining most appropriate to policy deliberation is operational definition. Platonic essences, Aristotelian genus-and-species, dictionary derivations, providing synonyms — all are relatively impotent in policy deliberation. One knows how a term is being used when one knows how the goal it describes would be put into effect. The cash value of a term is how it would work. Only when the policy goal is clearly defined can the goal itself be criticized.

At least three questions are fruitful in conducting rational goal criticism: (1) Is the goal factually well-grounded? (2) Can we seek this goal consistently? (3) What are the costs of achieving this goal?

Factual Grounding

Facts are related to policy goals in many straightforward ways. Consider the deliberation which took place in early 1965, when the post-Diem governments of South Viet-Nam were falling one after the other, and the Viet-Cong were rapidly taking control of the whole country. At that time American forces in Viet-Nam were theoretically just advising and training Arvin (Army of the Republic of Viet-Nam) units. One prominent policy proposal was to engage American troops actively in the fighting, and to increase our troop strength sufficiently to turn the tide of battle. One of the reasons given by proponents of the "get involved in the war" policy was that this action was necessary to fulfill our commitment to the Vietnamese. This argument might be structured this way:

> *Goal:* The United States should fulfill its commitment to the Vietnamese.
> *Position vis-à-vis this goal:* We are not now fulfilling our commitment to the Vietnamese since we are not fully engaged in the war.
> *Prediction:* Getting involved in the war will fulfill our commitment.
> *Conclusion:* Therefore we should get involved in the war.

Clearly there is much evidence relevant to this goal. What are the facts of our commitment? When and how was it made, to whom, what aid does it call for, what qualifications attach to it, what escape clauses are there?

The case for an American commitment in Viet-Nam is based primarily on two documents: the Eisenhower letter to President Diem of October 23, 1954, and the SEATO Treaty. Fortunately both documents are readily available to Monday morning quarterbacks, as they were to the Government decision makers in 1965. There is no dispute about their texts, and even a college sophomore could interpret them accurately.

Following the Geneva Conference of 1954, the French began to withdraw from Indochina. Eisenhower, anticipating the transfer of the United States aid from the French to Diem, wrote as follows:

> We have been exploring ways and means to permit our aid to Viet-Nam to be more effective and to make a greater contribution to the welfare and stability of the Government of Viet-Nam. I am, accordingly, instructing the American Ambassador to Viet-Nam to examine with you in your capacity as Chief of Government, how an intelligent program of American aid given directly to your Government, can serve to assist Viet-Nam in its present hour of trial, provided that your Government is prepared to give assurances as to the standards of performance it would be able to maintain in the event such aid were supplied.
>
> The purpose of this offer is to assist the Government of Viet-Nam in developing and maintaining a strong, viable state, capable of resisting attempted subversion or aggression through military means. The Government of the United States expects that this aid will be met by per-

formance on the part of the Government of Viet-Nam in undertaking needed reforms. It hopes that such aid, combined with your own continuing efforts, will contribute effectively toward an independent Viet-Nam endowed with a strong government. Such a government would, I hope, be so responsive to the nationalist aspirations of its people, so enlightened in purpose and effective in performance, that it will be respected both at home and abroad and discourage anyone who might wish to impose a foreign ideology on your free people. (**124**:100)

This is the sum of the formal and public Eisenhower commitment: *if* certain reforms are made, we will give aid. The letter does not say that we will maintain the Saigon Government in power. It does not say that *we* will defend that government against either an internal or an external enemy, that we will spend $25 billion a year supporting and defending that government, that we will put 550,000 American troops in South Viet-Nam. The conditional commitment is to give aid, and the qualification is that the Diem government can use that aid constructively and show effective performance. This is clearly no commitment to do what we are doing in 1968. This evidence — the Eisenhower letter — provides very little factual grounding for the commitment claimed.

The provisions of the SEATO Treaty are a more likely grounding for our later involvement in Viet-Nam. The Treaty is, after all, a mutual defense treaty, and we do appear to be defending South Viet-Nam with some degree of mutuality. Secretary Rusk invokes the Treaty to validate our commitment, as in this exchange during the Senate Foreign Relations Committee hearings of 1966:

Fulbright: You stated in your original statement that we have a very clear commitment. What is the origin and basis for a clear commitment to the action we are now taking in Vietnam?

Rusk: I think, sir, there are a combination of components in that commitment. We have the Southeast Asian Treaty to which South Vietnam was a protocol state.

Fulbright: What does that commit us to in that regard? This is where there is a good deal of confusion in my mind and I think in the public mind about the nature of that commitment. Does the Southeast Treaty, Southeast Asia Treaty Organization commit us to what we are now doing in Vietnam?

Rusk: Yes, sir, I have no doubt that it does. A protocol state has a right to call on the members of the organization for assistance. The obligations of the treaty are both joint and several. That is, they are both collective and individual. So that there seems to be no doubt that we are entitled to offer that assistance. (**228**:11)

But Rusk's apparently straightforward answer turns out, on inspection, to be an evasion of the facts in the treaty; to be *entitled* to offer assistance and to be *committed* to offer it are two different things. The Treaty itself is somewhat more convincing. The "action" clauses are in Article IV. Paragraph One of that Article deals with what Rusk calls "individual" actions to be taken against "aggression":

> 1. Each Party recognizes that aggression by means of armed attack in the treaty area against any of the Parties or against any State or territory which the Parties by unanimous agreement may hereafter designate, would endanger its own peace and safety, and agrees that it will in that event act to meet the common danger in accordance with its constitutional processes. Measures taken under this paragraph shall be immediately reported to the Security Council of the United Nations.

There has been, in the view of the United States Government, "aggression by armed attack" on South Viet-Nam (unfortunately, "aggression" is left undefined*). Viet-Nam is undoubtedly in the Treaty area, and is one of the designated protected states. Whether we have acted in accordance with our constitutional processes might be a matter of dispute, as also might be our reporting procedures to the United Nations Security Council.

There are factual grounds in the Southeast Asia Treaty for upholding Rusk's interpretation of our commitment in Viet-Nam. The Treaty itself, however, is not the only relevant factual evidence on which to ground a policy deliberation of our commitment to Viet-Nam. Many witnesses have testified about what the Treaty meant to the framers and how it has been interpreted since its signing. If the Constitution is what the judges say it is, so must a treaty be what the parties say it is. Perhaps the most interesting evidence about the place of the SEATO Treaty in our Viet-Nam involvement comes from Richard N. Goodwin, former assistant to Presidents Kennedy and Johnson, who wrote in 1966:

> Since there exists such a compelling case, resting, as Dean Rusk testified, "upon policy and strategic and geopolitical considerations that are of the utmost importance," it is baffling to find many supporters of

---

* For an excellent examination of the possible meanings of aggression, see Ralph K. White. (**235**:106–109)

the war offering justifications for our presence which have little foundation in history, reason, law, or the course of events. Perhaps it is simply
proof of the saying that in war truth is the first casualty. Most startling
of all is the recent claim that the United States has a formal and binding
commitment to use its armies to defend Viet-Năm — a commitment rest-
ing on the Southeast Asia Treaty, or, alternatively, on Presidential statements over more than a decade. . . . The language of the Treaty itself
is imprecise. In case of "armed attack" we agreed only "to meet the
common danger in accordance with [our] constitutional processes." No
nation is specifically required to go to war, although it is true that a
skilled lawyer could interpret the language as a commitment or as an
excuse for inaction, depending upon his instructions. The conclusive fact,
however, is that neither our fellow-signers, including France and Britain,
nor John Foster Dulles, who drew up the treaty, nor any American
President has believed or been advised that those words required us to
send fighting men to Vietnam. Under close questioning by Senator
Hickenlooper, who was eager to refute the slightest insinuation that this
was "Ike's war," General Taylor admitted, "No, sir. Very clearly we
made no such commitment. We didn't want such a commitment. This
was the last thing we had in mind. . . . Insofar as the use of our combat
ground forces are concerned, that [commitment] took place, of course,
only in the spring of 1965." One can search the many statements of
Presidents and diplomats in vain for any mention of the SEATO Treaty.
Time after time, President Johnson set forth the reasons for our presence
in Vietnam, but he never spoke of the requirements of the treaty, nor did
anyone at the State Department suggest that he should, even though they
surely reviewed every draft statement. The treaty argument is, in truth,
something a clever advocate conceived a few months ago. (77:17–19)

As cogent as they are, the facts provided by Goodwin are by no means
a complete rendering of the data available about SEATO and our alleged
commitment under it. To cover this one issue thoroughly would require
hundreds of pages.* But we hope enough has been given to show not
only how facts support or fail to support a policy goal, but also how the
psychological phenomena of selective inattention to facts can operate to
create, even in the United States, a "moral self-image" not justified by
the evidence. (235)

* For a discussion of the origin of the United States "commitment" to Viet-
Nam from a perspective even more skeptical than Goodwin's, see Bruce Ladd.
(121:160)

Consistency

A second question which can be asked of any policy goal is "Can we seek this goal consistently?" Being consistent in action is a virtue which moral philosophers have emphasized since Immanuel Kant. One of the most sophisticated treatments of the importance of consistency in the actions of an individual is that of R. M. Hare. (84) The same arguments which support personal consistency also support consistency on the part of nation states; there is no reason why we should not treat country A the same way we treat country B, other things being equal.

But can other things ever be equal? Can one really uphold consistency as a virtue of national action, when the facts of international life and internal politics are so complicated and constantly changing? If we arm the Germans, must we really arm the Japanese? If we call for free elections in Hungary, must we really demand them in Formosa? Can any two situations ever be the same?

Obviously, no two situations ever can be identical. The point at issue is whether two situations are the same in aspects relevant to a specific policy. The problem of relevance is monstrous; it will plague us again when we consider the use of evidence in historical analogies. But it has to be faced.

We believe that there are situations where public policy should be measured by consistency, where goals can be supported or criticized because they are consistent or inconsistent with what we have done in analogous situations. The United States, for instance, supports vociferously the principle of national self-determination. We hold that every nation should have the right to determine for itself the kind of government under which it shall live. Applying this principle to the nations of Eastern Europe, we hold their Communist regimes to be illegitimate because the citizenry has been denied the opportunity to choose between a Communist and a non-Communist government in open elections. We realize, however, that the people of Spain and Portugal have similarly been denied a clear opportunity for self-determination, and hence our rapport with the governments of those countries is generally poor. About Formosa we are also uneasy; the Formosans have never been given the opportunity to choose between being governed by Chiang Kai-shek and his rump mainlander government and establishing an independent state like Ceylon. (See 110.)

It is probable, even, that much of our uneasiness about the war in Viet-Nam is due to our knowledge that had the principle of self-determination been applied in 1956, as called for by the Geneva accords of 1954, Ho Chi Minh would have won, and there would exist at least one Communist state voted into power by the will of the people. (Those "experts" who claim that Ho had no intention of allowing the International Control Commission to actually supervise free elections are rationalizing our present difficulties. The evidence is clear. See **232**.) That Communism has been an irreversible phenomenon is up to this point an unfortunate but irrelevant consideration. The people of Russia, China, Cuba, Eastern Europe, and North Viet-Nam may not have chosen Communism freely, even though they are saddled with it, but this does not countermand the principle that if a people should choose it, the right is theirs. Our moral posture is compromised considerably by our advocating self-determination for territories controlled by our enemies but not for territories controlled by our clients.

We therefore hold it to be a legitimate criticism of the goals underlying such a proposal as "The United States should aid Portugal" that they are inconsistent with our professed support of the policy of national self-determination: Portugal simply is not self-determined, and yet she is a client of ours. Obviously, there must be *some* goal, inconsistent though it may be with the self-determination goal, behind the policy to support Portugal anyway. Perhaps we are compromising because we think our support will hasten the future possibility of self-determination in Portugal. Perhaps we just do not want to see Portugal "go Communist" and are afraid she would if allowed to decide for herself. Perhaps we need her as an ally at any cost. At any rate, we have compromised our present policy for a future goal at the expense of consistency.

Costs

The conclusion above leads us to a related question: What are the costs of achieving a goal? Clearly this is one of the most important considerations in policy deliberation. Must another goal be compromised or even sacrificed? Will the goal be worth the cost?

In April, 1965, underneath the camouflage about protecting American nationals and preventing bloodshed, the dominant reason for American intervention in the Dominican Republic was clearly this argument:

SUPPORTING GOALS 13
Goal: The United States should prevent Communist takeovers in the
    Western Hemisphere.
  Position vis-à-vis this goal: Communists are about to take over in the
    Dominican Republic (or "have taken over" or "will probably take
    over," depending on which of President Johnson's statements you
    select).
  Prediction: Landing the Marines will prevent this Communist takeover.
  Conclusion: Land the Marines.

Entirely apart from the truth of the positional statement and the prediction of this argument, there is serious doubt about the soundness of
the goal; the prediction invests it with the implication that the United
States should prevent Communist takeovers by military intervention.
But obviously there are other strategies which might be more acceptable
and less incendiary; *i.e.,* less costly.

One of the costs of our intervention was the loss of good will and
respect which we suffered in other Latin American countries. It is not
clear how great or how permanent a loss was sustained. Those who supported the intervention minimize the loss; those who opposed it claim
the loss was substantial. We do not attempt to evaluate the relevant evidence here; we cite the incident only as an illustration of how one goal,
preventing Communist takeovers in the Western Hemisphere, can conflict with a different goal, maintaining American influence in the hemisphere. If it can be shown that the intervention resulted in a serious
loss of influence, the cost was too great and the goal was depreciated.

Costs are also a major factor in the raging argument about whether
to build an antiballistic missile system. J. I. Coffey details them in this
discussion from *Foreign Affairs:*

  Anyone concerned with the security of the United States must, therefore, pay close attention to the potentialities of ballistic missile defenses
  for limiting damage from a nuclear strike, or, in a larger sense, for helping to deter such a strike. However, it is not enough to consider the case
  in so narrow a context, since national security embraces concerns other
  than that of damage limitation and may prescribe means of achieving that
  security other than large and costly expenditures for defensive systems.
  Thus, those deciding whether, how and when to deploy ballistic missile
  defenses must consider their broad effects, taking into account possible
  Soviet reactions, the impact on friends and allies of such a decision, and
  the political and sociological implications of such a move for the United

States. They must also consider other means of advancing our interests and security, the impact on the arms race, the implications for agreements such as the nuclear test-ban treaty, and the options open to the United States if it deems these factors important. (**36**:404–5)

The two goals of antiballistic missiles, deterrence and damage limitation, thus may be reached only by paying many costs: stimulating Soviet arms production, losing the confidence of allies, spending money which might better serve American interests elsewhere, discouraging further arms bans, and jeopardizing present arms agreements.

Surely the proposal for antiballistic missiles has provoked one of the most elaborate deliberations of all times. There is evidence that it has torn the Government as few disputes have. The intelligence activity preliminary to deciding whether an ABM system would cost further arms agreements with the Soviet would alone have taxed the evidence-gathering powers of several CIA's.

Two other obvious instances where one proposed goal would cost another goal deserve brief mention. Prevailing laws against euthanasia are supported by the desire to avoid unnecessary death. Medical evidence, however, establishes that one of the costs of avoiding unnecessary death is unnecessary suffering. If avoiding unnecessary suffering becomes a more important goal than avoiding unnecessary death, euthanasia begins to look like a less costly policy than prolonging life. (**95**)

Similarly, in Viet-Nam the goal of containing Chinese expansionism has great cogency; but as it becomes possible that achieving this goal may cost the physical destruction of the entire country of Viet-Nam, the importance of blocking the Chinese — assuming that we are in fact doing that by fighting in South Viet-Nam — begins to decrease.

The achievement of any goal will cost something, and the calculation of costs is clearly an evidential matter. Thus the deliberator, far from beginning his activity in the subjective realm of nonfactual values, is thrown immediately and conclusively into a struggle with evidence. No policy goal stands alone, unaffected by the evidential world surrounding it.

Summary

The first step in policy deliberation is analysis and criticism of goals. This is not an entirely subjective matter; facts impinge on policy goals in many ways. (1) Most goals incorporate a number of factual assumptions which must be inspected carefully. One of the goals of the American involvement in Viet-Nam depends for its validity on when and how a commitment was made, to whom it was made, what aid it calls for, and what qualifications attach to it. One must inspect the factual evidence to determine what the commitment is and how seriously we must take it. (2) Some goals can be challenged because we cannot uphold them consistently. To apply one standard here and another standard there is damaging to one's credibility, and the moral philosophers are agreed that consistency is a virtue not to be despised. The American goal of support for national self-determination, for instance, seems to suffer from inconsistent application. (3) Most goals cannot be achieved without extracting a "cost" of some sort; we may achieve damage limitation with an antiballistic missile system, but it may cost us another round in the arms race. Achieving any goal will cost the achievement of a goal incompatible with it; evidence must be brought to bear to determine the costs of a policy and their relative importance.

Suggested Readings

Bruce Gronbeck, "From 'Is' to 'Ought': Alternative Strategies," *Central States Speech Journal*, XIX (Spring, 1968), 31–39.

R. M. Hare, *Freedom and Reason*. Oxford: Oxford University Press, 1963, especially Chapter Eleven.

Roger Hufford, "The Logician, The Historian, and Rhetorical Criticism," *Journal of the American Forensic Association*, II (January, 1965), 14.

Wolfgang Kohler, *The Place of Value in a World of Facts*. New York: Mentor Books, 1966.

Eduard C. Lindemann (with T. V. Smith), *The Democratic Way of Life*. New York: New American Library, 1951, Book Two.

C. Wright Mills, *The Sociological Imagination*. New York: Grove Press, 1961.

Robert P. Newman, *Recognition of Communist China?* New York: Macmillan, 1961, Chapters Two and Seventeen.

President's Commission on National Goals, *Goals for Americans*. Englewood Cliffs: Prentice-Hall (Spectrum Books), 1960.

Karl R. Wallace, "The Substance of Rhetoric: Good Reasons," *Quarterly Journal of Speech*, XLIX (October, 1963), 239.

Ralph K. White, "Misperception and the Vietnam War," *Journal of Social Issues*, XXII (July, 1966), 1–164.

9028

2

Supporting Positional Statements

The looser the evidence concept appropriate to an area of enquiry, the more will the system of reasoning take the form of a cluster of interlocking propositions lending mutual strength and support for one another. Such systems can range from those based upon formal canons of evidential arguments, as with legal evidence, to systems admitting the most tentative and provisional modes of argument. However, no system of this type presents the aspect of a collection of chains of deduction. Rather, they are akin to crossword puzzles, each piece bolstering and interlocking with every other.

NICHOLAS RESCHER (181:94)

Positional Statements in Deliberation

When a deliberator has determined and criticized the goals of public policy; when he has answered the question "Where do we want to go?" the next logical step is to survey his position: "Where are we now?" Frequently the positional question may actually occur first, before an explicit consideration of goals. But whenever it occurs, asking about one's position is to ask for a statement based on evidence.

16

The answers of a deliberator to positional questions are either approving or disapproving. If, for instance, one is deliberating about the length of term Congressmen should serve, supporters of the status quo will argue that we should retain the present two-year term because it makes Congressmen highly responsive to the opinions of their constituents. The structure of this argument is:

> *Goal:* The House of Representatives should be responsive to the will of the people.
>
> *Position vis-à-vis this goal:* Elections every other year make Representatives responsive to the will of their constituents.
>
> *Prediction about a longer term:* A longer term will lessen Congressional responsiveness to the will of the people.
>
> *Conclusion:* Therefore we should retain the present system.

The positional statement here is approving: we are achieving the goal of responsiveness, we are accomplishing something important by the two-year term for House members. Positional statements of this sort are a kind of social measurement or evaluation.

Opponents of the present system, however, will advance a different argument:

> *Goal:* Members of Congress should be able to concentrate on the business of legislating.
>
> *Position vis-à-vis this goal:* Running for reelection every other year prevents them from concentrating on legislating.
>
> *Prediction about a longer term:* A longer term will enable them to concentrate on legislating.
>
> *Conclusion:* Therefore we should increase the Congressional term to four (or more) years.

Here the positional statement is disapproving. We are not achieving our goal, our social measurement is negative, and we therefore indict the present system.

If evidence supported both of these arguments, we would have two incompatible goals. We could achieve greater attention to legislating by increasing the Congressional term, but one of the costs of the new system would be decreased responsiveness to the will of the people.

These positional statements are typical of deliberation. They are inductive generalizations: "Elections every other year make Congressmen responsive to the will of their constituents," and "Running for reelection

every other year prevents Congressmen from concentrating on legislation"
are assertions about the past and present which must be based on historical evidence. Neither one of these statements can be derived deductively from a priori principles; they are derived inductively from
specific instances.

We must, therefore, discuss briefly the nature of such induction, and
the problems associated with it. Rescher and Joynt, in a perceptive study
entitled "Evidence in History and in the Law," state one of the important
characteristics of this type of reasoning:

> The central and fundamental character of the concept of evidence is
> that one statement or body of information can be evidence for another
> that goes *beyond* it in assertive content. A (correct) deductive argument
> can only elicit in a more overt manner certain facts already laid down
> in its premises, and consequently cannot extend our knowledge. A prop-
> erly conducted evidential argument, on the other hand, constitutes an
> inductive extension of the range of our information. . . . A deductive
> argument is either valid or not; there is no middle ground, for the con-
> clusion is either contained in the premises or it is not. In inductive, evi-
> dential argument we are merely concerned to give good (and not con-
> clusive) reasons for our conclusion. (**182**:562)

Hence no positional statement will ever be necessary or certain; it will be
derived from evidence by a fallible process.

Philosophers and some natural scientists have long been disturbed by
this nonconclusive nature of induction, which they call "the problem of
induction," and which they wrestle with interminably in an attempt
to make induction as certain as mathematics or the older branches of
physics and chemistry. Such fastidiousness need not concern us here.
Men do act, and will continue to act, more or less rationally on the basis
of inductive inferences which are adequate to their purposes, even though
they are not and cannot be certain. The problem for the student of evidence is not how to establish mathematical certainties and truths; it is
how to distinguish an inductive inference which is *probably true* from
one which is probably false.

Inductive inferences are of three main kinds: descriptive generalizations, causal explanations, and analogies. All three are constructed of
specific instances, or as the historians call them, concrete particulars.
The positional statement in one of the major arguments favoring withdrawal from Viet-Nam can be used to illustrate how all three function:

Goal: The United States should seek to decrease Chinese influence.

Positional statement: United States action in Viet-Nam is increasing Chinese influence by forcing Hanoi to accept aid from China.

Prediction: By withdrawing from Viet-Nam the United States will encourage Titoism in Hanoi.

Conclusion: Therefore the United States should withdraw from Viet-Nam.

This positional statement is complicated, and asserts three things:

    (1) Hanoi is getting aid from China.

    (2) This is happening because of American pressure on Hanoi.

    (3) It results in increased Chinese influence in Hanoi.

The first of these assertions is a descriptive generalization; the second is a causal explanation; and the third could be classed as causal even though it might be supported by analogy.

Descriptive Generalizations

"Hanoi is getting aid from China" is a descriptive generalization inferred from a number of specific instances. One such instance might be established by an eyewitness who saw Chinese weapons on North Vietnamese soldiers after a battle in the Central Highlands. Another might be that Chinese technicians were seen repairing a truck on a road near Hanoi. Another might be that a train loaded with military trucks was seen crossing the border from China into North Viet-Nam. In all these specific instances, no inferences are drawn; eyewitnesses are presumably reporting only what they see. They are not making generalizations or drawing conclusions.

These specific eyewitness reports do, of course, demand a certain amount of expertise on the part of the reporters. One would need to be able to identify a North Vietnamese soldier, a Chinese weapon, a Chinese truck. Some would say that making these identifications involves some degree of inference; we prefer to restrict the term inference to processes of generalization and comparison.

If one puts many specific instances together and claims "Hanoi is getting aid from China," one has gone beyond simple reporting and made an inference which carries a risk with it; this "inferential risk" is the danger of moving from the particulars to the generalization. Another way of saying this is that a generalization goes beyond the data which support it; it is, as Rescher and Joynt say, an inductive extension of the range of our information.

In using concrete particulars to form a descriptive generalization, one must make sure that this inferential risk is met. There are at least four questions to ask about any descriptive generalization:

(1) Is there enough evidence to support the generalization? A dozen Chinese weapons found on North Vietnamese soldiers and half a dozen Chinese trucks in North Viet-Nam would hardly be significant. On the other hand, Chinese aid would not need to be as massive as American aid to Saigon or Russian aid to the Arab states in order to be significant. Between mere token support and significant aid there is a large middle ground, and one can never answer the question "How much is enough?" with any precision. In some cases, one instance might be enough. (Many authorities contend that the single instance of Russian withdrawal of missiles from Cuba is sufficient evidence to support the generalization that "Russia backs down when confronted with the threat of American military action.") In others, several would be needed.

(2) Is there negative evidence which might destroy the generalization? North Vietnamese officials might be on record as complaining that China had not aided them. Chinese officials might be on record as advising fraternal revolutionary movements to make it on their own — as, in the summer of 1965, Lin Piao appears to have done. Perhaps the weapons and vehicles identified as Chinese are really Japanese, left over from World War II.

(3) Do the instances genuinely support the generalization? A shipload of Toyota trucks arriving in Seattle would not support the generalization that Japan was aiding the United States; if Chinese matériel was purchased and paid for by Hanoi, it could not be classed as aid. Nor would possession of American supplies by Viet-Cong troops support the generalization that we had been aiding the VC; the supplies could have been captured. One must always search for alternative hypotheses to the generalization being considered.

(4) Does the generalization go beyond the supporting evidence? Evidence that the Chinese were giving a substantial amount of matériel to the North Vietnamese would support the generalization that Hanoi is getting aid from China. But it would not necessarily support the generalization that China wants the North Vietnamese to push the Americans out of Indochina. Such a generalization goes beyond the data. The Chinese might find the Viet-Nam war useful to their propaganda ma-

chine and not want it to end; or they might be supplying Hanoi reluctantly to prevent Hanoi from turning to Russia for aid.

In the case we are considering, however, the generalization is valid. Evidence that the Chinese have aided North Viet-Nam is abundant, not contradicted in any significant way, and sufficient to support the generalization.

Descriptive generalizations which make no causal claims are sometimes known as "census evidence." One surveys the historical facts without attempting to explain them. In the above generalization, no attempt is made to say *why* the Chinese are aiding Hanoi. Some authorities on decision making seem to believe that census evidence is the only kind of data needed in deliberation; we can know what to do in Viet-Nam simply by taking a census and finding out what people want. (See **19.**) This program might be adequate in domestic affairs; in foreign affairs it assuredly is not.

Causal Explanations

"This (China aiding Hanoi) is happening because of American pressure on Hanoi." This second part of the positional statement presupposes that without the pressures of American action in Viet-Nam, Hanoi would not be getting aid from China; if the United States were not aiding Saigon, Hanoi would not need or accept Chinese aid. This translates into a basic Vietnamese fear of China. Here one claims to know the reason why something is true: mere census evidence is inadequate to support the claim.

The inferential risk in causal explanations is generally greater than in descriptive generalizations. One cannot directly observe causes at work; one can only infer them. Those who support the argument under discussion point to several "causal" factors at work in Sino-Vietnamese relations: previous Chinese invasions of Viet-Nam, small-power suspicion of a powerful neighbor, newly intensified Vietnamese nationalism, and so forth.

There are obviously different kinds of assertions here. To say, "Previous Chinese invasions of Viet-Nam have caused Vietnamese fear of China" is quite different from saying, "Because China is so powerful by comparison, the neighboring Vietnamese fear China." These two statements *explain* Vietnamese fear of China in quite different ways. Today it is recognized that there are many phenomena which can be classified together under the heading of "causal"; the old philosopher's division of causes into *necessary* and *sufficient* is no longer adequate. More flexible and subtle concepts of causes are required. Hart and Honoré, in the major legal work on causation, distinguish three different kinds of cause: (1) volitional human intervention in some affair, which initiates a series of physical changes — for instance, American chemical spraying of North Vietnamese crops to cause food shortages; (2) providing another person with a reason for doing something — one might say that American troops in South Viet-Nam cause the Chinese to supply Hanoi; (3) providing an opportunity for some action which is exploited by an agent; for example, Ambassador Lodge's cutoff of American funds to pay the security forces protecting Diem, causing Diem's fall.* Hart and Honoré do not pretend that these concepts exhaust the meanings of the label "cause"; they claim only that in legal and historical reasoning these meanings are prominent. (86:2)

Historiographer Louis Gottschalk warns against indiscriminate use of the label "cause":

> Perhaps historians ought to use the word *cause*, and even the word *causes*, sparingly and instead, breaking the concept down into its component parts, cultivate the more precise words — imprecise though they too may be — such as "purpose," "occasion," "antecedent," "means," or "motive," wherever possible. (78:227)

Focusing on previous invasions as a possible cause, or antecedent, of Vietnamese fear of China, one must determine the validity of the causal hypothesis by asking questions similar to those asked of a descriptive generalization.

First, are there enough instances of the cause at work? Would one Chinese invasion of Viet-Nam a millennium ago create a lasting fear? Possibly not; but there have been many Chinese invasions of Viet-Nam over the centuries. It is probable that enough instances are available to support the hypothesis.

Second, are the causal instances representative of relations between two countries? Or were they flukes, atypical Chinese behavior, and recognized as such by the Vietnamese? This question is more difficult to answer.

* The categories are those of Hart and Honoré, the examples ours.

Third, are there contrary causes at work which would nullify the hypothesis? Is similar ideology or mutual fear of Caucasian-imperialist nations more powerful than ancient feuds? Could one of these factors cancel out past fears?

Fourth, does the cause really account for the phenomenon, or is it merely tangential? This is analogous to asking whether the cause is sufficient. The relevant evidence here would have to come from a depth study of Vietnamese psychology. What forces in Vietnamese history have really affected Vietnamese attitudes toward China? Answering this would involve considerable inferential risk.

Historical Analogies

"Aid results in increased Chinese influence in Hanoi." This third part of our positional statement seems almost self-evident. After all, with 40,000 Chinese technicians helping to keep North Vietnamese military operations going; with Chinese food and manufactures appearing in North Vietnamese homes; with Chinese propaganda exhorting fellow Vietnamese revolutionaries to keep up the good fight, one would expect China to exert considerable influence.

But our specific evidence as to what is going on in Hanoi is slim. We really do not know how Ho and his people view the Chinese. Lacking direct-instance confirmation of Chinese influence in North Viet-Nam, one might attempt to establish this contention by invoking an analogy with American influence in South Viet-Nam: "Since United States aid gives us influence in Saigon, Chinese aid must give Peking influence in Hanoi." We are reasoning here from known data (American influence in Saigon) to unknown situations (Chinese influence in Hanoi.)

However, the statements that the United States wields influence in South Viet-Nam, and that this influence is because of aid, are themselves generalizations, and they are subject to the same kinds of critique as the historical generalizations and causal explanations considered previously. Our simple historical analogy turns into a very difficult judgment. Consider just the generalization that the United States does wield influence in Saigon.

(1) Is there enough evidence to support the generalization? Certainly the Saigon regime is little more than a client government of the United States. When we give the word, a dictator is assassinated. When we

press for land reform or pacification, ambitious schemes are proclaimed. When we call for elections, millions of people rush to the polls. This does demonstrate influence.

(2) But what about negative evidence? Among other negative data, we had to assassinate the dictator because he *would not* follow our advice. Land reform and pacification are chimeras; somebody goes through the motions, but little happens. When we call for elections, neutralists and pacifists are barred from running, and there are so many irregularities that 42.5 per cent of the *winners* believe themselves to have been elected by fraud. (**198**) Despite the optimistic front put up by the Johnson administration, this could not have been the kind of election we had in mind.

(3) Do the instances genuinely support the generalization? Perhaps a more appropriate label for our hold on South Viet-Nam is power, rather than influence. The ruling junta does what we say, in a fashion; they give lip service to our demands. But most of what has happened there is compatible with the contention that we do not really have influence, we merely have the strength to secure superficial compliance with certain requests. Perhaps the situation is really more like that of the Russians in Hungary in 1956.

(4) Does the generalization go beyond the supporting evidence? This question merges into the previous one: the evidence supports some statement about the American position in South Viet-Nam, but to say that it genuinely supports a contention that we have "influence" may be going too far.

Even this minor attempt to inspect an historical analogy has already led us to consider the position of another great power vis-à-vis one of its satellites. And if the experience of Russia in Hungary and other East European countries might be relevant, so might the experiences of Great Britain with her colonies, Rome with her empire, and so on. Thus analogical reasoning merges into straightforward generalization; an analogy is, in fact, a truncated generalization. We could consider the statement with which we began, "Aid results in increased Chinese influence in Hanoi," not just by a one-to-one analogy with American experience in South Viet-Nam, but by generalizing about the effects of giving aid in all known instances.

Analogies, when pressed, tend to expand into broader generalizations. An analogy is a comparison based on relevant similarities (see **164**:345), and few situations are without several relevant parallels. In the present case, the Peking-Hanoi relationship undoubtedly does have similarities to many other great power/small power relationships. And the statement that "aid results in increased Chinese influence in Hanoi" is a weak link in the argument we have been considering. Historical experience casts much doubt on the assumption that beneficiaries of bilateral aid have kindly feelings toward their benefactors, or grant them substantial influence. The whole argument may collapse on this single fallacy.

Along different lines, an elaborate analogy was recently used by *Consumer Reports* to further the argument that doctors should be periodically examined to force them to keep up with modern developments:

> The position of organized medicine has been, by and large, that quality control is almost exclusively the prerogative of the medical profession itself. As government and the public begin to oppose this point of view, there are some pained reactions. One official of the American Medical Association was recently (and typically) quoted as saying, "We don't want a bunch of commissars all over the country telling doctors what to do."
>
> No one, however, seriously wants to enslave the medical profession or strip it of its responsibilities. Members of the profession who nevertheless remain mistrustful might consider the regulation of another group deeply responsible for human lives: airplane pilots. If pilots were examined and licensed once, and then never re-examined; if continuing supervision were left to their own membership; if pilots trained in the era of the DC-3 were permitted to fly jets with no additional training; and if airliners and airports were not held to rigidly high standards of equipment, performance, and safety devices by an outside agency, it seems likely that far fewer people — including physicians — would be willing to take a chance on flying. (**47**:150)

As stated, this argument holds that since airline pilots are periodically reexamined because of their responsibility for human lives, doctors, who are also responsible for human lives, should be similarly reexamined. This is a one-to-one relationship. But notice that the characteristic of both these groups which warrants their comparison — responsibility for human lives — can be predicated of many other groups too. Military personnel handling dangerous weapons are responsible for human lives, and they are periodically reexamined, as are Atomic Energy Commission employees. Bus drivers are kept under continuous evaluation. In some states, even ordinary drivers are required to get regular examinations. One could generalize inductively that "Most occupations which involve responsibility for human lives require periodic examinations" and apply this to the case of doctors, who so far are exempt. The advantage of the analogy is that one is able to give more detail about each of two comparable situations than when one establishes a generalization and applies it to a new situation.

But even though one may be able to provide more detail in reasoning by analogy, it is vital to determine *which* details are relevant. In the analogy between doctors and airline pilots, one might claim that the only relevant consideration was degree of responsibility for human lives. Most historical analogies cannot be confined to such a narrow realm of relevant evidence.

When proponents of the American involvement in Viet-Nam invoke the analogy with Malaya to prove that we are achieving the goal of defeating the Viet-Cong, a wide realm of potentially relevant factors is apparent. Certain bench marks of British progress in suppressing the Malayan insurgency are perceived in Viet-Nam, and on the basis of these, the claim is made that we are winning. For instance, when the rural population provides intelligence against the enemy, when enemy desertions rise sharply, when the enemy develops shortages of food and lowered morale — any one of these occurrences can be cited as an index of victory, significant in the Malayan fighting, which has now also appeared in Viet-Nam.

Aside from the credibility of the evidence adduced to support these generalizations, there is a serious question as to *how many* relevant variables need to be taken into account. Perhaps the size of the enemy fighting force, the morale of our allies, the territory under enemy control, the ability of the enemy to penetrate our defenses, or the extent of outside assistance available to the enemy might be significant in deciding whether or not we are winning. When one compares the course of the wars in Malaya and Viet-Nam on all these dimensions, the analogy is difficult to establish.

Many historiographers, among them Garraghan (**70**:145), claim that analogy is used more often with invalid than with valid results. This charge may well be true. The inferential risk is great indeed when inferring that, since A, B, and C in Malaya were followed by victory, A′, B′, and C′ will be followed by victory in Viet-Nam. The formula for valid analogies is as difficult to carry out as it is easy to state: *are the two situations really comparable in all relevant variables?*

Evidence on a Capital Punishment Argument

One of the most durable policy arguments in the United States centers on capital punishment. Almost every year three or four states have a major legislative battle over the death penalty, and at least every three or four years some state abolishes or reinstates the penalty. As of 1968, thirteen of the fifty states had abolished capital punishment, the other thirty-seven retained it.

Probably the prime issue in the argument over the death penalty is its alleged deterrent effect on would-be criminals. The argument is developed as follows (stated as it would be in a death penalty jurisdiction):

Goal: We should have a penal code which prevents crime.
Position vis-à-vis this goal: The death penalty helps to prevent crime in this jurisdiction.
Prediction: Abolition of the death penalty will increase the crime rate.
Conclusion: Therefore we should not abolish the death penalty.

This argument is supported by every kind of reasoning. The positional statement is crucial, since there is general acceptance (by the public, but not necessarily by criminologists) of the goal, preventing crime. How do we know that the death penalty prevents crime? Among other evidence, we have the testimony of an eminent nineteenth-century British jurist, Sir James Fitzjames Stephen, who offers an ironclad inductive generalization covering the whole of human experience up to that century:

No other punishment deters men so effectually from committing crimes as the punishment of death. This is one of those propositions which it is difficult to prove, simply because they are in themselves more obvious than any proof can make them. It is possible to display ingenuity in arguing against it, but that is all. The whole experience of mankind is in the other direction. The threat of instant death is the one to which resort has always been made when there was an absolute necessity for producing some result. (**209**:753)

If one does not find this testimony convincing, there are refinements to the argument based on causal reasoning about two types of people: normal people and professional criminals. Normal people, though they may be sorely tried by life's tribulations and may contemplate murder at one or more times, are much too prudent to run the risk of capital punishment. Richard Gerstein, State Attorney of Dade County, Florida, said, "It is clear that for normal human beings no other punishment deters so effectively from committing murder as the punishment of death." (**72**:254) Normal people may not be entirely rational, but there is enough rationality in the average human being to cause him to restrain his impulses and reconsider his urges to kill. It is this process of contemplation which led the minority of the 1958 Massachusetts Commission to hold "that the death penalty threat is effective in preventing large numbers of wrongdoers from ever allowing themselves to reach that stage of criminality where they become victims of uncontrollable impulses. . . . It is in this early gray zone of murder premeditation that the death penalty threat is most apt to be operative and effective." (**146**:73)

Professional criminals are alleged to be even more sensitive to the existence of the death penalty than normal people since they have become familiar with the lesser punishment of prison, and it no longer has a deterrent effect of any consequence on them. But, say some experts, when life itself is involved, punishment becomes a matter of consequence. Sir Alexander Patterson, Director of British Prisons, testified to this effect in 1930: ". . . we who are in daily contact with professional criminals can safely say that with them the dread of the gallows is a strong deterrent. They have tasted prison and lost their fear of it. They may have misused their lives, but they are loath to lose them." (**79**:45)

The similar testimony of innumerable law enforcement officials and legislators backs up this assertion that the fear of death causes men to forego the act of murder in many instances. Not in all instances, certainly, or there would be no murders whatever where there was a possibility of capital punishment; but it would be effective in the vast majority of them. In fact, it is just this deterrent effect which cannot be adequately quantified. How can one know how many *potential* murders were prevented by fear of the death penalty? Judge Hyman Barshay of New York uses a figurative analogy to establish the point quite firmly:

> The death penalty is a warning just like a lighthouse throwing its beams out to sea. We hear about shipwrecks, but we do not hear about the ships the lighthouse guides safely on their way. We do not have proof of the number of ships it saves, but we do not tear the lighthouse down. (**72**)

This is only a small portion of the vast evidence supporting the deterrent effect of capital punishment. Inductive generalizations, causal explanations, analogies of all sorts support the positional statement. There is only one hitch to the argument: the primary particulars supporting the generalization that the death penalty prevents crime are fewer than those supporting the opposite generalization, that the death penalty *does not* prevent crime. The alleged causal connections between fear of death and law-abidingness cannot be proved: the analogies are faulty, and compelling statistics show the evidence to be inadequate.

For if one can compare the homicide rates in a number of states before and after the abolition of capital punishment; if one can compare the homicide rates in neighboring and sociologically similar states, some of which retain the death penalty and some of which do not; if one can plot the homicide rates before and after well-publicized executions — if these and other kinds of probative statistics are available, and if the story they tell is consistent and without exception over long periods of time, all the primary and particular evidence which goes into establishing the deterrence justification for capital punishment is undermined.

There are several elaborate and unexceptional studies relating homicide rates to the existence of the death penalty. They all tell the same story. Perhaps the most thorough study is that of Thorsten Sellin, Professor of Sociology at the University of Pennsylvania, who concludes, after reams of statistics:

> In preceding pages, one of the aspects of this issue has been considered, namely, the question of whether or not the death penalty appears to have any effect on homicide death rates. We have examined comparatively such rates in selected states that do and those that do not have the death penalty; we have compared the rates of capital crimes in specific states or countries that have experimented with abolition in order to observe the effect of the abolition or the introduction of capital punishment on such rates; we have noted the specific effect of highly publicized executions on homicides in a metropolitan city; and we have tried to learn if the claim of the police is true, when they say that their lives are safer in states that have the death penalty. Anyone who carefully examines the above data is bound to arrive at the conclusion that the death penalty, as we use it, exercises no influence on the extent or fluctuating rates of capital crimes. It has failed as a deterrent. If it has utilitarian value, it must rest in some other attribute than its power to influence the future conduct of people. (**197**:63)

One should, of course, examine Sellin's statistics and inferences for one-self. (We have. He is scrupulously correct.) One should also search for contradictory statistics put out by the supporters of capital punishment. (We find none.)

Where, then, does the evidence for the argument for deterrence fall down? In the first place, a plausible causal analysis may fail simply because the causal factors are not all known, or, indeed, even knowable. As Richard C. Snyder and colleagues state in their influential *Foreign Policy Decision Making*, "Simple notions of causality are no longer acceptable." (**205**:36) The notion of fear of death overriding all other emotions in one contemplating murder is too simple. There are other factors of equal or greater importance. As the Massachusetts Commission concluded, after studying the sociological evidence intensively, a person under great stress will not consider or not care about the consequences of his acts. (**146**)

In the second place, the homely lighthouse analogy does not apply to capital punishment, and it is false to begin with. One may not *hear* of the ships that pass safely, but one can count them in port authority records. The deterrent effect of capital punishment may be measured in the records, too: when Maine abolished the penalty, for example, the recorded homicide rate in that state simply did not go up.

Thus, in supporting (or attacking) the positional statement that the death penalty deters crime, causal explanation and analogy must yield to the inductive generalization produced by massive statistical analysis.

Summary

Positional statements are judgments about the present; they locate us in relation to a certain goal. The reasoning necessary to establish them is inductive or evidential. Such positional statements can never be certain, and they frequently involve considerable inferential risk.

There are three important ways of supporting positional statements. The first is descriptive generalization, where specific historical instances of a phenomenon are assembled without any claim to know why the phenomena function as they do. A positional statement of this sort would be "North Viet-Nam is accepting aid from China." In construct-ing or criticizing such a generalization, one must ask:

(1) Do we have enough evidence to support the generalization?

(2) Is there negative evidence which might qualify or destroy the generalization?

(3) Does the evidence directly support the generalization, or is it only tangentially relevant?

(4) Does the generalization go beyond the supporting evidence?

When the number of instances is large, the process of generalizing merges into statistics.

A second way of supporting a positional statement is with a causal explanation, where one claims to know why things happen as they do. The concept of cause is now recognized as extremely complicated. A causal statement would be one such as "The Vietnamese fear China because of the past Chinese invasions of Viet-Nam." About such a claim, one must ask:

(1) Are there enough instances of the alleged cause at work?

(2) Are the causal instances representative of the relevant phenomena?

(3) Are there contrary causes at work which nullify the claimed cause?

(4) Does the alleged cause really account for the phenomena?

The third way is by historical analogy, where two phenomena are alleged to be comparable in one unknown variable since they are comparable in several known variables. Thus one might make the statement "We are winning the war in Viet-Nam because the villagers are beginning to inform on the Communists, and this was the turning-point in Malaya." Analogy is frequently used and often valid, but it has great dangers; it is rarely possible to know that two situations are really comparable in all relevant variables. All types of positional statement require evidential support; they cannot be derived deductively from universal premises.

SUGGESTED READINGS

Gilbert J. Garraghan, *A Guide to Historical Method.* New York: Fordham University Press, 1946, Chapter Seven.

Louis Gottschalk, *Understanding History.* New York: Alfred A. Knopf, 1951, Chapters Ten and Eleven.

H. L. A. Hart and A. H. Honoré, *Causation in the Law.* Oxford: Oxford University Press, 1959, Chapter One.

Allan Nevins, *The Gateway to History*. Garden City: Doubleday (Anchor Book), 1962, Chapter Eight.

Alan Nichols, *Discussion and Debate*. New York: Harcourt, Brace, 1941, Part Three, Chapter Three.

Nicholas Rescher, "A Theory of Evidence," *Philosophy of Science*, XXV (January, 1958), 83–94.

Nicholas Rescher and Carey B. Joynt, "Evidence in History and in the Law," *The Journal of Philosophy*, LVI (June, 1959), 561–578.

3

Supporting Predictions

*Any decision we are now taking, any action we are now
undertaking, can bear results only in the future, be it immediate or distant: therefore any conscious activity of
necessity implies "looking forward"; and it is a telling
image, that of Lot's wife who, as she only looks back,
turns to stone.*

BERTRAND DE JOUVENEL (**104**:ix)

The Place of Prediction in Deliberation

Evidence has an important place in supporting goals, and it is indispensable in evaluating whether we are reaching them; but the greatest
cash value of evidence in deliberation is its use in predicting the consequences of present or proposed policies. To give a good reason for
adopting a certain policy involves providing evidence that the policy
will have desirable consequences, that it will gain more than it costs.

Most of the pressure points of deliberation are in predictions of consequences. The furious onslaught of the American Medical Association
against first Blue Cross/Blue Shield and later various medicare proposals
was based on predicted consequences of such "socialistic" measures:
the doctor-patient relationship would be destroyed, there would be fewer

33

recruits into the profession, the quality of medical care would deteriorate, and so forth. Only when these predictions ceased to frighten legislators and public health officials were forward-looking health insurance measures adopted.

In the economic area, prediction has become an important specialized activity; it is vital for a government to know what the probable effect of a tax increase or a change in the legal rate of interest will be. We argue that the Federal Government should reduce excise taxes because this will stimulate business; when stimulation has gone too far, we support an increase in taxes in order to cool off the economy. Economic predictions, as de Jouvenel notes (**103**), are much easier to make than political predictions.

But of the importance of political predictions there can be no doubt. When McGeorge Bundy, stung by Hans Morgenthau's charge that the government Bundy represented was psychotic about Viet-Nam, set out to challenge Morgenthau's credibility, he did so by attacking Morgenthau's predictive record: Morgenthau had been wrong about what would happen in Laos, he had been wrong about the effect of the Marshall Plan, and in predicting that the United States would not win a military victory in Viet-Nam he was simply giving vent to his congenital pessimism. Bundy saw Morgenthau's poor predictions as the major flaw in his factual armament and the major reason for not crediting his prediction about Viet-Nam.*

Again, Secretary of Defense McNamara, when he was challenged by Senator Ribicoff to defend the credibility of the Administration in 1966, first minimized, then acknowledged, the significance of prediction in the following interesting comment:

> Now I differentiate reports of events on the one hand from predictions or forecasts or hopes for the future on the other. I think we are only human and when we comment upon the future we are bound to comment within the limitations of a human being's ability to anticipate the future. Many of us have been wrong in making such comments in the past and many of us will be wrong in the future but I think the people have a right to expect from us comments on the future because it is only in recognition of the possible effects on the future of alternative courses of action that they can properly choose between alternatives. (**221**:202)

* On the CBS News Special Report, "Vietnam Dialogue: Mr. Bundy and the Professors," June 21, 1965. (For a somewhat biased analysis of this confrontation see **162**.)

In short, the prediction stage is the payoff stage in deliberation. A reason for doing something is no stronger than the probability that that action will accomplish what it is intended to accomplish. Predicting the consequences of a policy involves the same processes as evaluating the accomplishments of the status quo. The arena in which predictive reasoning takes place is more treacherous, though, as there are no facts about the future and extrapolation is inherently dangerous. But the bases for extrapolation are historical facts, which we can learn only by inspecting the best evidence. That evidence, as with positional statements, can be organized into descriptive generalizations, causal explanations, and analogies.

Prediction Based on Descriptive Generalization

Let us inspect again the most prominent argument offered by defenders of capital punishment:

Goal: We should have a penal code which prevents crime.
Position vis-à-vis this goal: The death penalty helps to prevent crime in this jurisdiction.
Prediction: Abolition of the death penalty will increase the crime rate.
Conclusion: Therefore we should not abolish the death penalty.

The same statistics which undermine the positional statement in this argument undermine the prediction also. Enough jurisdictions have abolished the death penalty without an increase in the homicide rate so that we can confidently predict that when Pennsylvania does so, the homicide rate will not be affected. This kind of prediction offers little challenge, since the base of the descriptive generalization on which it depends is extremely broad and the number of cases sufficient to insure reliability. Would that all the predictions necessary in deliberation were equally simple.

Predicting what China would do if the United States were to invade North Viet-Nam, destroy Hanoi, or blockade Haiphong is at the opposite end of the spectrum of difficulty. One could, of course, construct a descriptive generalization based on Chinese behavior in similar instances; but the number of instances would be so small that the generalization would be all but worthless. One would be forced to reason primarily by analogy, using Chinese behavior in Korea as the most likely indicator of what she would do in Viet-Nam.

One subject vital to the future of the world is prediction of population trends. One might think, because of the vast accumulations of data about population trends, that prediction could be almost foolproof, and that causal factors could be discerned which would allow prediction on the basis of causal explanation. It is unfortunately not that easy. We know *some* of the causes of increases in population: lowered death rates because of improved medical care, for instance. But birth rates also must be taken into account, as well as all kinds of psychological and social pressures. Since many of these factors defy adequate causal explanation, we must depend in attempting to predict population trends on extrapolation of past trends. These vary from region to region; a trend discernible in Sub-Saharan Africa will be quite different from a trend in industrial Europe; a trend in Japan will vary from a trend in Indonesia. Sometimes population trends go into reverse. Because of the myriad factors affecting population, prediction is hazardous; but it is nonetheless indispensable to anyone deliberating about birth control, resources which must be devoted to agriculture, and similar demographic topics.

Trend analysis is a variant of descriptive generalization which applies to many deliberative enterprises. Much of the structure of international economic relations is based on the prediction that developmental patterns in the industrialized nations will appear also in the underdeveloped nations. Economic advisors and trade commissions alike assume that specialization is the wave of the future, that in the developing countries planning will be separated from operations, production from distribution, purchasing from personnel, and so forth. (12:862) As the newly-independent nations begin to catch up with the twentieth century, many of the basic functions (education, recreation, production, welfare) that are concentrated in family and tribal units will be handled by specialized agencies. This is the assumption behind Rostow's *Stages of Economic Growth* (184) and similar predictive enterprises; but it is an assumption which needs to be critically inspected rather than taken for granted.

One of the most significant issues for American foreign policy is whether by intervention we can prevent insurgencies and social revolutions from "going Communist." The prediction of results of any proposed intervention is the most desperately important aspect of the deliberation which precedes decision. Herbert Dinerstein, in his book *Intervention Against Communism*, focuses on just this predictive problem, and concludes:

A striking generalization that emerges is that in the one case of un-
equivocally successful intervention (Greece), the Communists occupied
the antinational position. After all, it was they who wanted to turn over
Greek Macedonia to Yugoslavia. The conclusion seems fairly obvious
that intervention against communism has the poorest chance of success
if the Commuists can associate with the national cause. **(46:52)**

But even Dinerstein's generalization is now suspect. He wrote before
the right-wing coup in Greece in 1967, and it is no longer clear that the
American intervention of 1946 did in fact "save" Greece for democracy.
It may be that any intervention, even on the "nationalist" side, is counterproductive. But even this predictive generalization must be qualified to
apply only to underdeveloped countries; it is hard to see how the
Marshall Plan, which was also an intervention of an economic sort, was
unsuccessful.

Descriptive generalizations which predict the consequences of actions
must undergo the same searching questions proposed for generalizations
evaluating the present. A generalization can hold only

(1) if there is enough evidence to support the generalization,

(2) if there is no negative evidence which might qualify or destroy
the generalization,

(3) if the evidence directly supports the generalization, and

(4) if the generalization does not in any way go beyond the evidence.

Prediction Based on Causal Explanation

When predicting on the basis of causal analysis, one claims to know
why things behave as they do and projects past phenomena into the
future. One of the causal factors which sometimes supports successful
predictions is ideology. Hitler, for instance, in *Mein Kampf*, set forth
an ideological action code which was followed extensively by the Third
Reich. Few except his own countrymen believed he would really pursue
the policies he laid down in *Mein Kampf*, but those who took the message
at face value, and assumed that the ideology it contained would govern
Nazi action, had a sound basis for prediction.

Lenin, Stalin, and Mao have also provided an extended series of ideological writings which offer considerable guidance in predicting Commu-

nist actions, if due attention is paid to changes in the bloc power structure. The pioneering work on Communist programs was the RAND monograph by Nathan Leites, *The Operational Code of the Politburo*. (**128**) After sixteen years, this document can still be used as an aid in predicting what Ho Chi Minh will do.

Ideological analysis has been responsible for some significant successes in prediction. It was primarily on the basis of an evaluation of the series of articles "On Leninism" carried in the Peking press that Robert S. Elegant scooped the world of Sinologues in predicting the development of the Sino-Soviet split. (**55**) Other scholars and writers hedged and qualified: the Russian need for a strong ally in Asia, the Chinese need for Russian supplies and technological aid, the necessity for maintaining a common front against the capitalists all prevailed to induce caution among commentators in dealing with the developing Sino-Soviet rupture. Even that otherwise perceptive work, *Recognition of Communist China?* (**161**:229) tended to side with the cautious in rejecting the probability of a serious split. We were wrong, Elegant was right. He was right on the basis of an ideology which absolutely governed the Chinese operational code and allowed accurate prediction based on ideological causes.

One of the most vital predictive exercises in recent United States Government deliberation was that which estimated the results of bombing North Viet-Nam. The bombing strategy was justified on several grounds at various times: it would cut off infiltration from the North, it would prevent supplies going south, it would bolster sagging Saigon morale, and so forth. Some of the predictions panned out, others did not. But the most amazing argument for bombing the North went something like this:

> *Goal:* The United States should destroy the battle-readiness and morale of North Viet-Nam.
> *Position vis-à-vis this goal:* As a privileged sanctuary, North Viet-Nam now enjoys high morale and battle-readiness.
> *Prediction:* Bombing will destroy this morale and force Hanoi to seek peace.
> *Conclusion:* Therefore we should bomb North Viet-Nam.

This variant of the privileged-sanctuary argument was made by innumerable military and political experts. It depends on a causal analysis: bombing destroys the morale and will to resist of those on the receiving end. But close inspection of this prediction immediately exposes its fallibility. In searching for evidence to support the contention that bombing causes poor morale among the recipients, one first thinks of the use of nuclear weapons against Hiroshima and Nagasaki in World War II. These two bombs did seem to have a detrimental effect on Japanese will to resist. But this instance cannot be relied on too heavily, since the disposition to seek peace was already well advanced in Japan at the time the nuclear weapons were used, and it was not proposed to use nuclear weapons against Hanoi. Having considered this instance, one is hard put to find other support for the causal efficacy on morale of bombing. Hitler's strategic bombing of London was counterproductive: it made the British more determined to resist than ever. The official United States Strategic Bombing Survey in Germany after World War II indicated that too had misfired: it made German morale stronger than ever. (226) Moving to Korea, there is very little evidence that bombing contributed to the overwhelming success of MacArthur's forces in achieving a stalemate. In short, *the causal efficacy on morale of bombing simply cannot be established.* (See 237:24 ff.)

But this is only the beginning of the attempt to criticize this particular prediction. Even if, in certain circumstances, we could believe that bombing had adversely affected morale, there is still the question of the specific circumstances in North Viet-Nam. Forces were at work which clearly tended to offset the demoralizing effect of bombing. Ralph White, in *Misperception and the Viet-Nam War*, analyzed one of them: the "virile self-image" of the North Vietnamese which had been hardened by the bombing. In fact, there is evidence that the bombing strengthened morale and the will to resist. (235:52)

Those who made the bombing prediction simply had not done their homework. It is not even clear that the affable General LeMay, who wanted to bomb Hanoi back to the Stone Age, had fully weighed the evidence as to probable effects of such an activity, not only on the world at large but on Viet-Nam in particular.

Causal explanation, where intelligently carried out, can provide the basis for successful prediction of the consequences of an action. It requires attention to the same basic questions posed in the previous chapter:

(1) Are there enough instances of the alleged cause at work?

(2) Do the causal instances represent the relevant phenomena?

(3) Are there contrary causes at work which nullify the claimed cause?

(4) Does the alleged cause really account for the phenomena?

Prediction Based on Analogy

The simplest predictive method at first glance appears to be the analogy. Since A happened, A' will happen also — the circumstances are similar. It was partially on the basis of historical analogy that Senator Fulbright constructed his accurate prediction opposing the Bay of Pigs invasion. He pointed out the failure of our "cover" in the Castillo-Armas invasion of Guatemala in 1954, compared that adventure with the more difficult and elaborate Bay of Pigs project, and concluded that it would be difficult if not impossible to conceal the United States' hand. (**239**:43)

In deliberation about the type of narcotics control measures the United States should adopt, the analogy with British measures is extremely important. Their rate of addiction is very low; can't we achieve the same with the same program? Perhaps, if conditions are the same. But what conditions are relevant? Affluence? Racial composition of addict groups? Rural or urban addiction? Presence of an underworld narcotics distribution system? Mores? Mental health of the population in general? There is no formula to help one decide which historical facts, among the infinite number available about each of two potentially analogous situations, are vital to a prediction. For each variable one must ask, "Does this seem likely to affect the outcome under investigation?"

When one is attempting to predict the outcome of American efforts to defeat the Viet-Cong, for instance, one must consider the analogy with French efforts a decade ago to defeat the Viet-Minh. All the similarities and differences between the situation of the French in the 1950's and the Americans in the 1960's must be inspected. Many factors will support the conclusion that the two cases are similar, and that since the French lost, the Americans will too. Other factors will support the conclusion that the Americans have a better chance than the French did. Still other factors are irrelevant to a prediction.

The factor of race — that in both cases Caucasian armies are fighting an Asian people on Asian soil — is probative *for* the prediction that the Americans will suffer the same fate as the French. The factor of effective supply — the United States being able to produce more materiel at the battle sites — is probative *against* the analogy. The factor of language

— that the French speak French while the Americans speak English — probably is irrelevant. And so on. Making an analogy stick — or tearing one down — requires 99 per cent perspiration and 1 per cent inspiration. Deliberation on disarmament inevitably leads to the use of elaborate historical analogies, one of which attempts to predict the future course of Red China. Some argue that until the United States recognizes China and allows her to participate in world councils there is no prospect of effective disarmament. This argument might be put as follows:

> *Goal:* The United States should support all reasonable attempts to secure disarmament.
>
> *Position vis-à-vis this goal:* Our nonrecognition of China and our insistence that she be excluded from international conferences frustrate the possibility of disarmament.
>
> *Prediction:* Recognition would promote disarmament by bringing China into the negotiations.
>
> *Conclusion:* The United States should recognize China.

The first two stages of this argument can be passed by. Except for minor groups, disarmament is held to be a defensible goal; and the sheer mechanical exclusion of China from international negotiations does frustrate the possibility of genuine disarmament. But the prediction step is another story. It is not at all clear that bringing China into international negotiations would promote the prospects of disarmament. Is China not so rabidly aggressive and belligerent, perhaps, that she would be against disarmament even if included in negotiations?

One might grapple with this problem in many ways. Chinese ideology might be inspected, to show that while Peking approves of so-called wars of national liberation, she does not support a general war against her opponents and hence might approve of some measure of disarmament. A generalization about Chinese behavior based on her relations with neighboring states might be constructed, revealing that, propaganda to the contrary, actual Chinese behavior has been moderate and restrained — compatible with an approach to disarmament.

But the most plausible effort to substantiate the prediction that incorporation of China in disarmament negotiations would be fruitful lies in historical analogy — an extended comparison between the development of Russian Communism and the probable development of Chinese Communism. The focus of this analogy will be on the long-range future: to what extent China, like Russia, will grow out of her evangelistic revolu-

tionary fervor and develop a vested interest in peace and security. It is
the future of China, rather than the present, which assumes importance
in this analogy.

The historical facts on which this reasoning is based are those setting
forth Russia's development in internal stability and international cooper-
ativeness. In the early years of the Bolshevik Revolution, the insecurity
of the regime, caused to some extent by American, British, and French
invasions of Russia in an attempt to overthrow the Bolsheviks, led to
unbridled suspicion of capitalist states and to refusal to conceive of a
world in which Communist and non-Communist states could live amica-
bly side by side. The only conceivable security for the early Bolsheviks
lay in promoting revolution in all existing capitalist states, thus subvert-
ing their enemies and establishing nonthreatening regimes.

This fear on the part of Russia has now abated. The eventual withdrawal of foreign expeditionary forces from Russian soil, the diplomatic
recognition of the Soviet Government by most powers, even by the
United States in 1933, and the steady rise in the Russian standard of
living have changed the outlook of Russian foreign policy to the extent
that its revolutionary aims seem to be confined to "burying the West"
by economic and scientific competition. Russia's relations with her
neighbors, aside from the cushion of satellite states, are relatively pacific. Russia agreed to (and has scrupulously carried out) a peace treaty
for Austria, she plays a major though sometimes recalcitrant role in the
United Nations, and her behavior over Viet-Nam, where an ally is being
pummelled by the United States, is mild indeed. All this is not to say
that Russia is an ideal international citizen. Instances like the Cuban
missile crisis indicate that Russia is just as eager to have bases near
the United States as we are to have them in Turkey, Greece, and elsewhere. But the direction of Russian evolution is clear.

To what extent can China be compared with Russia? One could contend that China will in all probability follow the same developmental
path, provided she is recognized and enabled to achieve the same internal
stability and international respect which Russia has achieved. Clearly
the development in Russian attitudes would have been impossible had
she been indefinitely ostracized and isolated as we have attempted to
ostracize and isolate China. There is no reason to believe that Communist ideology is any more enduring in China than in Russia; revisionism
will follow Mao's passing from the scene just as it followed the death of
Stalin in Russia. The invasion trauma which determined early Russian

policy will largely disappear in China once the United States gives up its fatuous claim that Chiang Kai-shek is the rightful ruler of China. All successful revolutions settle down, despite such temporary aberrations as the Stalinist purges and the Red Guard movement; they become institutionalized and acquire stability. China will follow this path also. Therefore, recognition of China and inclusion of Peking in disarmament negotiations will ultimately promote disarmament.

Such reasoning from the past of Russia to the future of China is not easy to validate or criticize. There are no standard tests for analogical validity. It is banal to observe that the similarities in the two countries must outweigh the differences, or that the two countries must be analogous on all relevant points. The crucial item is precisely "What are the relevant variables?" There appear to be similarities in revolutionary origin, early insecurity of the regime, initial rejection by the family of nations, ideological character of the regime, growth of economic strength at tremendous humanitarian cost. But is the analogy disqualified by the Chinese belief that they have a purer form of Communism than the Russians? Is the greater chauvinism of the Chinese significant? Has the more prolonged American opposition to accepting China in the family of nations exacerbated her belligerence beyond repair? When the difficulties in making such an analogical judgment are laid bare, one is tempted to observe that only God would claim to have an answer.

Evidence on a Disengagement Argument

One of the major and still unresolved dilemmas of American foreign policy has to do with the question of German unity and the deployment of forces in Central Europe. George F. Kennan, the most articulate spokesman for a policy of containment of Soviet Russia in the 1940 decade,* came to feel, ten years later, that times had changed enough to warrant a new policy. He has come to be known not only as the author of containment but also of disengagement, the mutual withdrawal of the United States and Russia from Central Europe. One of the reasons Mr. Kennan feels we need a policy of disengagement might be outlined this way:

> *Goal:* The nations of Central Europe should be enabled to achieve independence of their present Russian masters.

* We are aware that Kennan's initial idea of containment differed substantially from the basically military policy which NATO adopted.

> *Position vis-à-vis this goal:* The presence of Russian troops in these na-
> tions prevents any real independence.
> *Prediction:* Disengagement would remove Russian troops and permit
> independent development.
> *Conclusion:* Therefore the United States should negotiate with Russia
> for a mutual withdrawal from Central Europe.

The uses of evidence in supporting this argument illustrate well the
predictive mechanisms we have dealt with in this chapter. Here again,
the pressure point is the prediction. The goal is rationally defensible,
even for Marxists, and certainly in the United States there is much support for freeing the satellite nations of Russian control. The positional
statement is also noncontroversial; Russian troops are as inhibiting in
East Germany as were Nazi troops in France. But the prediction is
where Kennan's argument has drawn much flak. Suppose both Russian
and American troops were withdrawn. Because Russia borders Central
Europe, she would retain a certain amount of control: it would be easy
for her to return rapidly and in depth, and the nations she borders would
be influenced by this knowledge. The United States, once out of Central
Europe, would have great difficulty returning. Two questions therefore
present themselves: (1) Will the Soviets honor a pledge of disengagement, or will they use the first pretext to return as occupiers? (2) Will
the proximity of the Soviet, and the pressures it can exert on its neighbors, be enough to inhibit or frustrate the drive for independence even in
the technical absence of Soviet troops?

(1) Will the Soviet honor a disengagement agreement? Once American forces have left Germany and are no nearer to Central Europe than
Britain, Spain, Italy, or wherever the treaty stipulates, will Russia not
feel wholly free to violate its own part of the bargain? There is, of
course, much talk of Russian violation of treaties. The operational code
by which Russia functioned twenty years ago would no doubt have made
her feel free to take any possible advantage of her neighbors. But times
have changed. Current Soviet behavior is strong evidence to support
a prediction that Russia would honor disengagement.

(2) Will the pressures which the Soviet can exert on its neighbors
stifle independent development of the (former) satellites? Here opponents of disengagement have made much of an analogy. Kennan states
this argument of those favoring continued American occupation of
Berlin and West Germany as follows:

They see Soviet forces accomplishing with ease, in the space of a few hours (12 to 18, if we accept Mr. Dean Acheson's figure), the re-passage of the area from which they might have been withdrawn. . . . From this, they argue that the political effects of a Soviet withdrawal would also be unsubstantial; the continued proximity of Soviet armed forces and the attendant fear of their imminent return would paralyze independent policy in the Eastern European countries. . . . In the shaping of this view, the experience of Hungary seems to have played a prominent part. (**105**:192)

The crucial question in this analogy is not whether Russia would in fact reinvade a country, but rather whether fear of such an event would paralyze movement toward independence. As support for the belief that such a fear would operate, opponents of disengagement point to Hungary and say, "See what happens when Russian displeasure is aroused. All the former satellites will be affected by this incident even if they were technically free of Russian troops."

But this is a faulty analysis. Hungary was at no time free of Russian troops. They were in Hungary (though not, for a period, in Budapest itself) on a treaty basis. This incident, therefore, is not analogous with conditions which would prevail if Russian troops were completely withdrawn from the satellites, so it could not serve as a deterrent to the development of independence in the event of disengagement. The true significance of the Hungarian revolt, as of the other East European incidents, is that it could occur despite the presence of the Russian troops. In this argument, the attempted projection of an historical analogy fails because significant factors in the proposed course of action are not similar to those of the instance invoked.

Having destroyed the Hungarian analogy as irrelevant to the probable consequences of disengagement, Kennan goes on to construct a descriptive generalization about the behavior of various nations of Europe which might well serve as a model of such generalizations:

It is all very well to say that these countries, appalled at the thought of the proximity of Soviet power, and at the absence of American forces from Germany, would fall over themselves to discover Soviet pleasure and make themselves the instruments of it, whether Russia actually re-invaded them or not. But experience simply fails to bear this out. The Finns have existed for years in a state of complete vulnerability to Soviet power and without the faintest reason to expect that anyone in the West would come to their assistance if the Russians put real pressure on them. This has not prevented them from leading an acceptable national existence and from cultivating institutions and practices wholly different from those of the Soviet Union. The Jugoslavs did not ask whether they had Atlantic Pact support when they made their break with Moscow. If the Poles have shown confidence and imagination in developing their own "path to socialism," a path which, again, departs materially from the Soviet example, it is certainly not an American guarantee which has given them this courage. The Turks did not wait for the formation of the North Atlantic Alliance before showing stoutness in the face of Soviet demands. In vain one seeks, in the Austrian scene, the evidence of that panicky running-for-cover before internal Communist pressures which critics of the concept of disengagement have portrayed as the inevitable result of leaving parts of Europe without the protection of American garrisons or of membership in NATO. (**105**:194)

Solid as this evidential reasoning ·is, it still must be inspected closely. There would seem to be enough instances, but there may also be contrary ones. And one needs to decide whether the evidence directly and adequately supports the generalization. Kennan's claim we have phrased as "Disengagement would remove Russian troops and permit independent development." This is not an extreme claim. Kennan does not predict that these nations will start a stampede toward alliance with the West, nor does he predict that they will cease to be "Communist." His evidence does support the belief that removal of Russian troops would "permit" independent development, and perhaps even a bit more. In fact, his very understatement and caution in generalizing mark Mr. Kennan as highly credible.

And, in 1968, the Czech program of liberalization, instituted in the absence of Russian troops, clearly validates his earlier prediction. One can only wish that a negotiated disengagement had been in effect, in order to test his hypothesis that Russia would respect it.

Even though we have used the question of disengagement to illustrate how evidence can support and challenge predictions, we do not offer the discussion as complete or up to date. The sporadic progress of the European Economic Community, the eccentricities of Charles deGaulle, and the changes within Central and Eastern Europe all complicate the problem of great power confrontation. But the principles of evidential reasoning used to substantiate Kennan's argument hold good though the data change. To bring the argument up to date would simply require more of the same.

The Importance of Expertise in Prediction

As we have indicated many times, the most serious problem in using evidence is deciding what evidence is *relevant* to a specific generalization, explanation, or analogy. In a descriptive generalization such as that of Kennan, cited above, much is made of the Yugoslav opposition to Soviet power, but nothing is said of Sweden, a small and nearby country scrupulously neutral, which has shown not the slightest sign of fear of Russia. Why the emphasis on one and the disregard of the other? In a causal explanation such as that which purports to predict the effects of bombing on North Viet-Nam, one has to decide whether the effects of nuclear bombing on Japan are relevant to one's reasoning about Hanoi, or whether they should be discarded as irrelevant. In an attempt to construct an analogical prediction about the effects of a possible United States intervention in Haiti or Panama, one has to decide what factors in previous interventions in Cuba, Guatemala, Mexico, the Dominican Republic, and others are relevant to the projected action and which are irrelevant.

The problem is of great practical import. In the latter half of 1941, it became increasingly likely that Japan would at some time launch an attack on the United States. Policy makers needed above all else to be able to predict the probable time and place of the attack. Again, in 1962, evidence began to accumulate that something extraordinary was taking place in Cuba. What this something was, and what it indicated for the future, was a matter of paramount importance to Washington officials. And yet the predictive mechanism available to the government left something to be desired in both instances, *precisely because of the problem of relevance.* The difficulties are set forth clearly in Roberta Wohlstetter's article, "Cuba and Pearl Harbor: Hindsight and Foresight":

> It is true for both Pearl Harbor and Cuba that we had lots of information about the approaching crisis. In discussing this information it will perhaps be useful to distinguish again between signals and noise. By the "signal" of an action is meant a sign, a clue, a piece of evidence that points to the action or to an adversary's intention to undertake it, and by "noise" is meant the background of irrelevant or inconsistent signals,

signs pointing in the wrong direction, that tend always to obscure the signs pointing the right way. Pearl Harbor, looked at closely and objectively, shows how hard it is to hear a signal against the prevailing noise, in particular when you are listening for the wrong signal, and even when you have a wealth of information. (Or perhaps especially then. There are clearly cases when riches can be embarrassing.) **(240**:691)

In the terminology of political science, relevant evidence is a signal; irrelevant evidence is noise. The problem of determining which is which is as acute for government decision makers as for Monday morning deliberators on policy matters. How, indeed, does one determine relevance?

We can give only a partial answer, and at that an oblique one. A determination of relevance can be made, if at all, only by an "expert," by one who has steeped himself in all the evidence potentially relevant to a prediction and has processed it and assimilated it to the specific predictive problem. The expert can function adequately only when his perspective is not colored by bias or interest — only when he is as objective as humanly possible. This doctrine of the dependence of prediction on expertise is most clearly dealt with in a RAND Corporation monograph by Olaf Helmer and Nicholas Rescher, entitled *On the Epistemology of the Inexact Sciences.* We cite it at length both because its insights are central to our subsequent development of principles of credibility and because it presents important doctrines rarely considered by logicians and rhetoricians:

> . . . a knowledge about past instances or about statistical samples — while indeed providing valuable information — is not the sole and sometimes not even the main form of evidence in support of rational assignment of probability values. In fact the evidential use of *prima facie* evidence must be tempered by reference to background information, which frequently may be intuitive in character and have the form of a vague recognition of underlying regularities, such as analogies, correlations, or other conformities . . . . This non-explicitness of background knowledge, which nonetheless may be significant or even predominantly important, is typical of the inexact sciences, as is the uncertainty as to the evidential weight to be accorded various pieces of *prima facie* evidence provided by underlying regularities. Hence the great importance which must be attached to experts and expertise in these fields. For the expert has at his ready disposal a large store of (mostly inarticulated) background knowledge and a refined sensitivity to its relevance, through the intuitive application of which he is often able to produce trustworthy personal probabilities regarding hypotheses in his area of expertness.

The important place of expert judgment for predictions in the inexact sciences is further indicated by the prominence of quasi-laws among the explanatory instrumentalities of this domain. Since the conditions of applicability of such generalizations are neither fully nor explicitly formulable, their use in specific circumstances presupposes the exercise of sound judgment as to their applicability to the case in hand. The informed expert, with his resources of background knowledge and his cultivated sense of the relevance and bearing of generalities in particular cases, is best able to carry out the application of quasi-laws necessary for reasoned prediction in this field. (**87**:30–31)

The significance of the Helmer-Rescher doctrine of the importance of expertise for prediction should be immediately apparent. It reinforces at a theoretical level the commonsense observation that the data necessary to a successful prediction may never be completely articulable, and that in the vital matter of determining relevance of explicit evidence, even the most knowledgeable expert must be guided by intuition. Far from increasing the subjectivity of the analysis of evidential reasoning, however, this doctrine merely shifts the focus. We must indeed, according to this doctrine, bow to expertise — but when the experts disagree, we must examine minutely their predictive records and the potential biases which might deflect their thinking.

The cash value of the Helmer-Rescher doctrine is this: prediction often involves evidence which cannot, despite our best efforts, be made explicit, and it often involves generalizations which are inarticulable. The critic of evidence must therefore go *behind* the articulated grounds of a prediction to analyze the reliability of the *predictor*. How this can be done is the subject of Part Two of this book.

SUMMARY

Predictions represent the payoff stage of deliberation; we approve or disapprove a specific policy because of its anticipated consequences. Predicting that a policy will have or will not have certain results may be more hazardous than making positional statements, but it involves the same kinds of evidential reasoning. Descriptive generalizations, causal explanations, and historical analogies are vehicles by which evidence can be brought to bear on the future. The tests for adequate use of these methods in prediction are the same as those given in the previous chapter. In prediction, however, the difficulties of determining what evidence is relevant are heightened. According to the epistemological doctrine of Helmer and Rescher, policy predictions usually involve inarticulable evidence and imprecise generalizations which call for intuitive evaluation, and this only an expert can do. How one evaluates expertise therefore becomes a major concern of the student of evidence.

SUGGESTED READINGS

Daniel Bell, "Twelve Modes of Prediction," *Daedalus*, XCIII (Summer, 1964), 845–880.

Irwin D. J. Bross, *Design for Decision.* New York: Macmillan, 1953, Chapter Three.

Olaf Helmer and Nicholas Rescher, *On the Epistemology of the Inexact Sciences.* Santa Monica: RAND Corporation, 1958.

Bertrand de Jouvenel, *The Art of Conjecture.* New York: Basic Books, 1967.

George F. Kennan, "Disengagement Revisited," *Foreign Affairs*, XXXVII (January, 1959), 187–210.

Nathan Leites, *The Operational Code of the Politburo.* New York: McGraw-Hill, 1951.

Robert P. Newman, "The Spectacular Irrelevance of Mr. Bundy," *Today's Speech*, XIII (September, 1965), 30–34.

Benno Wasserman, "The Failure of Intelligence Prediction," *Political Studies*, VIII (1960), 156–169.

The Credibility
of Evidence

PART TWO

4

Conditions Affecting Credibility

The first rule for understanding the human condition is that men live in second-hand worlds. They are aware of much more than they have personally experienced; and their own experience is always indirect. The quality of their lives is determined by meanings they have received from others. Everyone lives in a world of such meanings. No man stands alone directly confronting a world of solid fact. No such world is available. The closest men come to it is when they are infants or when they become insane: then, in a terrifying scene of meaningless events and senseless confusion, they are often seized with the panic of near-total insecurity. But in their everyday life they do not experience a world of solid fact; their experience itself is selected by stereotyped meanings and shaped by ready-made interpretations. Their images of the world, and of themselves, are given to them by crowds of witnesses they have never met and never shall meet. Yet for every man these images — provided by strangers and dead men — are the very basis of his life as a human being.

C. WRIGHT MILLS (**154**:405)

Perceptual Capacity

In this chapter we discuss the causal factors which affect credibility of evidence. This discussion is necessarily incomplete and inadequate. We can never fully understand why men perceive some things but not others, why some men break away from the socio-cultural perspectives with which they were raised while others do not, why some men are willing to lie while others are not. The most sophisticated theories of the social psychologists are often no better than guesses, and the historians, intelligence specialists, lawyers, rhetoricians, decision theorists, and others do not even achieve the sophistication of the social psychologists. In attempting to theorize about conditions affecting credibility, therefore, we are seeing as through a glass darkly.

It is obvious that some people perceive more than others, and that the perceptions of two people in the same situation may differ widely. The classroom experiments which demonstrate this phenomenon are by now well known. But perceptual differences should be obvious on a commonsense basis without any controlled experiments at all. We know that some people are colorblind. We know that a highly sensitive woman can enter a room and perceive tensions to which most males are insensitive. We know that a monolingual American cannot perceive meaning in a German conversation. We know that someone untrained in accounting cannot perceive irregularities in a corporation balance sheet. We know, in short, that our several perceptual capacities are determined partly by heredity but largely by training and experience.

In this discussion of perceptual *capacity*, we are not yet considering how that capacity is used — the perspectives which sometimes prevent even a capable observer from seeing crucial items. Perceptual *distortion*, or selective perception, the result of what historians call bias and what social psychologists call a belief system, will be discussed in the next section. At present, we are considering only the determinants of the perceptual field and the capacity of an observer to see what is to be seen. As lawyers and historians would put it, we are talking about the ability of a witness to tell the truth.

Courts of law, in determining the ability of a witness to tell the truth about a certain event, demand that the witness have been physically present at the time, be of sound eyesight, hearing, etc., possess adequate memory, and be capable of relating what he saw and heard. These physical conditions for credible testimony are just as important outside courts of law for those who would serve as *primary* authorities on a subject: who claim to have intimate firsthand knowledge of what is going on in Israel, or Panama, or Congress. Presumably, most of the authorities from whom the public intelligence draws its primary testimony are sound of sight, hearing, and memory, and are reasonably articulate. More important than these elementary characteristics are their background and training, and the sensitivity, industry, knowledgeability, and special skills which they bring to their task.

Since the ability to tell the truth about widely varying matters will depend on different circumstances in each case, there is much justice in Allan Nevins' contention that the tests of evidence are *ad hoc* tests. (**160**: **197**) In the intricacies of public policy problems, so much depends on a witness' ability to know *what* to observe and how to evaluate the importance of what he observes that training and experience, required in the courts only of "expert" witnesses, become all important. And as Roger Hilsman argues so powerfully in *Strategic Intelligence and National Decisions,* when an intelligence gatherer is wholly divorced from the policy apparatus and does not know what policies are being contemplated, *he does not know what to observe.* (**88**) The assumption that he is simply to accumulate "all the facts" is ridiculous. No printing press in the world could keep up with the output of one observer if he were indeed to report indiscriminately everything he saw and heard. It follows that even a "nonexpert" witness must know at least what to look for; he must have some idea of what to focus on, some sense of what questions to ask.

Therefore, the ability of a witness to provide credible testimony about conditions in the Near East, for example, would depend on factors such as these:

First, he must have enough historical, political, economic, and sociological knowledge of the region to provide a framework for his observations. If an authority offers his opinion on the strength of the Nasser regime, he must have enough background information on Egypt to know what to observe. An observer who sees nothing more than English-language news reports and has not studied the country extensively is in no position to generalize that the regime is stable or unstable. To this background knowledge must be coupled the ability to rise above his own value system, to see events as they appear to the Egyptians rather than to Americans.

Second, a competent authority on the events in a foreign area must be fluent in the local languages. Having to depend on interpreters clearly impedes the understanding necessary for accurate primary observations. Whirlwind tours by monolingual reporters and diplomats simply do not provide the necessary insight into local conditions.

Third, a competent observer will have the intellectual curiosity and motivation to get off the beaten track, to hear and see events outside a planned routine of interviews and official visits with people friendly to his point of view. Official visitors to a country often see only persons selected by the host government as "reliable." Businessmen rarely escape from the official round of conferences and cocktail parties in hotels and embassy compounds. Journalists and politicians on "fact-finding" visits acquire the same sort of superficial impressions, unless they are motivated to dig into the background conditions of a country and visit something outside the capital. For disheartening examples of lack of initiative, see Lederer's *Nation of Sheep*. (**126**)

Fourth, the most competent authorities about Near Eastern affairs will be those with extended residence in, and recent visits to, the areas they write about. Expertise rapidly becomes out of date. The Egypt of today is simply not the Egypt of ten years ago. The obsolescence of knowledge is sometimes greater even than the obsolescence of a machine. And while scholars entrenched in an academic listening post can contribute a great deal to knowledge about a situation, they cannot provide firsthand data; they cannot serve as primary witnesses.

All of this is but a crude delineation of the conditions necessary for a witness to be able to tell the truth about current events in the Near East. *The constellation of abilities requisite to expertise varies from topic to topic.* There is always the necessity to communicate; and if one is to be a witness to the world of labor-management relations, one needs, rather than knowledge of a foreign language, knowledge of the language of the docks, factories, and board rooms. If one is to be a witness to the problems of financing education, one needs to be able to speak the languages of taxation, statistics, and politics. If one is to speak truthfully about the detection and prevention of crime, one needs to have had "residence" in the precinct stations, the jails, and the courts.

Expertise is no casual acquisition. Ernst Halperin claims, about one area of great significance for the United States:

> There can be no such person as a "Latin American Expert," if we mean by this someone who is well acquainted with all the Latin American coun-

tries. For Latin America is vast, encompassing twenty independent states and several dependencies of foreign powers. Even if a writer decides to limit himself to a treatment of the Latin countries of the South American mainland, he is still faced with the problem of having to deal with ten separate countries, all different from one another. It would take a scholar about five years to become reasonably well acquainted with the history, literature and politics of any of them. To study them simultaneously, to prevent one's knowledge from becoming superannuated, one would have to devote about fifty years to become an expert on all of South America alone. (**83**:36)

Ideally, trained reporters with adequate backgrounds should produce similar accounts of happenings they have witnessed. Because of perceptual distortion, this rarely happens. When, therefore, one runs across two accounts of a crucial event which correspond closely, produced by expert writers with totally antagonistic perspectives, one sits up and takes notice. This appears to be the case with two narratives of the war in Viet-Nam during 1963, one written by David Halberstam of *The New York Times* (**82**) and the other by Australian Communist Wilfred Burchett. (**22**) These reporters witnessed, from opposite sides, a number of battles for the Mekong Delta during 1963, including the much-publicized battle of Ap Bac. Their accounts of these events are basically similar. It is only when they describe matters which they did not personally observe that they diverge; thus Halberstam's account of the Buddhist crisis of 1963 appears to be superior to that of Burchett, who was not an eyewitness.

Sometimes expertise founders on uncontrollable conditions. With all the expertise in the world, it is sometimes impossible for Caucasian newsmen or scholars to get the full picture of what is happening in non-Caucasian areas because of foreign suspicion and mistrust. In an extensive survey of American correspondents working in Asia, John Hohenberg of the Columbia University School of Journalism found that, while the language barrier was listed as the most prominent difficulty in their work, the second most important barrier was hostility on the part of news sources. (**91**:11) This is hardly surprising. In an area only recently released from white domination, one would hardly expect intelligence gathering by white agents to be easy or cordial. The unwillingness of the United States to fully exploit *foreign* sources of intelligence, which in many instances are vastly superior to anything we can produce, will be discussed in Chapter 6.

Such inherent incapacities as one's race, social status, linguistic habits,

or even more intangible cultural characteristics are probably more important than most people realize. The study of cross-cultural communication, now only in its infancy, can be expected to make a significant
contribution to the study of perceptual capacity in the future. For the
present, one can only claim that there are great gaps in our intelligence
because *people won't tell us things we want to know.*

Perceptual capacity, in most cases, involves physiological normalcy,
training and experience in the area under study, mastery of foreign languages or technical jargon, intellectual curiosity and initiative, and, in
the case of primary authorities, eyewitness status. But all these characteristics combined do not add up to complete credibility. The witness
must also overcome the many factors disposing to perceptual distortion.

Perceptual Distortion

A bias, belief system, or perspective is a set of lenses which focuses
the attention of an observer so that he perceives certain phenomena and
disregards others, thus distorting reality. When the bias is strong
enough, an observer may even perceive something which is not there at
all, simply because he expects to see it. No one is completely free of
such distortions. The task of the student of evidence is to identify distorting biases and either discard the evidence which contains them in
favor of better evidence or compensate for the probable bias sufficiently
to make the evidence usable.

One of the earliest analysts of the effects of perspective on perception
was the sociologist Karl Mannheim. For him, the problem of "unmask-
ing" a witness was all important; perhaps his clearest statement is this:

> . . . in certain areas of historical-social knowledge it should be regarded
> as right and inevitable that a given finding should contain the traces of
> the position of the knower. The problem lies not in trying to hide these
> perspectives or in apologizing for them, but in inquiring into the question
> of how, granted these perspectives, knowledge and objectivity are still
> possible. (**144**:296)

To be forewarned is to be forearmed. The groundwork for objectivity,
obviously, is some knowledge of the major biases which affect perception. There is no better place to begin than with a statement of George
Kennan about the Soviet belief system and how it colors the entire Russian view of the world:

From the time of their seizure of power, forty years ago, the Russian Communists have always been characterized by their extraordinary ability to cultivate falsehood as a deliberate weapon of policy. They began by adopting an attitude of complete cynicism about objective truth, denying its value if not its existence, declaring the lie to be no less useful and respectable than the truth if only it served the purposes of the party. Departing from this premise, they have systematically employed falsehood not just as a means of deceiving others and exploiting their credulity, but also as a means of comforting and reassuring themselves. It has seemed to them at all times easier, and in no way improper, to operate a militant political movement on the basis of convenient falsehood than on the basis of awkward truth.

I think we have to recognize today, particularly on the basis of Khrushchev's recent statements and policies, that the effects of this systematic abuse of the human intellect are deep-seated and troublesome. Forty years of intellectual opportunism have wrought a strange corruption of the Communist mind, rendering it incapable of distinguishing sharply between fact and fiction in a single segment of its experience, namely in its relationship to any external competitive power. Let me stress that it is only in this one sector that the Communist mind is thus affected. In other respects it is extremely shrewd and discerning.

I have been asked hundreds of times in recent years how it could be that men of such great native intelligence as the Soviet leaders, commanding so elaborate and costly a network of intelligence-gathering agencies, could be anything else but excellently informed about ourselves and everything having to do with us. I should like to suggest an answer to this question.

In everything that can be statistically expressed — expressed, that is, in such a way as not to imply any judgment on our motivation — I believe the Soviet Government to be excellently informed about us. I am sure that their information on the development of our economies, on the state of our military preparations, on our scientific progress, etc., is absolutely first-rate. But when it comes to the analysis of our motives, to the things that make life tick as it does, I think this whole great system of intelligence-gathering breaks down seriously. It breaks down because over all these forty years the Communist party has made it impossible for the people who collect factual information to accompany that information with any really objective analysis of the nature of Western society. Some of the fictions dearest and most basic to Russian Communism's view of itself would be jeopardized at every turn by that sort of analysis. The Soviet diplomatic representative or journalist abroad has no choice but to cast his analytical report in the terms of Marxist-Leninist ideology whether this is applicable or not in the given instance. In this way the Soviet leaders find themselves committed to a badly distorted image of the outside world. (**106**:20–22)

This was written by Kennan in 1957. There is some reason to modify it in 1968, but it clearly pinpoints the number-one bias which vitiates the intelligence of the Soviet Union, and which we will later find to vitiate American intelligence also: ideology. Daniel Bell and others who have celebrated the "end of ideology" are somewhat premature; there is considerable reason to believe that the most intense ideologues in the world now occupy high office in Washington.

The effects of ideology on the testimony of Soviet officials who travel in the Western world can be documented exhaustively. Ideologies are the most potent of the many factors which distort perception. Whether Marxist-Leninist, Christian-capitalist, racist, nationalist, or millennialist, the lenses which direct the perceptions of the ideologue are usually dangerously flawed.

Particularly where conflict has set in, the misperceptions of ideologues subvert credibility. As Ralph K. White documents for both sides of the Vietnamese conflict, the "diabolical enemy-image," "virile self-image," "moral self-image," and similar distortions of the combatants have made balanced intelligence all but impossible. (**235**) Even when wars begin for reasons other than ideology, conflict itself stimulates ideological justifications; "we" become holy and justified, "they" become evil and contemptible. Witnesses caught up in the rationalizations of either side are undependable. As White says, "Any group that is emotionally involved on one side of a conflict suffers handicaps in balanced perception of the situation as a whole and of itself. Onlookers have the immense advantage of need-free perception." (**235**:69)

Even where there is no emotional commitment to an ideology, group or national interest can have a deflecting influence on perception. Frenchmen will always *want* to believe that their conduct of war in Indochina was more humane than that of Americans. Englishmen will always *want* to believe that the policies of their Colonial Office were more enlightened than those of the Belgians, French, Dutch, and Portuguese. Americans will always *want* to believe that their hold over the Latin American nations is more benevolent and disinterested than the colonial policies of their predecessors. And intelligence from agents holding these national points of view will be distorted to some degree because they want to see their own nations come off well.

John Mecklin, former information officer in the American embassy in Saigon, describes this wish-fulfillment psychology as it operated during 1963–1964. Newsmen had been reporting a quite different story from that forwarded to Washington by the Mission of which Mecklin was a part, and the bad blood between the two had built up to substantial proportions:

> The root of the problem was the fact that much of what the newsmen took to be lies was exactly what the Mission genuinely believed, and was reporting to Washington. Events were to prove that the Mission itself was unaware of how badly the war was going, operating in a world of illusion. Our feud with the newsmen was an angry symptom of bureaucratic sickness. (**150**:100)

In domestic as well as in foreign affairs, a financial interest often causes major perceptual distortion. Ideology may be the greatest corrupter of intelligence, but the Almighty Dollar is not far behind. Any man will see the world through eyes which are sympathetic to the source of his livelihood. Labor leaders and their employers will perceive the same set of phenomena quite differently. The tobacco industry and its employees will not find causal links between cigarettes and cancer. Import-vulnerable industries will perceive different economic facts from those perceived by exporters. The "traces of the position of the knower" are usually found where economic interest is present.

Economic interest, of course, is not always visible. Many of the sources of public intelligence are not clearly linked with an economic interest which would bias their testimony. Even Senator Paul Douglas did not know, for instance, that an article he allowed to go out over his signature touting the virtues of Nationalist China had been written by a payroller of the public relations firm employed by Nationalist China. And if a United States Senator did not know this, how could the general public have known? (**219**:697, 825) It is often very difficult indeed to uncover the financial interests behind "news" stories of various sorts. The CIA concealed its channels of support from the public for more than a decade.

One can find concrete instances of corruption of public intelligence caused by financial interest. Ben Bagdikian, writing in the *Columbia*

Journalism Review of Spring, 1967, cites several: Trujillo paid Mutual Broadcasting System $750,000 for regular favorable broadcasts about his regime in 1959. When the government of Mexico was about to expropriate 2,500 square miles of Mexican property owned by Hearst in the 1920's, Hearst ran a spectacular series condemning the government of Mexico, based on fraudulent documents claiming Mexico had bribed four United States Senators with $1,115,000. The *Manchester* (N. H.) *Union-Leader*, as conservative as they come, rebuked Barry Goldwater during the 1964 campaign for once criticizing Jimmy Hoffa. The Teamsters had a $2,000,000 investment in the *Union-Leader*. (See **9**:8–9.) And these are but some of the foibles of the mighty; lesser men are just as amenable to the power of the purse. He who holds the purse holds not only power; he holds evidence.

Sometimes the influence of economic dependency is relatively subtle. A bureaucratic disease known as "career involvement" afflicts many of the functionaries in large organizations, causing them to see things the boss's way and report phenomena which will be pleasing to him. Hypocrisy is not involved. Loyal employees, whether of U. S. Steel or the Federal Bureau of Investigation, absorb the corporate outlook — and bias — which reinforces morale and, incidentally, leads to promotion. They genuinely "see" what it is in their best interests to see.

Less economic in derivation, but also career-related, is the bias historians call the "partiality of paternalism." (**101**:164) Those who originate ideas, who develop and publicize theories, acquire a parental affection for them. Subsequent confirmation of the theory will be exaggerated, disconfirmation played down. Professors are especially susceptible to this disease. Any organization, however, will develop attachments to theories and explanations, once these have been identified with the organization. To acknowledge contrary evidence is to acknowledge having made a mistake; powerful psychological pressures therefore constrain the partisans of a committed organization to see only those phenomena which support its continuing good judgment.

Students of legal evidence discern a kind of bias which Wellman calls "unconscious partisanship":

> What is it in the human make-up which invariably leads men to take sides when they come into court? In the first place, witnesses usually feel more or less *complimented by the confidence* that is placed in them by the party calling them to prove a certain state of facts, and it is human

nature to try to prove worthy of this confidence. This feeling is unconscious on the part of the witness and usually is not a strong enough motive to lead to actual perjury in its full extent, but it serves as a sufficient reason why the witness will almost unconsciously dilute or color the evidence to suit a particular purpose and perhaps add only a *bit* here, or suppress one there, but this bit will make all the difference in the meaning. (**233**:152)

It takes but little imagination to see how the same phenomenon works outside the courtroom. Reporters "complimented by the confidence" of a high government or corporation official will try to prove worthy of this confidence. Friends of long standing find it hard to believe ill of each other; complimented by the confidence of the association, they testify to the virtue of the associate. (Thus Dean Acheson was "unwilling to turn his back" on Alger Hiss.)

Similarly, journalists, politicians, and academics who have been wined and dined by Franco or Chiang Kai-shek, General Motors or the Air Force, or who have received a deep freeze or vicuña coat from some public relations-conscious impresario will probably be reluctant to repudiate the patron. Gratitude for favors rendered colors a vast amount of the fact and opinion which flood the channels of public intelligence. Were it not so, there would be no need for conflict-of-interest statutes and news media policies against accepting free trips and vacations.

One frequently alleged cause of biased testimony is what is known as the "refugee mentality," or "exile mentality," explained by Marquis Childs this way:

> Ever since the Russian revolution of 1917 and increasingly in the past two decades exiles have influenced American policy and the American appraisal of critical situations. These are in most instances patriotic, dedicated, freedom-loving men and women. But by the very terms of exile they are more likely than not to be wrong in their estimates of what is happening in their former homeland. And quite understandably they want to believe that the forces of repression which drove them out can be overthrown. (**32**)

Thus they feel compelled to picture the situation blacker than it is to justify their departure and the renunciation of their birthright.

As plausible as the hypothesis is, and as confirmed as it may have been in the case of refugees from the Russian and Chinese revolutions (**133**; **161**:199), there seem to be at least two prominent instances where refugees have not been noticeably biased. After World War II, Inkeles and Bauer conducted extensive research among the refugees from behind the iron curtain then living in Western European camps. These investigators were highly sensitive to the problem of exile bias, and constructed tests of flattery and distortion to measure the extent to which their respondents were biased. The results were generally favorable to the refugees' credibility. (99:Part One)

Again, the best evidence seems to indicate that the refugees from Castro's Cuba, who have often been blamed (by Marquis Childs, among others) for misrepresenting the situation in their homeland, have actually been reasonably accurate. Some of the early refugees, Batistianos and dispossessed middle-class conservatives, were not completely credible, and their testimony diminished in value with the passage of time. Later refugees, however, told what proved to be a highly accurate story. The intelligence failure which underlay the Bay of Pigs was probably due not to the biased evidence of refugees but to the selective attention of the CIA, which listened to what *it* wanted to hear and disregarded the rest. It seems to have been the belief system of the CIA, not the belief system of the refugees, which caused distortion.* Because of contradictory findings from separate historical incidents involving refugees, therefore, we regard the "refugee mentality" hypothesis as not universally valid.

A similar principle which seems to indict the credibility of a significant group of witnesses is what we choose to call the "reaction principle." By this we mean the bias or perspective of ideologues who have become disillusioned and abjured their former affiliation. The particular group to which this principle most applies, in considering public intelligence in the United States, is the ex-Communists who have made a career of exposing their former comrades. They seem simply to have reversed the lenses with which they formerly viewed the world; the doctrines they opposed under the old Communist ideology are their new truths.

On the face of it, when a Communist has left the party and is no longer subject to discipline, he is "free" to tell the truth. But in place of the stringent demands of ideological conformity, a whole host of new pressures begins to operate. As Herbert Packer points out in his exten-

---

* For an extensive seminar paper on the problem of the Cuban refugees we are indebted to Mary Brigid Gallagher.

sive study, *Ex-Communist Witnesses*, these people profited handsomely from ratting on their old associates; naturally they wanted what they had to say to be useful to their new sponsors, the FBI and the Department of Justice. They also, according to Packer, "experience a strong reaction against their old allegiance and, in many cases, manifest an intense desire to do everything they can to abjure it." (**171**:216) Having been conditioned to authoritarian beliefs, they found it difficult to adopt a moderate view of the world. Of the four witnesses whom Packer dissects, Elizabeth Bentley and Louis Budenz emerge as largely incredible, while John Lautner and Whittaker Chambers seem to be less subject to distortion. The credibility of ex-ideologues seems to be a cut above that of active partisans, but it is still suspect.

Concluding our list of factors predisposing to bias is what might be called the "power syndrome." We refer here not to the official participants in a governmental or institutional power structure, whose bias is obvious and direct, but to those outside the ruling circles who yet aspire to them, and whose testimony is distorted by the necessity of pulling punches, or avoiding offense, of maintaining a public image compatible with a future governmental position. The "shadow cabinet" of the Kennedy dynasty, for instance, is committed and compromised to the extent of the individual members' ambitions. It is more than cocktail party humor to observe that X is "bucking for Secretary of State in the next Kennedy Administration," or that "Y has his eye on the Supreme Court." We know of cases, particularly in certain university circles, where private opinions are publicly modified because of ambition for high office. This, also, is career involvement of a sort; but because a witness does not at the time of his testimony hold an official position the perceptual distortion may not suggest itself. It may, nonetheless, be as real and as severe as that of fully committed cabinet members. Not only the fact of power but the anticipation of power can be corrupting.

No possible discussion of the causes of bias, of the origins of distorting belief systems, could be complete or perhaps even adequate. Our discussion is informed by a decade of attention to the credibility of public intelligence in the United States, with special emphasis on intelligence about foreign affairs. The biases we have mentioned are the ones which have seemed most vitiating and most prominent. Another generation or another area of concern might call for a quite different list. Despite this, we are confident that ideology, national interest, self-interest, unconscious partisanship, and power are human motives which have always been and will always be significant in focusing the eyes and ears of intelligence sources. The nuances and refinements which might be appended to these will, as Nevins contends, grow out of the situation.

Willful Distortion

So far, our discussion of perceptual distortion has dealt primarily with the effects of ideology, national interest, self-interest, etc. We have considered only situations where faulty evidence is *believed by its purveyors to be true*, where the bias of the reporter flaws his perception but not necessarily his integrity. But there is another kind of distortion to consider: willful distortion, the deliberate reporting of untruths. Kennan's description of Soviet behavior noted the large amount of deliberate lying in which the Communists indulge, not capriciously or sporadically, but systematically and for ideological reasons. In the Western world, fortunately, there is no similar widespread attempt to poison the sources of public intelligence; but lies are dispensed from prominent sources, and it is the business of the student of evidence to uncover as many of them as possible and to point out their implications. Mostly, they result from tensions of a crisis, an organizational gag rule, or exaggerated career involvement; sometimes, however, they appear to be the result of individual pathology.

Crisis situations always produce deviant behavior, even on the part of otherwise honorable men. And just as one may be tempted to say that one likes his wife's new hat in order to save a marriage, a President may be tempted to prevaricate in order to save the world, or save his country's reputation. Thus Eisenhower denied that U-2's were overflying Russia; Kennedy told Adlai Stevenson (who subsequently reported it in good faith to the United Nations) that the United States had nothing to do with the Bay of Pigs invasion; Johnson denied in 1964 that there had been peace feelers from Hanoi. We are passing no moral judgment on this behavior; we note it only because one who is seeking the material truth must learn that, in crisis situations where tension is high, he cannot assume that the parties involved are candid and truthful.

Organizational gag rules also result in much prevarication. Newspapers, business corporations, labor unions, governments, and pressure groups of all kinds have institutional perspectives which their employees are required to support, even to the extent of misrepresenting the truth.

In touchy situations, there is usually a "cover story" which spokesmen for the organization are required to enunciate. Arthur Schlesinger, Jr., passed such a cover story on to *The New York Times* in April, 1961, about the nature and size of the Cuban refugee landing in the Bay of Pigs. It seems quite clear that Mr. Schlesinger was not at liberty to tell the truth in this situation.

Less dramatic, but more pervasive, are the intelligence distortions which result from career involvement or from the "Dale Carnegie principle" — telling others what they want to hear. United States aid officials, reporting on projects they have carried out in the field, are frequently unwilling to acknowledge failure, corruption, pilferage; that would harm their careers. Troop commanders on the battlefront will report enemy casualties that did not occur, since high enemy casualties will please their superiors. Lies told for such reasons may seem justifiable, but they poison the public intelligence nonetheless.

Finally, there are cases of pathological lying, of individuals who seem unable to tell the truth even when the truth would not hurt them. The lies of Senator Joseph R. McCarthy seem to be of this sort. Marat, the famous French revolutionary, was a pathological liar. Catherine de' Medici, says historian Herbert Butterfield, "was so untruthful that we must not believe her too readily even when she is giving evidence against herself." (**27**:22) Such individuals may be few and far between. But when their lies coincide with a strong popular prejudice, as did McCarthy's, much falsehood can be incorporated into the belief structure of an entire constituency.

The difference between simple perceptual distortion and willful distortion may be highly significant to a moralist, but in the study of evidence, false information originating from a powerful bias is just as useless whether the witness knew he was telling an untruth or was merely mesmerized by his own perspective.

Authenticity — the Cheating Document

Any user of evidence must be aware of the chance that a document he acquires may not be authentic — it may not actually be what it purports to be. Such spurious documents have long been the bane of historians. Allan Nevins, in *The Gateway to History*, lists a whole series of forged documents which have misled both laymen and experts: Parson Weems's *Life of George Washington;* the Morey letters, falsely attributed to

James A. Garfield; the Lincoln-Rutledge letters palmed off on the *Atlantic Monthly* in 1928; the Donation of Constantine; the Protocols of the Elders of Zion; the diary notes of Maxim Litvinov, and dozens of other fraudulent items. (**160**:Ch. 6)

Twentieth century technology may make it easier to detect forged signatures, to determine if a certain piece of paper could have been made in the sixteenth century, and to solve some of the mechanical problems of determining authenticity. It has done nothing, however, to decrease the disposition of men to cheat. Television quiz show riggings, De Angelis's receipts for nonexistent salad oil, ghostwritten Ph.D. dissertations, Billie Sol Estes's faked fertilizer tanks, exam cribbing at major educational institutions — all represent modern documentary fraud. The student of evidence has to assume that sometime he will come up against a fraudulent document.

Needless to say, the credibility of a document which does not come from the source to which it is attributed is impaired. Spurious documents may tell some truths; if they were completely false, their chances of fooling anyone would be slight. But as a whole, they cannot be trusted.

One kind of nonauthentic document is that which is fabricated, manufactured, made up out of whole cloth, and then attributed to some prominent authority. Such manufactures have been detected in academic debating, where the pressure to win is enormous, and where a key piece of evidence on a crucial issue may mean the difference between a three-foot trophy and a two-foot one. Since, unfortunately, most (99 per cent) academic debates are heard by judges not expert in the subject being debated, and since they are not recorded, possibilities of fraud are extensive. In the 1964 National Collegiate Championship Debate, which was recorded, one speech contained three pieces of evidence which, after careful investigation, turned out to be fabricated statements attributed to prominent authorities: Lee A. DuBridge, the *Wall Street Journal*, and Dick Netzer. (**163**:8–10) Academic debates, like the *Congressional Record*, are undiscriminating vehicles in which pure sublimities are interspersed with utter trash. No student tempted to quote from either one should do so without checking the *original* source.

Another kind of nonauthentic document is the one that is plagiarized. To plagiarize is to pass off someone else's work as one's own. One might assume that plagiarism would occur only in the "underworld" of scholarship, and yet a book published by a respectable university press in

1965, about the late President Diem of Viet-Nam, contained extensive passages plagiarized from Donald Lancaster, Ellen Hammer, Bernard Fall, and Sirdar Ikbal Ali Shah. (28) The "author," Anthony Bouscaren, obviously warrants an entirely different credibility rating from that of the distinguished people from whom he lifted much of his text. Still another kind of nonauthentic document is the one that is ghostwritten. A document carrying A's name, but actually written by B, may or may not warrant the same credibility rating one would give to A's word alone. A real instance of this problem is best given in Allan Nevins' words:

> A peculiarly irritating problem of responsibility is presented by such a book as *MacArthur 1941–1951: History in the Pacific*, by Major General C. A. Willoughby and John Chamberlain (1956). Its preface states that it is "not to be regarded as in the nature of General MacArthur's memoirs." Yet it is based on material which he read and annotated, and one of the two authors was MacArthur's intelligence chief throughout the Pacific fighting, thereafter his official spokesman, and a close personal friend. The numerous controversial assertions in the book . . . would possess values if they came from MacArthur, very different from those they bear as coming from Willoughby. It is not clear from whom they *do* come. (160:169–170)

In the present hectic pace of American life the ghost-writer is becoming more and more prominent. Dozens of editorials which appear in weekly papers represent not the considered opinion of your good friend and trusted guide, the local editor, but a prefabricated editorial service in Oregon. The speech your congressman makes at a community clambake may not be his speech at all; it may represent the work of his administrative assistant, to which the congressman gives but half-conscious assent.

There are other problems which, while not classifiable as problems of authenticity in the strict sense, nonetheless relate to the *bona fide's* of a document and hence affect its credibility. There is, for instance, much evidence from writers whose sponsorship or institutional affiliation might lower their credibility, and hence who appear under false colors. One such instance is an article entitled "The Faceless Vietcong," by George A. Carver, Jr., which appeared in the prestigious *Foreign Affairs* of April, 1966. This was the lead article of the issue, and it supported Government policy down the line. Carver was identified by *Foreign*

Affairs as "student of political theory and Asian affairs, with degrees from Yale and Oxford; former officer in the U.S. aid mission in Saigon; author of 'Aesthetics and the Problem of Meaning.'" In actuality, Carver is a CIA agent, a fact which gives his testimony an entirely different weight than it would warrant if he were only what *Foreign Affairs* claimed of him. This deception, rapidly exposed, caused much turmoil in the academic community. A succeeding issue of *Foreign Affairs* carried an article by Bernard Fall substantially contradicting Carver.

Similarly, much government propaganda is issued between the covers of legitimate publications by reputable publishers. Few innocent readers would know, for instance, that the most incompetent work about the Dominican intervention of 1965, Jay Mallin's *Caribbean Crisis: Subversion Fails in the Dominican Republic,* published by Van Nostrand, was commissioned by the United States Information Agency at a fee of $2,368. **(212)** Even if Mallin, a former *Time* correspondent, had been able to tell the truth about the Dominican intervention, his willingness to do so would have been compromised by the fact that he was "sponsored."

A similar problem lies in the deliberate creation of events which are then reported unwittingly by otherwise credible writers. Incidents are staged, documents are "planted," interviews are mistranslated. William Lederer reports a story of a Thai village evacuated of its original inhabitants and re-peopled with exemplary Thai officials so that a team of American anthropologists who lived there for a year "confirmed the fact that American assistance was just about perfect. Everyone was happy, and the Thai aid program continued." **(126:36)**

Another problem arises from censored documents. Where testimony of a witness has been tampered with, something less than the full truth emerges. Many government reports are censored for security reasons, a sometimes necessary restriction. Where censorship takes the form of clearly indicated deletions, readers know that the material does not represent the full story and can make allowance for what might have been in the gaps. But censorship does not always reveal itself in this way. Who would know, for instance, unless he happened across a knowledgeable review, that the most prominent book on Liberia, written by four outstanding Northwestern University economists, was delayed in publication several years until the authors made revisions to the liking of the Liberian Government and the United States Agency for International Development? (**130**) A censored document may still be credible in some of its particulars; but it is not the authentic whole it would be without tampering.

Uncovering documentary fraud is largely a matter for experts. Just as making sound predictions demands a refined sensitivity based on inarticulable background information, so sensing fraud in a document demands having a "feel" for authenticity in the subject area. Here the book reviews are often useful. The student wanting to know how to weigh a book can start with the *Book Review Digest*. This volume will indicate where many of the reviews appear, and will give brief excerpts from some of them. Superficial reviews, like these carried in *Library Journal* and *Kirkus Service*, need not be pursued further. Reviews in *The New York Times Book Review*, *The New York Review of Books*, *The Saturday Review*, and *Book Week* should be looked up and read in their entirety; they will likely be competent and substantial.

The most thorough reviews, however, and the ones most likely to assess authenticity, will appear in the professional journals: *American Historical Review*, *American Political Science Review*, *Trans-Action*, and so forth. Unfortunately, since these often do not carry reviews until the year following publication of a book, *Book Review Digest* may not list them. A very useful review of Felix Greene's *A Curtain of Ignorance*, for instance, appears in the March, 1965, *American Political Science Review;* the book was published in 1964, and *Book Review Digest* lists only reviews of Greene's book which came out in 1964.

The authenticity of articles is best established by reading periodicals of hostile persuasion. Whatever one's ideological slant, one should read journals at both ends of the ideological spectrum. The *National Catholic Reporter* will keep sharp watch on *America; National Review* will attempt to poke holes in *Commentary*. The *Columbia Journalism Review* carries valuable comment on the daily press.

The public intelligence is shot through with evidence which is not authentic, which does not really come from the source alleged. Where authenticity is in doubt, credibility suffers.

SUMMARY

People exposed to the same events will often give widely divergent testimony about them. One reason for this is that *perceptual capacities* differ. In law courts, an eyewitness must be able to see and hear clearly, be able to remember accurately, and be able to relate what he saw and heard. On most of the topics about which students need evidence, considerable expertise is needed for testimony to be useful. Witnesses must know what to observe: they need training and experience in the area under study, mastery of relevant languages or technical jargon, and intellectual initiative. Even when all these qualifications are present, testimony may still be misleading. *Perceptual distortion* may cause observers to see what really is not there. Ideology, national or other group interest, individual self-interest, career involvement, unconscious partisanship, exile mentality, reaction against one's past, and desire for power are some of the biases which distort perception. And there is sometimes *willful distortion* of evidence — plain lying. This may be caused by a crisis during which an organization tries to protect itself, by an organizational gag rule which forces subordinates to put out a cover story, by the Dale Carnegie principle of telling people only what they want to hear, or by the pathology of congenital liars. In Western society, since lying is frowned on, pressures to tell the truth are strong, and men hesitate to lie for fear of being caught. Ideologues suffering from severe perceptual distortion have no such inhibitions, hence their testimony is generally as dangerous as that of pathological liars. Finally, the *authenticity* of a document which one uses for evidence may not be clear, in which case the credibility of the testimony will be impaired. Some documents are fabricated; others are plagiarized; some authors claim false credentials; occasionally a document reports a staged incident; some documents are censored; and when documents are ghostwritten, the relevant credibility is difficult to estimate.

Suggested Readings

Ben H. Bagdikian, "News as a Byproduct," *Columbia Journalism Review*, VI (Spring, 1967), 5–10.

Peter L. Berger, *Invitation to Sociology*. Garden City: Doubleday (Anchor Books), 1963.

Paul F. Boller, Jr., *Quotemanship*. Dallas: Southern Methodist University Press, 1967, Chapters Seven and Eight.

R. C. H. Catterall, "The Credibility of Marat," *American Historical Review*, XVI (October, 1910), 24–35.

R. G. Collingwood, *The Idea of History*. New York: Oxford University Press, 1956.

Ole R. Holsti, "Cognitive Dynamics and Images of the Enemy," *Journal of International Affairs*, Number 1 (1967), 16–39.

Allen Johnson, *The Historian and Historical Evidence*. New York: Charles Scribner's Sons, 1926.

William Lederer, *A Nation of Sheep*. New York: W. W. Norton, 1961, Parts One and Two.

Herbert L. Packer, *Ex-Communist Witnesses*. Stanford: Stanford University Press, 1962.

Ralph K. White, "Misperception and the Vietnam War," *Journal of Social Issues*, XXII (July, 1966), 1–164.

5

Indices of Credibility

Obviously, asseverations of honesty do not always carry conviction. More than the avowed purpose of telling the truth is needed. The tone and spirit of an historical writing must be taken into account. And if other writings than the one under consideration can be found, these too should be given a careful scrutiny. An author who betrays his willingness to sacrifice the truth in one instance can hardly be trusted in another.

ALLEN JOHNSON (**101**:80–81)

Situational Tests

The situation in which evidence is generated is certainly one dimension on which it may be evaluated. Although Anglo-Saxon courts require that evidence must be given under oath and subject to cross-examination to be admissible before a tribunal, no such requirements can be imposed on the vast bulk of public intelligence. Without hearsay evidence, the structure of human knowledge would collapse. Nonetheless, there are certain common conditions which affect the probable worth of public testimony.

1. DEGREE OF TENSION. In general, *the lower the tension associated*

with an event, the higher the credibility of reports about it. Common-sense observation of wartime periods contrasted with periods of "thaw" will soon lead to the conclusion that propaganda, managed news, censorship, and other such information pathologies are more often associated with wartime. Furthermore, the Dale Carnegie principle operates more firmly in periods of high tension. Robert C. North and his collaborators applied the techniques of content analysis to the historical events preceding World War I. After months of team-conducted coding, scaling, evaluating, analyzing, and feeding into their computer the data from hundreds of diplomatic reports, reports of attachés, consular reports, reports of private agents, communications between heads of states, memoranda, minutes and marginal notes, instructions, circular letters, and formal communications to ministers of foreign affairs — after, in short, a monumental scholarly effort — they reached a number of conclusions. One of them states what we call the crisis principle:

> The higher the tension, the stronger the tendency of agents in the field to report — consciously or unconsciously — the information which they perceive as desired or expected by decision-makers at the center. (**168**:170)

The North study found other principles operating in periods of tension, some of them also significant for evaluation of evidence: rumor tends to be transmitted as fact, decisions are made on the basis of affective feelings rather than cognitive calculations, habitual images and stereotypes are increasingly relied upon, and suspicions and fears are accepted as fact.

Conversely, when things are calm and routine, the credibility of reporting rises. This seems to be true not only in relations among nations, but in many areas of social concern. A spy trial will call forth all kinds of alarmist testimony. Urban riots will heighten fear, and rumors will be accepted as fact by those predisposed to accept them. A fight over medicare will increase tensions in the community of physicians and lower the credibility of intelligence emanating from the American Medical Association. Truth appears to be incompatible with crisis. We will find this principle very useful in the discussions of major sources of evidence following this chapter.

2. ACCESSIBILITY. *The more accessible the situation being reported on, both to the reporters and to the consumers of reports, the more credible the reports.* This is true not only of situations far removed geographically compared with others closer to the target audience; it is

also true of physical and linguistic access. Arthur M. Schlesinger, Jr., for instance, has stated that newspaper accounts of decision making in the White House are not to be taken seriously; such reports, he claims, have no more relation to reality than the shadows in Plato's cave. (**192**:493) Reporters do not have access to what goes on in the White House, except to the extent that the occupants thereof choose to describe their deliberations.

Similarly, American intelligence about Britain is better than about the non-English-speaking countries of Western Europe because the language barrier is not so great. American intelligence from all Western European countries is probably better than current (1968) intelligence from Cuba; in Cuba we are faced not just with barriers of culture and language, but with the physical barrier of ruptured diplomatic, cultural, commercial, and tourist relations. But even Cuba is, in many ways, more accessible than Viet-Nam. Distance and cost make personal observation by all but agents of the government and reporters nearly prohibitive. The cultural-linguistic gap is enormous and is complicated by the hostility barrier discussed in Chapter Four. Opportunities for an interested party to investigate controversial intelligence about Viet-Nam are hardly greater than they are in the case of Cuba, and both are more inaccessible than Western Europe.

Most domestic matters are, by contrast, highly accessible. This does not mean that intelligence concerning strikes, riots, or peace marches is uniformly accurate; it means only that sustained and major deception about them is less likely. Other things being equal, evidence about accessible events is more trustworthy than evidence about inaccessible events.

3. Freedom to report — absence of gag rule. *The more freedom a witness has to report things as he sees them, the greater his credibility.* Organizations frequently have ideological positions or financial interests which require agents to produce results congruent with the prevailing "line" or ideology. Even where there is no overt rule, agents often sense that the boss will not tolerate dissent and hence report only what is consistent with the organization's policy.

Many times organizational ideologies are so powerful that agents see only what the organization wants them to see; this is a problem of perceptual distortion. But even when there is no perceptual distortion agents may be forced or seduced into reporting what they know to be false.

Documentary Tests

4. AUTHENTICITY. *The greater the presumption of authenticity, the higher the credibility of a document.* If one has a reasonable acquaintance with a subject, fraudulent documents will convey a sense of phoniness. Sometimes they can be checked in the many indices of current literature; if the alleged author is living, he may respond to a letter. Marked changes of style in a document suggest the work of two different authors.

Probably the major clue to nonauthenticity is exaggeration or claims to have observed something which other witnesses were in a position to observe but did not. One can check a document against other works of the alleged author; if they are not compatible, authenticity may be questioned. In the case of some of Joseph McCarthy's forged documents, his refusal to allow other Senators to see them was pretty conclusive indication of their fraudulence. (**17**:321) Documents "sailing under false colors" are extremely hard to detect; publishers are not eager to reveal facts about their authors which would detract from the acceptance of their writing.

5. INTERNAL CONSISTENCY. *The higher the internal consistency of an author, the more credible his testimony.* As with most generalizations, there are times when this principle does not hold. The whole problem is again one of relevance. Credibility would not necessarily be damaged in the case of a witness who approved of war against Nazi Germany but who disapproved of war against Communist China. The cases are different, and the whole panoply of goals, evaluations of the status quo, and predictions of consequences make different responses appropriate.

On the other hand, when a source such as the Navy or the State Department takes inconsistent positions on whether or not it possesses a classified file on Amelia Earhart, the agency credibility is severely damaged. (**73**) Some of the public rejection of candidate Goldwater in 1964 seems to have been based on his apparently contradictory positions. For instance, at the San Francisco convention he stated that "extremism in the defense of liberty is no vice." Later at the Hershey strategy conference, however, he stated, "I seek the support of no extremist — of the left or the right." It was difficult to believe that Goldwater both approved of extremism and repudiated the support of extremists. (**17**:371) Whether or not lack of consistency in an author damages his credibility must always be a matter of judgment.

6. CAREFULNESS OF GENERALIZATION. *The more careful the generalizations of a witness, the higher the credibility of his testimony.* Allan Nevins has a simple test for bias: "The clearest mark of the biased witness is his desire to oversimplify historical events; to distort them by giving excessive emphasis to some single factor." (**160**:223) Nevins' examples make it clear that oversimplification is what we would call inadequate descriptive generalization and causal explanation. We agree that carelessness and oversimplification in generalizing are damaging to credibility, though we do not go so far as Nevins.

Oversimplification may well result from bias. When one finds a claim that all the world's troubles, or even all American troubles, result from the income tax, or the Communist conspiracy, or "the dirty capitalists," one ought to be suspicious. Law enforcement officers and prosecuting attorneys constantly overgeneralize from the instances where a criminal has killed an officer on duty. Each such incident brings forth the argument that capital punishment must be applied more often to prevent such crimes. But statistics show that they occur with approximately the same frequency in death penalty states as in abolitionist states. The generalization is too easy, too simple-minded; the attempt to make it brands a witness as biased. By contrast, an authority like George Kennan shows all the characteristics of moderation and caution which indicate objectivity. This does not make Mr. Kennan wishy-washy or inconclusive; one can be firm without going overboard.

We do not believe that all cases of overgeneralization or oversimplification derive from bias. We have found otherwise credible witnesses to oversimplify on matters peripheral to their sphere of expertise without compromising their basic credibility and accuracy. One needs to be suspicious of careless generalization, but we cannot agree with Nevins that it is the most significant liability of witnesses.

The problem of carefulness of generalization relates to how an author deals with inferential risk. One of the crucial areas here is crime statistics. Little inference is involved in simply collecting crime statistics. So long as reporting units are honest and understand the FBI definitions of various crimes, the testimony of that agency to the effect that gross felonies went up 7 per cent last year involves little inference. What is done with this figure is another matter. When one claims that the increase in felonies proves that the United States is less law-abiding, a host of complications appears. One has to assume that previous felony statistics were based on the same definitions, collection procedures, and integrity of processing which applied in the most recent year. One has to assume that detection of felonies was similar in the past and the present. For the statement to be taken at face value, one has to show that the most recent year was typical or representative, *i.e.*, not a wartime period or a depression period, when crimes have always shown an increase. "The United States is less law abiding" is, in short, a conclusion some distance removed from the data on which it is based. Clearly, the inferential risk in reaching such a conclusion is great.

An extreme risk would be presented by the claim that recent Supreme Court decisions have *caused* the increase in crime. The proof requirements for this conclusion, to any but the simple-minded, are almost overwhelming. One can observe a felony; one cannot observe Supreme Court decisions causing crime. Other things being equal, the farther removed a statement is from the perceptions on which it is based, the more suspicious one must be.

7. RELUCTANCE. *The greater the damage of his own testimony to a witness, the more credible it is.* The principle of reluctant testimony is ancient and esteemed in jurisprudence. It is assumed that sane individuals will not say things against their own interests unless such testimony is true beyond doubt. Thus, when the Chinese Communists claim that a steel production quota has been overfulfilled, one must take it with a grain of salt. When, on the other hand, they state that the Red Guards are not obeying orders to go back to school, or that there is a food shortage in Shensi Province, or that the enemies of the state are making trouble in Sinkiang, one can accept this as highly probable. Peking would probably dispense such damaging facts only if they are true.

Similarly, when the State Department reversed itself in September of 1965, admitting what it had previously denied — that a CIA agent had offered a $3,300,000 bribe to Prime Minister Lee Kuan Yew of Singapore — one could be sure that such a bribe was in fact offered. State would have no motive for thus certifying American ineptitude.

Reluctant testimony is not common, but it does occur. Where it can be had, its probative value is considerable.

Characteristics of the Writer

8. EXPERTISE. *The greater the relevant expertise of an author, the higher his credibility.* The qualification "relevant" is a stumbling block with this principle also. Our previous discussion of what it takes to be an expert on Latin America pointed out the limitations of scope of expertise in any one person. It is a moot point whether a writer who was highly knowledgeable about Brazil, Peru, and Guatemala could qualify as a general authority on Latin America; certainly he would be more of an authority on it than a Western European scholar. But does close acquaintance with Japan make one an authority on Viet-Nam? Is a Cuban expert by the fact of his expertise more able than laymen to testify about events in the neighboring Dominican Republic?

Formal training is by no means necessary for expertise. Politicians, journalists, businessmen, and diplomats, with no college credits whatsoever in subjects to which they later devote their attention, have become highly respected authorities. The formal training and career experience of a writer, both of which can be checked in biographies, may provide data helpful to estimating his expertise. But no source whatever will reveal how much time someone has put into studying a subject.

Internal analysis, gauging how much an author knows about a subject from examining his writing, is unavoidable but treacherous. He may pretend to know things that are not so. He may have borrowed most of his material from others, and plagiarized or merely paraphrased it. Therefore, despite the importance of perceptive capacity and firsthand experience in developing expertise, we do not put great weight on estimates of an authority's "qualifications" when this means merely formal training or reputation with the general public.

A man's standing with a professional group in his area of claimed competence, if it can be found out, is a firmer base for judging expertise. It would be difficult for an incompetent historian to become president of the American Historical Association. The president of the Association for Asian Studies likewise could not easily be a fraud. But the proliferation of organizations devoted to every subject under the sun muddies the waters. How would a layman know that the China Institute of America, for instance, was little more than a propaganda outlet for Chiang Kai-shek, and that the criterion for affiliation with it was not necessarily expertise? An expert's expert is probably pretty well qualified in his field, but one cannot always discover who is competent to pass on another's expertise.

9. OBJECTIVITY. *The greater the objectivity of an author, the more credible his testimony.* Any man will have biases, or "convictions," which will distort his perceptions at times. The most the user of evidence can hope for is to find witnesses whose biases are under control.

But it is necessary to identify bias in order to compensate for it. Obvious bias will go along with commercial sponsorship. How could one expect a "scientist" on the payroll of the Tobacco Research Institute to expose any fact which would harm his employer? How could one expect an employee of United Fruit to be candid about the revolutionary movements in Central America? How could one expect a Teamsters Union lawyer to tell the whole truth about Jimmy Hoffa? If, therefore, one knows who is on what payroll, a big step in identification of bias has been taken.

Determining ideological biases is more a matter of internal analysis than of exterior affiliation. One would know, of course, the bias of a card-carrying Communist or a John Birch Society member if these memberships were public. At the extremes of the political spectrum, loaded language will usually give a writer away; words such as "atheistic Communist" and "imperialist aggressor" obviously indicate partisan testimony. But in between the extremes is a vast area where hidden bias can be debilitating.

Sophisticated writers in controversial areas are coming to realize the need for declaring biases, not only so they will themselves be on guard but so readers may be warned. Thus Douglas Pike, in the preface to his detailed study *The Viet Cong*, includes an impassioned plea for saving the Vietnamese from Communism. (172:xii) Having warned readers where he stands, he settles down to the dry details of his history. Similarly, Harold C. Hinton indicates clearly in the preface to *Communist China in World Politics* how he feels about the men in Peking, and he identifies himself as a member of the Institute for Defense Analyses. (89)

This is an encouraging trend. We share with Ralph K. White the belief that candor is necessary to sound testimony:

> We psychologists are at last learning that a partial reduction of one's own misperceptions (which is all that fallible human beings can hope for in any case) is achieved better by candidly admitting one's own biases,

to others as well as to oneself, and then consciously combatting them, than by pretending that they do not exist. (**235**:85)

When the day comes that tendentious writings are marked by such disclosures of interest and perspective, the study of evidence will be much easier. Meanwhile one must dig for institutional connections, and infer the rest.

10. ACCURACY RECORD. *The more accurate the description and prediction record of a source, the higher the credibility of his testimony in general.* We believe accuracy record to be the single most important index of credibility. Historiographer Allen Johnson says, "An author who betrays his willingness to sacrifice the truth in one instance can hardly be trusted in another"; and it is equally true that an author who was unable to call the shots in past instances is not to be believed in future ones. The training and experience of an authority may be superb; he may have access to all the relevant data, may appear to be scrupulously objective, may be careful and consistent in his statements, and may satisfy all the criteria one might impose — and still be wrong. Masses of data do not mean anything in themselves. It is only when they are assembled and interpreted, focused on a specific problem, and noise or irrelevant data discarded that successful prediction is possible. The unarticulated premises and subliminal perceptions which distinguish the expert with a "feel" for his subject from one who is a simple collector of facts come to the fore most clearly when one is predicting.

To put it another way, descriptive accuracy is easier to achieve than predictive accuracy. One can describe an event more or less successfully without making sophisticated judgments about its significance. In prediction this is not possible; one immediately takes inferential risks. It takes so much more perception, wisdom, and objectivity to predict than to describe that when an expert has established a claim to successful prediction, he has established a claim to the highest credibility. As Helmer and Rescher point out, "Thus the ultimate function of expert advice is almost always to make a predictive contribution." (**87**:38)

Since prediction is the highest and most difficult dimension of expertise, predictive failure is not as damning as descriptive failure. Secretary McNamara, as a predictor, failed miserably in his efforts to anticipate what would happen in Southeast Asia. But this is not a derogation of such magnitude as pointing out that Secretary Rusk in 1951 described the Peking regime as a "Russian puppet," and said it was "not Chinese." (**187**) Such a monumental error makes his colleague's sanguinity about our success in the Vietnamese war seem a minor failing.

Of course, young and untested experts must be evaluated by other indices of credibility, as they do not yet have predictive records. But for the rest, those whose records are on file, trustworthy judgments are often possible. Some writers, of course, hedge their statements in such a way that little can be gained, ten years after they wrote, from attempting to determine their accuracy in the light of history. But the probabilities are that if such writers were not saying anything checkable ten years ago, they are not saying it now, and their testimony will not, for that very reason, be useful to the consumer of evidence.

In the chapters that follow we shall make much use of predictive records in evaluating the credibility of some of the more prominent authorities on major American problems. Digging into a writer's record is time-consuming, but it is nonetheless indispensable. The man who has been right in the past is likely to be right in the future.

Tests of Primary Authorities

11. EYEWITNESS PRINCIPLE. *The greater a witness' personal observation of a matter to which he testifies, the higher his credibility.* To be a primary witness, one needs not just the perceptual capacity discussed in the first part of this chapter and a high rating on the general tests of evidence discussed in the second part; he needs to have been where the action was. It is not enough to observe from the outside, to read what documents are available, to interview participants or refugees. One needs to have been inside the chambers where decisions are made to furnish primary particulars; inside ghettos when riots were going on to testify to their spirit and specifics; inside Indonesia during the Communist coup attempt to describe it and its implications accurately.

The crucial question to ask any witness about the specifics on which he builds his generalizations is, "How do you know?" If he answers "Because I was there," he claims primary status. If he answers "Because Bernard Fall, Jean Lacouture, and Robert Shaplen say so," he is a secondary source, and one must then make different demands of him.

We do not in any way intend to derogate secondary sources. As Bernard Fall notes, one of the most valuable works on Viet-Nam is Victor Bator's *Vietnam: A Diplomatic Tragedy,* which was entirely a

"product of research in New York's libraries, while several books liter-
ally written in the rice paddies were just trash." (**59**:24) But Bator, as
does any secondary source, had to depend on eyewitnesses.

The cash value of this principle is that brief inspection tours or
temporary journalistic assignments are not worth the candle. We refer
again to the account of the shortcomings of such expeditions in Lederer's
A Nation of Sheep. Two weeks' eyewitnessing in the Dominican Republic does not provide a journalist with sufficient background to know
what to look for or to evaluate what he sees, particularly if he is short
on the kinds of training discussed earlier in this chapter. The useful
eyewitness is more than a flying-tripper.

12. CONTEMPORANEITY. *The more contemporaneous the report of a
witness, the more credible his testimony.* This is an ancient historiographical truth, based on both reason and experience. The greater the
time-lapse between observing and recording, the greater the possibility
of inaccuracy.

Memory is as fallible as any other human faculty. Thus General
Joseph W. Stilwell's account of World War II in the Asian Theater,
which consists of a private diary and letters written to his wife during
the fighting (**211**), is superior to General Claire L. Chennault's account
of the same events, which was written some years later and in a climate
of opinion which could have seriously distorted his memory. (**31**)
Both men were biased, and the user of evidence from either one needs
to adjust for this bias; but Stilwell's account is better raw material
because of its contemporaneity.

Tests of Secondary Authorities

13. SELECTION OF PRIMARY SOURCES. *The more discerning a writer's
selection of primary sources, the more credible his testimony.* An obvious assumption underlies this principle: when a writer depends on the
testimony of others, he is obligated to reveal that dependence. This is a
fundamental tenet of scholarship. The whole apparatus of scholarship
is designed, among other things, to enable readers to check out assertions and trace them back to their original sources. Acknowledgment of
the use of others' work is a *sine qua non* for credibility. If there is no
acknowledgment of dependence, we are entitled to assume that the basic
data and observations are original with the writer.

After a period of study in any specific area, a student will have made evaluations of many of the primary sources. When he turns to a secondary source, one of the criteria on which he can judge that source is the selection of primary authorities. It is clear, for instance, that an account of the Dominican revolution based on the newsweeklies and official communiqués is inferior to an account based on the work of Tad Szulc, Philip Geyelin, and Dan Kurzman. (48) It is likewise clear that an account of the Vietnamese war based on *Time*, Marguerite Higgins, and Secretary McNamara is inferior to one which relies on David Halberstam, John Mecklin, and Malcolm Browne.

In many cases, seriously biased writers will lean over backwards to establish their contentions from the words of their opponents. This seems, in fact, to be a characteristic of extremist literature. It is not without rationale. If an enemy can be made to condemn himself out of his own mouth, his reluctant testimony has tremendous weight.

14. ACCURACY OF CITATION. *The more accurate the citations of a writer, the more credible his testimony.* Some polemical writings, designed usually for the already converted, deal only in very general assertions which the author does not feel need to be backed up by anything approximating evidence. Other writers dealing with controversial subjects regard themselves as primary authorities, at least in part, and present few if any sources of data. Government authorities base much of their rhetoric on secret intelligence to which the public is not privy. But most writers about serious subjects acknowledge that some if not all of their material was provided by someone else. Where recorded (printed, written, taped, filmed) sources are cited, a student can always go to the original to see if it really says what the secondary source claimed.

There are three primary ways of misrepresenting material one quotes: citing contrary to context, omitting significant words or phrases, and altering words.

Quoting "out of context" is frequently condemned by writers on logic and similar topics, but the phrase is misleading. Any quotation which is less than the original whole is in that sense out of context. The real index of misrepresentation is quoting *contrary* to context. For example, in his review of Frank Trager's *Why Viet Nam?* Bernard Fall says:

> First of all, let me say immediately two things: his academic credentials are impeccable, his background on domestic issues is liberal, . . . and as a former head of the Point Four program in Burma, he has had firsthand

experience in the Far East, even though his stays in Vietnam were limited to a very few weeks spread over three occasions. The latter fact is hardly inhibiting. . . . **(59)**

From this excerpt, which is accurately reproduced, one would assume that Fall was generally favorable toward Trager. Not at all. The citation is contrary to context, since the rest of the review is devoted to establishing of Trager that "As a Vietnam scholar, he is a total failure." (This latter quotation, which is also taken out of context, is not misleading in the slightest; it sums up clearly and precisely Fall's attitude toward Trager.)

One cannot, in quoting, reproduce the entire context, else there would be no room for one's own material. But one can, and credible writers do, quote according to context. This does not foreclose using reluctant testimony. One could introduce Fall's favorable citation about Trager in this fashion, without violating the context.

Although he is vigorously opposed to Trager, Fall nonetheless admits that "his academic credentials are impeccable, his background on domestic issues is liberal," etc.

The introduction here acknowledges Fall's basic position, and therefore does justice to the context. The reader is warned that, to fully understand Fall's position, he must read the original.

The second common technique of misrepresentation is the omission of significant words or phrases. A common omission is the prefatory "If . . . ." Frequently "not" is omitted to reverse an author's conclusions. Qualifiers such as "some," "possibly," and "perhaps" can be left out of a quotation, making it wholly misleading.

The third technique is substitution: "would" for "might," "knew" for "believed," and so forth.

These errors occur in various combinations. Blame for them is not always self-evident. Printers do make errors, but they are random; an error which reinforces the bias of a writer must be regarded suspiciously. Sometimes it is difficult to judge whether a quotation is used contrary to context, as the context may be involved and ambivalent. But on the whole, analysis of accuracy of citation is one of the most telling and objective techniques to use in determining the credibility of secondary sources.

Summary

There are no hard and fast *rules* of evidence in everyday life to correspond to the legal rule against hearsay. *Principles* of use to the consumers of evidence are as follows. In each case, it must be assumed that the principle holds, other things being equal; that is, unless the evidence is disqualified under some other principle.

SITUATIONAL TESTS

1. *Tension.* The lower the tension associated with an event, the higher the credibility of reports about it.
2. *Accessibility.* The more accessible the situation being reported on, both to the reporters and their audience, the more credible the reports.
3. *Freedom to report* — absence of gag rule. The more freedom a witness has to report things as he sees them, the greater his credibility.

DOCUMENTARY TESTS

4. *Authenticity.* The greater the presumption of authenticity, the higher the credibility of a document.
5. *Internal consistency.* The higher the internal consistency of an author, the more credible his testimony.
6. *Carefulness of generalization.* The more careful the generalizations of a writer, the higher the credibility of his testimony.
7. *Reluctance.* The greater the damage of his own testimony to a witness, the more credible it is.

CHARACTERISTICS OF THE WRITER

8. *Expertise.* The greater the relevant expertise of an author, the higher his credibility.
9. *Objectivity.* The greater the objectivity of an author, the more credible his testimony.
10. *Accuracy record.* The more accurate the description and prediction record of a source, the higher the credibility of his testimony in general.

TESTS OF PRIMARY AUTHORITIES

11. *Eyewitness principle.* The greater a witness' personal observation of a matter to which he testifies, the higher his credibility.
12. *Contemporaneity.* The more contemporaneous the report of a witness, the more credible his testimony.

Tests of secondary sources

13. *Selection of primary sources.* The more discerning a writer's selection of primary sources, the more credible his testimony.

14. *Accuracy of citation.* The more accurate the citations of a writer, the more credible his testimony.

Suggested Readings

Louis Gottschalk, *Understanding History.* New York: Alfred A. Knopf, 1951, Chapter VII.

Olaf Helmer and Nicholas Rescher, *On the Epistemology of the Inexact Sciences.* Santa Monica: RAND Corporation, 1958.

Allen Johnson, *The Historian and Historical Evidence.* New York: Charles Scribner's Sons, 1934, Chapter IV.

Allan Nevins, *The Gateway to History.* Garden City: Doubleday (Anchor Books), 1962, Chapter VII.

The Sources
of Evidence

PART THREE

6

Government

Then the rulers of the state are the only persons who ought to have the privilege of lying, either at home or abroad; they may be allowed to lie for the good of the State.

PLATO (**173**:211)

Indeed, if one were designing an organization to produce pathological results, one could hardly do better than an information system dependent mainly on spies and diplomats.

KENNETH E. BOULDING (**18**:10)

Legislature and Judiciary

Writers of term papers, dissertations, and arguments will have much to do with the Federal Government as a source of evidence. This is not only because the Government spends billions yearly on intelligence gathering, research projects, and the most extensive list of publications in the world, but also because it employs twice as many public relations men as there are reporters in Washington in an effort to see that the Government side of any issue is fully presented to the public. Government not only makes news, it dispenses news.

State and local governments, of course, also originate intelligence,

91

but we do not deal with such intelligence in this chapter, interesting and important as some of the local issues are — education, crime, housing, mass transit, riots. One has to concentrate somewhere; and because American misperception is most likely to be lethal at the national level, we confine our discussion of the credibility of Government sources to the Federal area.

As a further limitation, we discuss the judiciary and legislature only briefly. Executive intelligence dominates the Federal output and largely determines our relations with the rest of the world. The President and his assistants, the cabinet officers and their departments, and the semi-independent bureaus and regulatory agencies claim most of the expertise in the Federal Government.

The other branches of government, however, do contribute to public intelligence. Members of the judiciary are primary witnesses on crime, constitutional rights, separation of powers, and many other legalistic topics. When judges are quoted on such matters, inspection of their credibility is very much in order.

To the extent that we have inspected the credibility of the Federal judiciary, especially Supreme Court judges, the judiciary comes out well. The background and experience of Federal judges is generally impressive; appointments may be political, but standards of judicial expertise are maintained nonetheless. There is strong resistance to the appointment of unqualified jurists to the Federal bench. Opponents of integration and "hard-line" law enforcement officers have contended that some judges were appointed without adequate experience in the law, but such attacks invoke a very narrow interpretation of what constitutes relevant experience.

On the dimension of perceptual distortion, the provisions for pay and tenure in the Federal judiciary do about as much as can reasonably be done to assure that judges will be freed from political, social, and economic influences, and will speak with sincerity and candor. We cite the record of Justice Hugo Black, whose appointment was challenged on the grounds that he had been a segregationist. Whatever racial and cultural biases he may have had in his younger days disappeared in the atmosphere and security of the Court.

A Federal judge, more than any other public servant, is free to call a spade a spade. Justices are human. They make errors, both of fact and judgment. Occasionally one finds bribery and influence-peddling in the lower-level judiciary. But placed on the broad spectrum of human performance, their word is as consistently credible as the most rigorous critic could expect.

A somewhat different situation arises when judges depart from legal concerns and testify to nonlegal matters. There is no reason why judges cannot make themselves into authorities on nonlegal matters; but when they move outside the area of their primary expertise, their perceptual capacity is not inherently superior to others. At least one member of the current (1968) Court has drawn fire because of his extralegal writings. Justice William O. Douglas, a man of many talents, has written on policy matters far afield from his judicial concerns. He writes on everything from foreign policy to conservation. Is he, on the extra-judicial topics, a credible authority? We suspect that the vast range of his concerns may preclude the possibility of genuine expertise and credibility in all the fields he writes about.

The impact of Congressional opinions is widespread and significant. Can one believe the testimony of senators and representatives, the results of their investigations, the conclusions of the many research reports which they commission?

There is, first of all, a problem of authenticity. One cannot always tell whether the statements of a member of Congress are really his own. They may present data he is personally responsible for, or they may merely present what has been dug up for him by a research assistant. With the crushing demands on members of Congress, it is hard to see how they can avoid depending on ghost-writers for the vast majority of statements they must make on matters of public policy. We referred earlier to the spurious nature of an important article published over the signature of former Senator Paul Douglas. Since no public figure wants it known that his speeches or books are not his own, it is difficult to find out what proportion of the statements of legislators is original and what proportion is ghostwritten. Legislators do tend to specialize: Fulbright on foreign affairs, Richard Russell on tax policy, Wright Patman on small business, for instance. A rule of thumb commends itself: a statement by a member of Congress is more likely to be his own, rather than ghostwritten, if it deals with his major interest.

Considerable insight into the nature of Congressional expertise is provided by Ralph K. Huitt's classic study of a Congressional hearing. The bill under consideration was the proposed 1946 extension of the wartime price-control act; the hearing was held by the Senate Committee on Banking and Currency. Huitt observes:

The Committee members seemed most impressive when they were act-ing as representatives of specific constituency interests in their states. Here they seemed to speak as experts in their own right. The clichés fell away, the fuzziness and amateurishness disappeared; here the facts were clear and the grasp sure. As a consequence, when the senators talked details of the products and industries of their states with each other they could get together on what they meant, the frustrations of contradictory figures and shifting frames of reference relieved for the moment. Mitchell on the dairy industry in Washington, Murdock and Millikin on dairy cattle in Utah and Colorado, Hickenlooper on land prices in Iowa, Ful-bright on strawberries and poultry in Arkansas — these are but a few examples of members speaking easily and with authority on the interests of their states. (**96**:347)

But expertise in one field is not contagious in politics any more than elsewhere. The solon most sophisticated on taxes may know nothing at all about civil rights. On specific areas of foreign policy, the experts are rare. What legislator, for instance, knows the history, sociology, manners, and mores of Viet-Nam, or has had extended residence there? In fact, to the extent that a Congressman has actually been to a non-English-speaking country, he is probably afflicted with considerable *mis*-information. Congressional junkets, which may help to attract better men than would be in politics if no such fringe benefits existed, are nonetheless dangerous to the fabric of legislative intelligence. It is best to let Lederer tell the story of Congressional junketeers:

What frequently happens to them is an outrage to common sense. They get what is known as "the business." Every foreign minister and agency insists on having the honor of entertaining and briefing the distinguished visitors. The ambassadors and generals stationed overseas advise the American VIP's that they must accept invitations or the natives will lose face. And so the few days "inspecting" are spent in a mad rush of brief-ings, parties, and dinners, usually interspersed with shopping. Result: the American departs in a state of fatigue and ignorance — but with a happy collection of mementos — a silver cigarette case suitably inscribed by the prime minister, native art, etc. His total time has been spent in two or three official mansions, a couple of briefing rooms, and several stores. He has neither seen nor learned much new about the country except what his own — and what foreign officials, which is often the same thing — want him to. Occasionally there are VIP's such as Senator Mansfield, Congress-men Porter and Lindsay, to name a few, who do superb jobs of investi-gating an overseas area. They are unusual. (**126**:99)

Some legislators have made themselves experts, some have done considerable homework, some have conducted admirable hearings. But election to Congress does not automatically carry with it the ability to testify truthfully on crucial policy matters.

We come now to bias. Does politics impose upon its practitioners an overriding perceptual distortion? Certainly the necessity to go along with public opinion, to say what is likely to please one's constituents, is a debility of some moment. Legislators, being human, range all the way from the late Joseph McCarthy, an outrageous liar, to Robert Taft, whose integrity was substantial.

On matters where public opinion is evenly divided or indifferent, there is little more problem for legislators than for other would-be experts; but it is precisely the controversial topics with which we are concerned: Cuba, China, Israel, Viet-Nam, HUAC, the military, capitalism, socialism, God, mother, country. On these issues and many more, politicians are not completely free to testify as they believe. And it *is* an impeachment of a Congressman's testimony to show that he said something because he had to get along with his constituents. There is nowhere a better description of the debilitating pressures on Congressmen than the first chapter of John F. Kennedy's *Profiles In Courage*. (**107**)

But there are more subtle problems of bias. Neither constituent pressures nor mink coats and deep freezes tell the whole tale of attempts to influence Congressmen. There are parties and publicity, speaking engagements and back scratching, hospitality at country houses, and today even a kind word said in the ear of a strategic college admissions officer. A Senator who goes too far in opposing the party line may find his home state short on defense contracts or his patronage otherwise curtailed. Of factors disposing to bias in politicians there is no end. Clearly members of Congress must be evaluated as individuals. No generic credibility can be assigned to them.

It is worth mentioning that on the most decisive index of credibility, predictive record, Senator Fulbright has scored solidly. On the Tonkin Bay resolution his foresight failed, but in the words of Tristram Coffin, one of his biographers,

Fulbright's overall record of prophecy is pretty good. He warned President Truman that unless atomic energy were put under international control, there would be a monstrous arms race and proliferation . . . He told Secretary Dulles that arms shipments to India and Pakistan would lead to war between the two. He argued that the Eisenhower Doctrine was an unwise grant of unlimited power to the President, and would lead future Presidents into war on the basis of patriotic generalities in a Senate Resolution. He warned President Kennedy the Bay of Pigs would be a fiasco. (**37**:259)

Just as it is impossible to generalize about individual members of Congress, it is impossible to generalize about Congressional hearings. They have great potentiality because of the power and purse of the Congress. Packer, at the end of his long study of ex-Communist witnesses, points out that because they are open-ended and nonadversary, Congressional hearings can elicit a coverage of controversial topics denied to court trials and administrative hearings. But he concludes:

> These advantages, while theoretically impressive, are in practice rarely exploited to their full extent, and are in any event more than offset by several crippling disadvantages. Chief among these are politics and publicity. . . . As long as the Congressional inquiry serves as an instrument of politics, a means by which political points are won and lost, its utility as a fact-finding institution in a highly charged context is bound to be sharply limited. Less obvious but equally disadvantageous is the flimsy structure of the typical investigation. The committee members are busy men. They are forever having to leave the hearing room to go to the floor of the House or Senate, or to some other, equally pressing committee meeting. Members wander in and out. The presiding officer may change several times during a single session. Sometimes the new man does not quite catch the drift of what has gone before. The whole business is apt to be quite unsystematic. The cure for all this is supposed to be the committee staff, particularly the committee counsel. But, as we have seen, staff members are not always adequately prepared. And the caliber of personnel, while outstanding in some cases, often leaves something to be desired. (**171**:228)

Huitt's picture of the OPA hearings is basically similar. In addition to the disorganization and aimlessness, he emphasizes the highly partisan nature of the hearings and the disposition of Democrats to perceive a side of price control which would justify its continuance while Republicans perceive the opposite side. Obviously, as a source of testimony, witnesses before such a hearing are not likely to be objective. The witnesses called by the Democrats would be encouraged to tell one side of the story; witnesses called by the Republicans would be prodded to tell the opposite. In the OPA hearings there was no objective or impartial mediator or evaluator to produce a coherent end result: "Thus contradictions need not be resolved, and in these hearings they were not resolved. The hearings could be said not to have progressed. At the end the same questions were being asked as at the beginning, and were receiving the same sets of answers." (96:354)

Bias affects Congressional hearings. Evidence contrary to a committee's beliefs can be omitted from the record. Hostile witnesses can be grilled, friendly ones babied. Third-rate authorities can be called, first-rate ones neglected. Awkward matters can be postponed, strategic ones trumpeted. What matters, from a political standpoint, is the headlines of the moment. Few will pore over the record to register a judgment of truth or falsehood, and even when they do, events have moved past the moment of relevance. William Allen White is reported to have said that the American public usually gets the truth, but by the time it does, the truth is cold potatoes and does them no good.

When, on the other hand, a well programmed and directed hearing takes place, much of value emerges. Fulbright's investigation of foreign lobbyists was such a hearing. The subject matter of this investigation was less controversial, less likely to produce merely hardened commitment to a preconceived opinion. Staff work was well planned and coordinated. One chairman presided over the entire proceeding. Far from being able to predict the outcome, the reader of the transcript finds himself being led along an inductive path which wanders but always returns, slowly points to a generalization, and at the end leads him to believe that the Foreign Agents Registration Act is inadequate. The attitude of the Committee is one of inquiry; the mutual suspicions and hostilities of the OPA investigators are absent. (219) The *report* of such a committee is therefore more credible than the report of a partisan hearing such as the OPA generated.

But there is a more significant problem in evaluating testimony from Congressional hearings than distinguishing between good hearings and bad ones. The tendency of students and the general public is to clothe all testimony given before the hearings with the prestige of Congress, disregarding the difference between the conclusions of a committee and the testimony of individuals who appeared before it, and further disregarding the fact that people of all shades of competence appear. The hearing room is simply a forum in which witnesses express their opinions; the transcript is no more than a vehicle which conveys that thought to the public. The thought is not improved by being carried in a transcript of a Congressional hearing. The vital thing, then, is the integrity of the individual witness, which is even more important than the integrity of the committee before which he appeared.

Before we leave the subject of Congress, we must look at the ubiquitous *Congressional Record*. This frequently quoted journal is not what it purports to be, a record of what takes place on the floor of Congress. Revisions, insertions, inaccuracies abound. Walter W. Stevens, concluding a thorough discussion of "Inaccuracies in the Texts of Congressional Speeches," says:

> What has not been said in Congress has been printed as if it had been said; proof-readers and editors have freely altered statements made by Congressmen; the inevitable confusion in which the reporters have worked has resulted in human error; Congressmen have revised their remarks after delivery; and statements made on the floor of Congress have been expunged from the record. (**210**:187)

From the standpoint of a rhetorical critic, who must know exactly what Senator Jones did say in his Senate speech on apportionment, revisions of the text made afterwards by the Senator to make himself look better preclude accurate assessment. From the standpoint of a policy deliberator, however, who wishes to use the Senator's remarks as evidence, the revisions may more closely represent the truth than the original statement. This kind of "inaccuracy" does not compromise the credibility of Congressional testimony taken from the *Record*. Insertions, alterations by proofreaders, and human errors in transcription are another story. Clearly the *Congressional Record* is not the best quarry from which to mine the testimony of national politicians. *Any* statement gleaned from the *Record* should be checked against the original source for accuracy and, if possible, checked with newspaper accounts.

But the major credibility "problem" associated with the *Congressional Record* does not arise from its corruption at all. It arises instead from the kinds of materials which find their way into it, some of which have the highest credibility, some of which are monstrous fabrications, but all of which take on the popular prestige of the Record. The *Record* is a hodgepodge outdoing even the *Reader's Digest*. In it are to be found editorials, home-town news items, Gallup statistics, magazine

articles, all included by the "leave to print" mechanism. The Holy
Scriptures, which are alleged to furnish the Devil with hortatory materials, are monolithic compared with the *Congressional Record*. Any
scoundrel who wants to prove the most incestuous blasphemy can find
support for it somewhere in the *Congressional Record;* inspect "citations" in *The Worker* (Communist) or *None Dare Call It Treason* at
the other end of the spectrum.

Consequently, an unexceptionable rule — a singular situation in the
study of evidence — must be applied to citations from the *Record: no
quotation taken from the Congressional Record has any weight unless
the original source of the quotation is given and qualified.* Nine times
out of ten, one can secure the original document from which to quote
directly.

Members of the Congress, Congressional hearings, reports of Congressional committees, and the *Congressional Record* supply much of
the evidence used in policy deliberation, but one may not presume that
this testimony is accurate. Its purveyors are forced to speak on innumerable topics about which they cannot hope to be expert, and they
are obliged to stay within the parameters of permissible opinion-range
or lose their jobs. We do not here denigrate the members of the U.S.
Congress, most of whom are outstanding; what we do is emphasize that
Congressmen are in a situation where truth on controversial matters
cannot generally be expected from them.

The Executive

An across-the-board study of evidence fed into public intelligence
channels by the Executive branch of the Federal Government would require a lifetime to accomplish and take many books to contain. Some
delimitation is essential; for purposes of this study, we have narrowed
our consideration to Federal testimony on foreign affairs, and within
that area, to recent conflict situations. *We do not pretend that this gives
a balanced picture of Executive department intelligence;* we do claim
that this is the one area on which the student and the public desperately
need more accurate evidence.

It is not just the importance of the subject which causes us to concentrate on foreign affairs; it is the mystique of Government officials
when pronouncing about them, the wiser-than-thou attitude assumed
on the basis of access to a multi-billion-dollar intelligence-gathering

operation whose product is largely denied to outsiders. That this mystique contributes greatly to the deference accorded high Government officials there can be no doubt. When a Government official is challenged, he can always fall back on the claim that no one who is not privy to the national intelligence estimates can possibly speak authoritatively about foreign affairs.

Such a claim to omniscience is difficult for journalists or academics to refute, as difficult as it is to argue with a religious fanatic who claims that his pipeline to the Almighty is the only one in working order. The decision makers in the White House do not have to tell those on the outside how they know what they claim to know. Since there is always the possibility that some secret agent *has* penetrated the Kremlin, and that the Government knows something people on the outside cannot know, the Government claim to superior knowledge is not easily challenged — *at the time*. With the aid of history, one can show where the Government of three years ago or five years ago was misinformed; but this is little help in dealing with an intelligence system which claims to have all the answers *now* and will not tell how it got them.

Despite the shield of secrecy behind which the Federal intelligence network operates and the billions spent on it, there have been challenges to its credibility. This is what is referred to by the press as the "credibility gap" — the gap between what the Government says is happening and what enterprising reporters uncover for themselves. We emphasize again that we do not pretend that this credibility gap applies to all Federal agencies on all topics. The Departments of Interior, Agriculture, Labor, and so on do not primarily deal with areas as sensitive as foreign affairs, and the intelligence which they produce is not to be classified with foreign intelligence. Federal agency data, by and large, seem to be trustworthy. The Bureau of Labor Statistics and the Bureau of the Census, to name only two, have been so constituted as to enable professionals free from political pressures to compile basic data about the country.

There are, of course, instances in which Government statistics which are basically sound are distorted for political reasons. McGaffin and Knoll report one such case:

> Six days before the 1962 Congressional elections, for example, Secretary of Labor W. Willard Wirtz announced that unemployment had reached a three-year low during October and that the number of unem-

ployed had declined by 2,000,000 since the Kennedy administration
had taken office. . . . After the election returns were in, Wirtz admitted to
James McCartney of the Chicago *Daily News* that his statement had contained "invalid" statistical comparisons because the figures had not been
adjusted for seasonal variations. Wirtz had also claimed, before the elections, that "4,500,000 more Americans have jobs than when this administration took office in January of 1961." This total, too, required seasonal
adjustment and shrank, after the votes were in, to 1,224,000. (**142**:22–23)

But such patently political distortions of Government evidence are minor
compared with the problems of foreign policy intelligence which are our
main concern.

It is worthwhile to look at Executive branch testimony about the
crises of the 1960's from the standpoint of all of the indices of credibility, noting which ones apply and which do not, and evaluating the
credibility of the Government on the indices which are relevant. We will
consider accuracy record last. By crises of the 1960's we mean the two
Cuban incidents, Viet-Nam, Santo Domingo, and minor cold-war skirmishes. Occasionally we will find it enlightening to go back a decade or
two, but generally our concern is with the functioning of the current
global intelligence network.

We begin with the observation that since tension is high in most of
these crucial areas, there will be a strong "tendency of agents in the
field to report — consciously or unconsciously — that information which
they perceive as desired or expected by decision-makers at the center."
(**168**:170) This perceptual distortion will be greatest in the case of
Viet-Nam, where most of our chips are on the table, plus many of the
Russians' and some of the Chinese'; it will decrease as we consider
areas of lesser tension, reaching a minimum where United States relations with Andorra are concerned. Where tension has fluctuated within
an area, such as the Dominican Republic, Government testimony will
be less credible at the peak of a crisis, returning slowly to normal afterwards.

Next comes the matter of accessibility. None of the tension areas
are highly accessible, because they are at some physical distance from
the intelligence consumers, because they possess different cultural and
linguistic systems, and because they are off limits in general to casual
visitation. In the early days of the Dominican crisis, the airports were
closed and reporters could not get into the country. Cuba was for many
years closed to all but aerial surveillance and undercover spying. As

noted in Chapter 5, intelligence about none of the crisis areas is likely to be as reliable as intelligence about Western Europe.

Incredible as it may seem, government intelligence is even plagued with nonauthentic documents. During World War II, the British Operation Mincemeat planted a large number of fake documents where they would find their way to the German high command; the result was complete surprise about Allied invasion plans in the Mediterranean. (**158**) Frequently since that time, double agents have misled both sides in the cold war with fraudulent documents. (**15**) We predict that when the full history of Viet-Nam is known, some of the captured documents on which American intelligence has based its consistently deprecatory conclusions about enemy morale will be exposed as deliberate plants. Nor is the transgression of authenticity all unintentional; the prevailing belief among private intelligence experts is that CIA's *Penkovskiy Papers*, published in 1965 by Doubleday, are largely fictitious. (**238**: 283) Where secrecy prevails and government refuses to reveal its sources, exposure of unauthentic documents is all but impossible.

We come now to the freedom of government agents to report. Two distinct operations are included here: (1) freedom to talk to reporters and the public, and (2) freedom to transmit findings upward within the intelligence network without fear of reprisal.

All governments and many other organizations operate under gag rules. Agents are often not free to tell reporters what they have found without clearance from the top. There may be certain drawbacks to this rule in practice, but in theory it is hard to see how any government can allow itself to speak with conflicting voices. When this happens, as it did in Laos recently, with State, Defense, and CIA going three separate ways, only confusion can result. Truman was right in firing MacArthur; an appeal to political forces over the President's head cannot be tolerated. Especially on vital matters, the Government must speak with one voice, so a gag rule is necessary.

How far such a rule should be carried is open to dispute. One can conceive of tolerating disagreement within the government on many nonsensitive issues. The State Department generally will not even tolerate this. Senator Fulbright took the measure of the gag rule in 1959, when the Senate Foreign Relations Committee undertook to obtain the advice of *retired* foreign service officers, asking them to comment anonymously on aspects of foreign policy they felt competent to deal with. Their responses were collected and published by the Committee.

The document containing their advice is one of the most searching and stimulating tracts on foreign affairs in existence. Gratified by the outcome of this effort, the Committee sought to extend it to include the candid opinions of active diplomats. As Senator Fulbright tells it,

> In an effort to provide a balance to this collection of views, the committee asked the Department of State to cooperate in obtaining similar comments from chiefs of diplomatic missions now on active duty, with similar anonymity as to individual identification of views. The Department of State was not willing to agree to the committee's request. (**220**:4)

In other words, no curious Senator is going to be allowed to outflank the Establishment. This is carrying the gag rule too far.

Sometimes prohibitions on release of information are of short duration, sometimes they last interminably. The secret diplomatic communications of the Chinese Civil War period were released in the China White Paper of 1949, almost before the events they reported were over. The gag rule prohibiting disclosure of the facts of Amelia Earhart's mission of 1937, on the other hand, has persisted for more than thirty years. (**73**)

The significance of the gag rule for the student preparing an expository or argumentative essay lies not just in its tendency to restrict information, but also in its imposition of uniformity on Government testimony. When reporters representing different organizations give similar observations, their dispatches reinforce each other. When two Government officials make identical statements, their combined testimony is not usually more credible than the single witness of one of them. It is useless to "fortify" the testimony of the Secretary of State with the testimony of an Assistant Secretary and a military spokesman. Barring unusual crossing of wires, they will tell the same story — a story whose basic outlines are determined at the top. A country desk man in the State Department is simply not allowed to contradict his superior the way Homer Bigart can contradict David Halberstam or James Reston. One of the most inept uses of evidence by students, and one of the most widespread, is the assumption that if they can only keep piling up testimony from Government officials, they will prove their point. This is simply not reasonable; the testimony of one Government official does not necessarily fortify that of another.

Freedom of agents to transmit findings upward without fear of reprisal is equally significant in evaluating Government intelligence. The

Dale Carnegie principle — telling others what you think they want to hear — has probably operated to some degree in all societies. Sometimes this is called providing "congruent" information. Anthropologists report the existence of cultures where this practice is universally followed. In a twentieth-century intelligence apparatus, it can only result in disaster.

We presuppose the necessity for candor in an intelligence system. In a world coming to be more and more mechanized, thus eliminating the factor of human judgment at many junctures of intelligence processing, the necessity for candor would seem to be increased. Computers may be deadly accurate in receiving, storing, sorting, translating, and reproducing "information," but they cannot judge it. If the data with which a machine is programmed are faulty, the whole communication system is bankrupt. As the operators of the machines say, the GIGO principle applies — Garbage In, Garbage Out. Therefore the question "To what extent are Government agents free to report what they find?" is vital to an evaluation of intelligence. The answer is not encouraging.

We might begin with the case of the pre-1950 China experts. Because of America's fascination with China, and the numbers of American missionaries sent there, there was excellent raw material for a first-class corps of China experts. By 1940, the State Department had built up a group of China specialists who were "the most envied corps of diplomatic experts in the Orient." (5:45) They were frequently sons of missionaries, had spoken Chinese since childhood, were intimate with the customs and thinking habits of the Chinese. There were twenty-two of them before World War II, and the data they furnished Washington were highly accurate and insightful. (Their reports were also frequently disregarded during the war, when someone like Ambassador Hurley chose to believe Chinese government sources instead. See 126:100.)

Almost to a man, these experts predicted that the Communists would take over China unless there was major reform in the Kuomintang. For these accurate but unpalatable dispatches they came under the fire of McCarthy and the professional anti-Communists, and every conceivable technique was used to discredit and harass them. By 1952, this corps had all but disappeared. Twenty of the twenty-two were scattered around the world, and only two remained in Government posts dealing with China. One of the twenty, John Stewart Service, was cleared six times in succession by the State Department Loyalty Board, only to be finally dismissed. He was not reinstated until June, 1957, as the result of a Supreme Court order.

This dismemberment of the China Service alone demoralized the diplomatic corps for a decade and vitiated State Department evidence on China as well. Only because of the trauma of the Korean War period and the McCarthy purges was it possible for American officials to believe that Russia had taken over China, then that the Peking Government was about to fall, and throughout that Chiang Kai-shek could somehow regain his former domain. The influence of State during this period was considerable on other branches of Government service; one cannot expect men willing to tell the truth to gravitate to Government service when political forces can thus mercilessly crush them.

The powerful impetus given to congruent reporting in the 1950's has never really subsided. In early 1967, Dr. Chris Argyris, Professor of Organizational Behavior at Yale, reported on an extensive study he conducted of State Department managerial techniques. Dr. Argyris held long interviews with ninety-one American diplomats. He found the State Department to be dominated by a social system that discourages frank reporting:

> When he asked the diplomats what they would do if they disagreed with the position of a superior, the majority replied: "Be careful about disagreeing openly." Many younger diplomats, they said, quickly learn that "to make real changes you must be a wave maker and that's dangerous. It could harm your career." A senior diplomat is quoted as saying, "If I were to be very honest, I think that one reason I have succeeded is that I have learned not to be open, not to be candid." (**45**)

The thought of a substantial portion of American intelligence originating with such people is disturbing.

Yet sycophantic reporting is encouraged all down the line. Secretary McNamara's many fact-finding trips to Viet-Nam are cases in point. As Mecklin reports, "McNamara was rightly famous for a steel-comb mind that specialized in weeding out fluff, and he was probably as good, or better, than anyone else in the Pentagon at that kind of on-the-spot inquiry." But for him to expect those whom he interviewed on the Vietnamese battlefields to be candid when he interviewed them in the presence of their superior officers, who would remain behind to punish them when he had gone back to Washington, was "contrary to human nature."

(**150**:214) Most of his interviewing was done in the presence of the Commanding General. In 1963, this was General Harkins, a "see-no-evil" supporter of the Saigon regime and the last man who should have been present if one wanted accurate reporting.

Ultimately, the ground rules for transmitting information from field agents to the top is determined by the man at the top. The attitude of President Johnson toward "team play" was probably stricter than that of his predecessors. The Associated Press version of the rules is reported in this dispatch of August 20, 1965:

> President Johnson lunched with the State Department's high command Thursday and said he told them he expects "frank and private advice before decisions are made, and unified support" once they are reached. The best of policies, Johnson informed reporters, cannot be carried out unless people are for them all the way. (**6**)

The call for "frank and private advice" before decisions are made sounds laudable, until one reflects that there are few areas that have not already been covered by some decision. And what does it mean to be "for them all the way?" As perceived by agents in the field, this can only mean reporting what will appear to show a decision as correct. "All the way" can be a very long way indeed. Are present policies to last forever? Once the official mind has been made up, has it been made up for good? Can no new evidence, no new development on a controversial front open the way to reconsideration of a policy? And what will be the fate of an agent who hints to the boss that all is not sweetness and light? Supporting a policy "all the way" may mean all the way to disaster.

It would, of course, be unreasonable to think that the whole realm of foreign policy, much less domestic policy, is closed to reconsideration, and that only favorable developments are to be allowed in the channels of communication. As we indicated at the beginning of this discussion, the strictest requirements for providing congruent information apply to the high-tension situations. This is confirmed by the analysis of Clayton Fritchey, writing in the January, 1967, *Harper's*:

> The President tolerates, at times even encourages, lively argument and some dissent among his principal advisers on many of his policies, including such important ones as taxation, labor-management problems, monetary issues, and civil rights. Also, diversity of opinion on some phases of foreign policy is not taboo. But Asia is out-of-bounds. With the departure

of Under Secretary George Ball, the No. 2 man at the State Department, the last dissenting voice on Vietnam is gone from the President's inner circle, which from now on will be hermetically sealed against any fresh thinking on the war.

What is true of State is also true of the President's chief advisers in the White House, the Cabinet, the National Security Council, the Joint Chiefs, the CIA, etc. On Vietnam, a hundred minds with but a single thought. If a stray critical thought should ever get loose in this company, it will be shot down long before it reaches the boss. (**66**:92)

If disagreement is not tolerated in top councils, it is unreasonable to expect that the intelligence network will be free of distortion on the highly sensitive topics.

There are, of course, strong-willed men and men of uncompromisable integrity in any organization — at least for a while. David Halberstam, who had reported from the Congo during Ambassador Edmund Gullion's tenure there, compared Gullion favorably with the Nolting-Harkins-Richardson team which headed the Saigon mission in the early 1960's:

> Sometimes during those months I used to wonder what would have happened if someone like Edmund Gullion had been ambassador to Vietnam. Gullion seemed to me to be the epitome of what an American diplomat should be. He always tried to find out exactly what was happening in the country where he was posted, and he had a reputation for being blunt both with the State Department and the White House. This frankness was tolerated at State and permitted at the White House because Gullion personally had President Kennedy's respect; he had gained this when, as a high political officer in Indochina, he had frankly told visiting Congressman Kennedy in 1951 that the French were not winning the Indochina war and could not win it under the present circumstances. Gullion convinced Kennedy both that American policy should be changed and that he was a young diplomat who was willing to speak out despite what the rest of the mission was saying. I still find it hard to believe that Gullion would have deluded himself or his superiors very long about what was happening in Vietnam at the time. (**82**:74)

Thus there are some agents in the field willing to feed into the intelligence network data which will not please their superiors. But Edmund Gullion resigned from the diplomatic service to head the Fletcher School at Tufts. Under Johnson's rigid rules, mavericks were silenced or driven out; the field was left to the "team players." (See especially **201**:Ch. 12.)

After Eugene McCarthy's spectacular showing in the early 1968 Presidential primaries, President Johnson seemed to change course somewhat. He allowed Clark Clifford, described by one of his friends as "a very clear-headed man [who] has the ability to see things as they are and not as he would like them to be" (**199**), to open up channels for noncongruent information on Viet-Nam in his first months as Secretary of Defense. One swallow does not make a summer, and the state of Government intelligence cannot be rehabilitated overnight; but Clifford appeared to make a start.

This brings us to the documentary tests of evidence. First, on the matter of consistency: given the gag rule, one could expect that no obvious inconsistencies would be allowed to come from Government sources. Occasionally, when a general in Saigon has not yet heard what the Pentagon put out on a certain battle, there will be conflicting reports. These are soon corrected. The interesting problems of consistency arise from changes in the official position over time.

Many critics make much of the fact that the Government line on Viet-Nam has changed so fundamentally. Until 1965, the war was considered internal subversion, supported by Hanoi but still plain insurgency. This view abruptly changed. The best evidence indicates that the Government's new line, aggression from the North, *preceded* actual involvement of North Vietnamese units in the fighting. At the least, however, North Vietnamese units did move south of the demilitarized zone. As a response to the involvement of American troops, the label "aggression" applied to this movement may be unwarranted; but there has been a high degree of consistency, since 1965, in the Government line.

There is further reason to suspect the credibility of Government intelligence on the basis of the wildly fluctuating stories put out during the Dominican revolution. The number of Communists claimed at various times to have been involved in the revolt jumped from two to three to fifty-three, fifty-four, fifty-eight, and finally seventy-seven. An intelligence service which could not decide within a week whether Communist participants in a revolution which we were then policing numbered three or seventy-seven seems derelict. (See **48**:53–55.) Inconsistencies do indict the credibility of Government evidence about the Dominican affair. When an organization's "knowledge" fluctuates so vastly from one day to the next, one may presume that the intelligence it disseminates is unreliable.

So we come to inspect expertise, the perceptual capacity of Government agents to see the truth. Government service, no less than politics, has suffered in this country from low prestige in relation to other professions, from low pay, from poor opportunity to advance, from political appointments made as political favors rather than as rewards for meritorious service, from bureaucratic regulations, and from other handicaps. It is no wonder that constant complaints come from Washington that the caliber of entrants into Federal service is not what it should be. These problems are particularly pressing in the Department of State where, despite the glamor of some overseas posts, political pressures have been most deadening. We have already cited the instance of the pre-1950 China specialists.

Nor is it clear that recruits into Government service acquire the proper training and experience. Some of them have been well trained before they enter Government employment. The departments dealing with domestic and economic affairs are probably best off in this regard, those dealing with foreign affairs worst off. (**201:10**) We are only now beginning to obtain the specialized talents, including linguistic competence, for world-wide operations, but all the mistakes and faults will not be corrected in this generation and perhaps not in the next.

This is somewhat surprising, given the upgrading of the educational system which resulted from Russian launching of the first satellite in 1957. However, the primary emphasis in this educational speed-up was on science; other areas still lag. As late as 1966, George M. Kahin of Cornell, probably the foremost American authority on Indonesia, had this to say before the House Committee on Foreign Affairs, Subcommittee of the Far East and the Pacific:

> *Kahin:* . . . We need much greater knowledge than we have of the political factors that govern the situation in Asia. To that end we ought to provide adequate funds to the Department of State so that it can develop a sufficient number of regional experts who are endowed with a really substantial knowledge of particular Asian countries and their current political milieu and with a real ability to speak the languages of these countries. At the same time this Congress and your committee should be supplied with a sufficient number of specialists who are independent of the executive branch and capable of assisting Congressmen such as you — I hope you won't take this amiss if I say it —
>
> *Mr. Zablocki:* I agree with your point that Congress does need enlighten-

ment. That is why we are holding these hearings. I do hope you are
not trying to imply that the State Department is devoid of language and
other specialists?

Kahin: Grossly undernourished, sir. It is not devoid, but in many critical
areas it is seriously lacking in really capable people. It is vastly undernourished with regard to this. . . . (**218**:116)

Part of the difficulty in obtaining accurate intelligence about Viet-Nam
has been due to the shortage of qualified personnel. James C. Thompson,
Jr., who was for five years an intimate of the Government policy-making
process, in explaining how we became so deeply involved, notes:

In the first place, the American government was sorely *lacking in real
Vietnam or Indochina expertise*. Originally treated as an adjunct of Embassy Paris, our Saigon embassy and the Vietnam desk at State were
largely staffed from 1954 onward by French-speaking Foreign Service
personnel of narrowly European experience. Such diplomats were even
more closely restricted than the normal embassy officer — by cast of mind
as well as language — to contacts with Vietnam's French-speaking urban
elites. For instance, Foreign Service linguists in Portugal are able to
speak with the peasantry if they get out of Lisbon and choose to do so;
not so the French speakers of Embassy Saigon. (**215**:48)

And because of the crisis nature of the Vietnamese affair, there was
no time for the lengthy training necessary to make American agents
fluent in Vietnamese (as opposed to French). The three-month or nine-
month courses, as Lederer says, may teach "enough to order a meal in a
restaurant or tell somebody where to carry a bundle; but it is not
enough to discuss the nuances of politics and security with the peasants,
let alone the generals." (**127**:20) As a result, our prisoner interviews
depend on Vietnamese interpreters, who are often Viet-Cong sympa-
thizers, usually deficient in English, and frequently hostile toward white
foreigners.

Intelligent people who are stationed for a long time in a foreign
country and have the initiative to learn local history, culture, and
languages can always do so. Unfortunately, the set of the foreign
service is often *against* this development of expertise. Tours of duty
are usually short. In order to advance in the ranks, officers must win
kudos from their superiors. This means keeping up with Embassy
gossip, attending all the parties, becoming adept at political infighting,
keeping one's relations with visiting VIP's untarnished, and in general

keeping one's nose clean. But these activities, while necessary to survival and membership in the in-group, are incompatible with developing any real expertise on the country. (**201**:33–37) Our own experiences with the mutual-admiration-society aspects of the American diplomatic establishment number only three or four instances, but they confirm in each case the difficulties in the path of a foreign service officer who tries to break away from the clique and get close to the people.

Even worse, foreign service personnel are sometimes forbidden to make contacts which might increase their knowledge of the countries in which they serve. Immediately after World War II, when the Dutch were trying hard to hold on to Indonesia, Americans attached to the Embassy in Jakarta were forbidden to associate with Indonesians; they were to get their intelligence from the Dutch or the British. (**241**) This may have led to a commendable Caucasian purity, but it made no contribution to accurate reporting on the Indonesian situation. Similarly, in the last days of the Batista regime, Ambassador Arthur Gardner issued orders that no one in the Embassy was to have any contact with those elements in the Cuban political spectrum who opposed Batista. (**113**:157)

Thus, despite the widespread belief that a massive intelligence-gathering apparatus such as that of the Federal Government must possess a high concentration of skilled operators, there is considerable evidence to the contrary. The actual expertise of Government agents leaves much to be desired. Not only is the intake of personnel less than optimum, but the climate of conformity discourages learning and repels the more capable, *in the area of foreign operations.*

We come now to the question of objectivity, of how much the Government intelligence system is subject to perceptual distortion from belief systems or biases. As was pointed out with the Kennan analysis of Soviet intelligence in Chapter 4, the most crippling distortions are due to ideology. What has been true of Russian perceptions of the United States has been true, to a lesser extent, of American perceptions of Russia. The early decades of the Soviet Revolution are perhaps too far back to have great relevance to the 1960's, but students of evidence who want to take the measure of ideological distortion by American officials in recent years should read the description of John Foster Dulles' perceptions of Communism in Ole Holsti's "Cognitive Dynamics and Images of the Enemy." Dulles was the ideologue par excellence. His "theological" view of the world, and his hostility toward the Soviet, not just because it threatened American interests but because it was atheistic, introduced an element of distortion into American diplomatic thinking and policy which persists to this day.

Holsti describes the misperceptions to which Dulles' ideology gave rise: that Soviet hostility toward the United States was a party phenomenon and did not represent basic divergence of national interests; that the men in the Kremlin had little or no popular support; that the Soviet was near economic collapse; that scuttling the Aswan Dam loan was in the best interests of the United States. Naturally, this ideology affected the whole intelligence apparatus; Holsti notes that "the Dulles-sanctioned 'purge' of foreign service personnel during the zenith of Senator McCarthy's power was a deterrent to accurate reporting by any but the imprudent or the very brave." (**92**:37) Those who were purged probably had been reporting facts which were incongruent with Dulles' ideology.

Dulles was succeeded, in 1961, by a Secretary of State more moderate in personality but equally intemperate in ideology. Rusk found the devil incarnate in Peking rather than Moscow; he couched his flamboyancies in soft Southern accents; and he left the spotlight to his strong-willed presidents. But the basic ideology is the same: Christian capitalism versus atheistic Communism. All the psychological defenses against incongruent information are well manned at the State Department: the diabolical enemy-image, the virile self-image, the moral self-image, selective inattention, absence of empathy, military overconfidence.

When, in 1965, Ralph White made a value-analysis of North Vietnamese and American statements contained in a prominent book about the Vietnamese War, he found the American officials to be less rigid than their counterparts in Hanoi. One hundred per cent of Communist characterizations of us were in terms of evil rather than good, whereas only 97.7 per cent of the characterizations by Johnson and McNamara of the Hanoi leadership were in terms of evil. (**235**:48) From this we may take some comfort. Pressures on American agents to provide congruent information are presumably 2.3 per cent lighter than those prevailing in the establishment of our current enemy. This is small comfort to the person seeking sound evidence.

In the lower echelons of the foreign intelligence apparatus, the importance of ideology decreases and the importance of career involvement increases. In 1961, after seven long years of touting Ngo Dinh Diem as the right man to fight Communism in Viet-Nam, when evidence began to accumulate that he was losing that fight — militarily, politically, economically, in every way — the agents who had been reporting could obviously not tolerate an admission that they had been wrong. For three more years, official releases flooding from Defense and State Departments denied, concealed, and repressed losses to the Communists in Viet-Nam. John Mecklin, Public Affairs Officer in the Saigon Embassy during these years, describes the situation:

> One of the spectaculars of the American performance in Viet-Nam was the compulsive official optimism about the state of the war. This was partly explained by the common ailment of "career involvement," a man's natural inclination to make his work look good. . . . There were some memorable extravagances. Lyndon Johnson, who visited Viet-Nam in 1961 as Vice-President, compared Diem publicly with Winston Churchill. Secretary McNamara called him "one of the great leaders of our time." After a visit in 1962 General Taylor claimed to have found "a great national movement" that was crushing the Viet Cong. Ruefully I must confess helping to draft a speech by Ambassador Nolting in 1962 forecasting that "the Republic of Viet-Nam will take its place in history as the country where the tide of Asian Communism was reversed and the myth of Communist invincibility forever shattered." (150:116–117)

Mecklin does not draw the conclusion that because things were bad in Viet-Nam we should precipitately have gotten out. Nor do we. His conclusion, and ours, is that Government intelligence was totally worthless; worse, if possible, than no intelligence at all.

Even in 1968, there can be no admission of previous error, no recognition of fallibility. Whether due to ideology, interest, career involvement, unconscious partisanship, or whatever, once a government has developed commitments to certain policies and views of the world, subsequent events have to be seen as supporting those commitments. The satirical *McLandress Dimension* epitomizes this:

> . . . the truly sophisticated man argues not for the wisdom or even the prudence of a foreign policy but for its continuity. Few things more clearly mark the amateur in diplomacy than his inability to see that even the change from the wrong policy to the right policy involves the admission of previous error and hence is damaging to national prestige. (57:67)

Even Clark Clifford's pessimistic review of the progress of the war in Viet-Nam, presented to the cabinet on March 13, 1968, which resulted in Johnson's peace proposal two weeks later and which was described by other cabinet members as "the most comprehensive and candid statement of the war they had ever heard," (**58**) did not bring forth any hint from the Administration that anything had gone amiss. The new "bombing halt" was presented as if entirely in accord with previous policy. The American Government, no less than others, regards the admission of error as a mortal sin. The whole intelligence apparatus is adjusted to this principle. The intelligence product suffers accordingly.

Thus, the lenses through which Government foreign intelligence agents, their superiors in the transmission chain, and the spokesmen at the top view the world are heavily colored. It would be surprising if perceptual distortion did not occur. And the stronger the ideology, the greater the feeling of commitment, the greater the distortion.

Occasionally, in the vast output of Government intelligence, one finds reluctant testimony. The State Department reversal on the bribe to Lee Kuan Yew was mentioned in Chapter 5. There have been others. McNamara admitted that bombing North Viet-Nam was doing little to halt the flow of men or supplies to the South, whereas stopping this flow was the original goal of the bombing; this testimony must be regarded as reluctant.

But such departures from the expected are rare, and they never concern central or fundamental doctrines. Dulles, for instance, could tolerate and eventually accept evidence that the Soviet Union was actually quite strong economically, since the belief in Soviet economic weakness was not the core of his ideology. Hence, one can find reluctant testimony in Dulles' speeches about the growth of Soviet economic strength. But an acknowledgment that Soviet attitudes toward the United States were softening would have dealt a mortal blow to his belief structure and forced him to discard the inherent bad-faith model he held for the Soviets. Hence one can find nowhere any testimony from Dulles to the effect that the Soviets were anything but our implacable enemies.

Several of the tests of evidence which have considerable purchase in evaluating the testimony of individual authorities outside the Government are largely useless for checking Government intelligence. Because the system is monolithic, it hardly makes sense to apply the criteria for credible *secondary* sources. The intelligence system as a whole contains so many primary sources that one could hardly require of the Secretary of Defense, for instance, that he himself be an eyewitness for most of the events he testifies about. He hires and controls his eyewitnesses: they are an integral part of the network for which he is the penultimate spokesman. Naturally, because of the urgency of day-to-day conduct of foreign affairs, there is a premium on contemporary reporting; Government cannot be faulted for depending on much-delayed reports.

Since the primary source material which goes into the final intelligence product is secret, one cannot inspect the accuracy of citation, or the adequacy of selection — except insofar as the whole network can be indicted for low perceptual capacity and high bias. But these two tests of evidence cannot be used to gauge individual testimony as they can be for non-Government authorities. Carefulness of generalization also falters as an independent check because of the impossibility of finding out how much evidence lies behind which generalization. There are multitudes of high-level generalizations in Government news releases; but when one is disposed to question the adequacy of the primary particulars on which they are based, the usual response is "Sorry, but that's classified." Only when a major indiscretion like the "White Paper" on Viet-Nam comes to light can one see through the inferential process and penetrate its vitals. For this document, the evidence of a handful of Chinese weapons captured on the Viet-Cong did not begin to support the generalizations about "invasion from the North." But white papers are temporary aberrations. In general, Government intelligence is released in a summary fashion, with inferential processes obscured and sources well protected.

One little-noted problem of Government intelligence is the tendency for Washington to trust only reports by American nationals. Both Hilsman and Wasserman, two recent critics of Government intelligence, feel that the American system shuts out anything reported by foreigners, even when the foreigners would be in a better position to sense critical items than native Americans. (The liabilities of strangers, particularly those of an alien race, in attempting to find out strategic items of information have already been described.) As Wasserman puts it,

> The structure, techniques (e.g. 'piecing together the picture'), and re-
> cruitment of intelligence are conducive to its uncritical submission to the
> policy framework. For instance, the practice of favoring 'ideal' repre-
> sentatives of a society and discriminating against the foreign-born or
> educated — who might be more receptive to, and capable of, understand-

ing foreign societies — in recruitment for diplomatic and intelligence positions is undoubtedly conducive to uncritical intelligence. (**231**:163)

Hilsman notes a similar finding, the "tendency to discount cultural difference," one result of which is the feeling among intelligence operatives that "for practical purposes one could assume that the basic motivations of Americans were almost universal." (**88**:104, 105) This is a mistake. In the more critical areas, the sources of intelligence will not only think differently from Americans, they will hesitate to confide in Americans. To the extent that this nativist prejudice pervades the intelligence network, the product of that network is suspect.

Unfortunately, this "nativist" prejudice permeates both State and CIA. In the State Department, the Foreign Service has long viewed itself as élite, superior to consular officials, Washington operatives, and attachés whose blood is not so blue. (See **201**.) CIA grew out of the World War II Office of Strategic Services, many of whose leaders were of Brahmin origin. To this day the twenty top CIA officials are largely drawn from the Ivy League colleges. (**238**:141) Given such aristocratic pretensions at the top, it is not surprising that the American intelligence agents abroad are conditioned to solicit informaton from local élites and disregard what is in the minds and hearts of the *descamisados*.

But the final test, the ultimate payoff of intelligence, is its accuracy record, both in description and prediction. By their fruits ye shall know them. Here a word of warning is essential. Absolute accuracy is not to be expected of any human intelligence endeavor. One cannot demand of an expert that he know everything or be able to predict everything. One can only demand that, to warrant our trust, an authority be more successful in describing and predicting than alternative sources of information, and that it not claim knowledge when in fact it is grossly ignorant.

Year in and year out, the credibility of the United States Government on foreign affairs has probably not been much different from that of other North Atlantic governments. All governments have sensitive areas where they do not perceive accurately and have cover stories to conceal things they do not want to get caught at. At the time of the Suez invasion, the intelligence output of the British Government was particularly untrustworthy. During the Algerian War, the same was true for France. If a much greater credibility gap has been attributed to the American Government in the years of our Viet-Nam involvement, it is perhaps because we have become more ideological, more crusading, more self-righteous than in the past, and more of all these things than contemporary governments of Europe.

Prior to the 1960's, there was no talk of a credibility gap on the part of the American Government. There were, of course, intelligence failures, and occasionally a Government lie was exposed; but there was no bunching of incidents, no pervading belief outside the Government that Government officials could not be trusted.

In order to maintain perspective on Government credibility, one should recall pre-1960 intelligence failures. General MacArthur assured President Truman at the Wake Island Conference in 1951 that under no circumstances would the Chinese Communists enter the Korean War — this at a time when Chinese troops were already far across the Yalu. Clearly no great merit attaches to Government credibility for that prediction. Similarly, in 1951, Rusk, Acheson, and assorted State Department functionaries were describing Manchuria as annexed to Russia, claiming that the Peking regime "is not the Government of China. It does not pass the first test. It is not Chinese." (**187**) Whatever one may say of Mao Tse-tung, one of his obsessions does not seem to be Russophilia. Some years later, Dulles was describing the Russian economy as about to collapse, writing off the Peking regime as a "passing phenomenon," and belittling Nasser's chances of building his Aswan Dam. Later in the decade, our diplomats read about the overthrow of governments in Iraq and Turkey in the morning newspapers; Eisenhower, otherwise a pillar of rectitude, was caught slightly off base with a story denying that any American spy planes had been overflying Russia. Such a miscellaneous collection of intelligence failures is probably par for the course. The American Government probably saw neither more nor less clearly, and lied neither more nor less, than other governments.

The tempo of failures began to pick up in the 1960's. Cuba provided a memorable start. The planned Bay of Pigs invasion was a CIA operation from start to disaster, and because of this it was classified. During the Kennedy-Nixon campaign, Nixon, who apparently knew all about CIA's plans, denied the rumors floating around as the cover story required that he should. Kennedy learned the truth of what Nixon had so vehemently denied only after his election.

Two aspects of the Bay of Pigs debacle are significant for an analysis of Government credibility: internal Government intelligence was largely false, and statements issued to the public were largely false. On both counts, the decade got off to a bad start.

One cannot know how much of what the Government "knows" in general it learns from CIA. In the case of the Bay of Pigs, however, CIA intelligence was dominant. And on this operation, the CIA was right about only one thing: its belief in the courage and willingness to fight of the Cuban refugees whom it enlisted in the invasion army. On every other dimension it was wrong. CIA was wrong in believing that such an operation could be hushed up, in the first place; knowledge of the Guatemalan training camp was widespread, having reached even Castro's ears. CIA was wrong in believing that Castro's army would not fight. It did fight, not with any great finesse, but doggedly and loyally. The CIA was wrong in believing that conditions in Cuba were ripe for revolt, and that the invasion would trigger a mass uprising and whole-sale defections. There was no uprising, and only two or three defections. The CIA was wrong in making no provision for an alternative plan in case the frontal assault failed. CIA told the President that such a plan had been made, when in fact it had not. CIA was wrong in selecting the Bay of Pigs in the first place — the terrain was wholly unsuited to a guerrilla landing. It would be hard to be more wrong than this.*

There was, officially, a complete shake-up of CIA after the Bay of Pigs. But what changes could really be made? Could large numbers of incompetents be fired? Hardly, since disaffected former intelligence agents roaming the streets would be an open invitation to the Russians to obtain priceless secrets. Whatever happened to improve CIA, there could have been no thorough housecleaning. CIA's own attitude was demonstrated when it awarded a secret intelligence medal to Richard M. Bissell, chief architect of the Bay of Pigs, just before his separation from the service. (**239**:232)

So much for internal Government intelligence. What about the releases which were fed to the press and the public? During the Cuban invasion, the whole Government public relations network was drawn into disseminating the cover story: Adlai Stevenson, McGeorge Bundy, Joseph W. Reap, Pierre Salinger, Dean Rusk, Arthur Schlesinger, Jr. What they stated was uniformly false, whether or not each individual knew the whole truth: the United States was not financing the affair; it had not been staged from Opa-locka Airport in Florida; American na-

---

* For a substantial account of the Bay of Pigs affair see **102**.

tionals were not involved; the State Department was unaware of any invasion; all the Government knew was what officials read on the wire services; and finally, there was no invasion, only a landing of a few guerrillas. (See **239**:64)

We do not deny CIA successes in overthrowing the governments of Guatemala and perhaps Iran, or in gathering accurate intelligence (mostly photographic) during the missile crisis, by pointing to CIA failure at the Bay of Pigs. We simply claim that in this one, crucial, close-to-home operation the agency's intelligence was worthless, and the Government's cover story was worthless, too.

But did the press do any better? Admittedly a lot of nonsense appeared in such journals as the *Miami News* and *U.S. News & World Report*. And the performance of the press in pursuing and publishing the facts of the CIA training camp in Guatemala left much to be desired. (**14**) But by and large, from the beginning to the end of the whole affair, press accuracy was good enough to make the Government look very sad indeed. Even if half of what appeared in the newspapers was false, the percentage of truth published by the press was so far ahead of that admitted by Government that no conscientious student of evidence could resist chalking up a big score in the press column.

Part of the reason for press superiority was the general superiority of open sources. Government intelligence operatives who can hide behind the cloak of anonymity and who are protected against exposure by secrecy do not have to be as accurate as those who know that their mistakes will be bared to the world. When one considers that Government operatives have much stronger ideological and career commitments ruling them than rule most newsmen, journalistic superiority is hardly surprising. Wilensky affirms this judgment, especially in light of the Bay of Pigs:

> For these reasons there is some truth to the common assumption that a sophisticated reporter working with open sources is better than an agent working with top-secret information. On the key question of whether an invasion of Cuba would touch off an organized insurrection against Castro by the Cuban resistance, reporters such as Joseph Newman of the New York *Herald Tribune*, fresh from the scene, had better estimates than Allen Dulles and Richard Bissell of the CIA, whose thoughts suffered from the burden of secrecy. (**237**:180)

We turn now to Viet-Nam with the warning that our four- or five-page discussion about Government intelligence on that ill-fated country will necessarily exclude a great deal of relevant data. The United States has been involved in Viet-Nam in one way or another since 1943, and the total amount of publicly available, Government-supplied evidence about events there is so vast that it defies comprehensive study. The student of evidence has one toe-hold on this monumental output, however. The real test of the Government accuracy record, after all, is how it compares with that of alternative sources; the student can therefore justifiably limit his investigation to intelligence disputed by other sources, testing it against the truth as it emerged from subsequent events. But even the territory of disputed events is impossibly vast. Much of what has happened or what has been alleged to happen in Viet-Nam during the past decade has been and still is bitterly disputed by Government agents and non-Government observers. Our criterion for selecting incidents to inspect is therefore subsequent agreement among authorities on what actually happened.

Let us look first at reporting for the period of 1956–1960. These were the years during which the American Government claimed, in the 1961 Viet-Nam White Paper, that South Viet-Nam had produced something close to an economic miracle. Wesley Fishel, one of the discoverers of Diem, a kingpin in the Michigan State-CIA Mission to train Vietnamese police, and senior American civilian adviser to Diem, declared in 1958 that South Viet-Nam "can be classed as one of the most stable and peaceful countries of Asia today." (**60**) Wolf Ladejinsky, Government expert on land reform, dismissed early insurgency as the work of "local Viet-Minh agents in remote areas." (**122**) Government "fact-finding" missions to Saigon were indeed getting the "business"; they returned with a hymn of praise to the strong-willed mandarin who had made a nation out of the shambles left by the French.

Others writing during this period, however, did not focus on exactly the same objects perceived by Government emissaries. Foremost among them, and foremost on any list of those with a claim to accuracy about the last two decades of Vietnamese history, was Bernard Fall. In the September, 1958, *Pacific Affairs*, under the title "South Viet-Nam's Internal Problems," he took a long look at the prevailing optimism and posed some awkward questions. Far from finding an economic miracle, he found mostly difficulties. The aid program was out of balance, and merchants were faced with a glut of unsaleable goods. Indeed, the Federation of Vietnamese Industrialists (equivalent to the National Association of Manufacturers) complained that the heavy importation of foreign products had almost paralyzed local production. Rice exportation, which had averaged 1,500,000 tons annually between 1913 and 1941, was less than 190,000 tons in 1957, and rice exports were stopped in 1958. Industrialization attempts were ludicrous: a watch assembly plant operated intermittently, a petroleum company was scandal-ridden, a coal mine was expected to produce 15,000 tons a year. Land reform had seen scarcely a tenth of the available acreage distributed; and after occupying a meager plot, many farmers found they had not been "definitely granted" the land, but still owed rent or purchase payments to the "rightful" owners. Most significant of all, in this most peaceful of Asian nations, violence was increasing, in a pattern indicating an attempt by the rebels to isolate Saigon from its hinterland. Thus, while the American Government believed Diem to be a miracle-worker and to have pacified the country, Bernard Fall was writing, "The conclusion is inescapable that there must be some coordination between the rebels and the North Vietnamese government. . . . By early spring, 1958, insecurity had made sufficient strides for the reappearance of the once-dreaded pattern of desertion of isolated villages." (**61**:255–7) Fall was right, the Government was wrong.

In the 1956–1960 period, while the Government was painting a rosy picture of what was happening in Viet-Nam, information was available to independent observers which proved that the picture was anything but rosy.

The next period, leading up to the fall of Diem on November 2, 1963, continued the same contradictory pattern: the Government, operating under a "sink or swim with Ngo Dinh Diem" rule, displayed what Mecklin calls "compulsive official optimism." Most of the press, untouched (except for *Time* and Hearst men) by any kind of gag rule or official position, saw things going from bad to worse.

This was the period of Lyndon Johnson's reference to Diem as a Winston Churchill, of General Taylor's "great national movement crushing the Viet-Cong," of McNamara's finding that the war was going so well that the bulk of American forces would be out of Viet-Nam by the end of 1965. More indicative even than these generalities was the treatment given to specific battles, such as the crucial encounter at Ap Bac, forty miles southwest of Saigon. This was the first major encounter between Viet-Cong forces and Saigon troops supplied with helicopters and amphibious tanks. This was the battle described by General Harkins as "a victory for our ally." When the claim of victory raised reporters'

eyebrows, Admiral Felt reinforced the judgment: "It was a victory —
we took the objective." (**116**:91)

Eyewitnesses to the battle of Ap Bac on January 2, 1963, agree on
what happened. A battalion of Viet-Cong were dug in along a tree line.
Three battalions of Saigon troops, an armored company, and a large
reserve force attempted to surround and annihilate them. Artillery bom-
bardments of the Viet-Cong positions alternated with futile attacks on
the ground. The Arvin armored force, after its commander refused
initial orders to attack, finally crawled to within range of VC guns where
it stalled. Five helicopters of a dozen landing reinforcements were
destroyed. At night, having exhausted most of their ammunition, the
VC withdrew, having suffered twenty-one dead and seventeen wounded.
Arvin losses were sixty-one dead and one hundred twenty-three wounded,
including three American advisors. (See **116**:Ch. 4, and **82**:Ch. 10.)

Arvin troops did occupy the village of Ap Bac when the VC had fled,
but only for twenty-four hours. By the time General Harkins and Admiral Felt were announcing the victory, the VC again flew a Communist
flag over the village. The military aspects of the battle, however, are
really less important than the intelligence aspects. In the intelligence war
between Government and press, Ap Bac was only one of thousands of
skirmishes. Halberstam describes part of the action involving Neil
Sheehan of UPI:

> The battle of Ap Bac was followed by a second battle — a press battle.
> Two days later Admiral Harry Felt, Harkins' superior officer, arrived in
> Saigon on an inspection trip obviously precipitated by Ap Bac. At the
> airport Sheehan asked Felt if he had any comment. The admiral replied,
> "I'd like to say that I don't believe what I've been reading in the papers.
> As I understand it, it was a Vietnamese victory — not a defeat, as the
> papers say." He turned to Harkins, who said, "Yes, that's right. It was
> a Vietnamese victory. It certainly was." As they turned away Harkins
> apparently identified Sheehan, for Felt turned around and said, "So you're
> Sheehan. I didn't know who you were. You ought to talk to some of the
> people who've got the facts."
>
> Sheehan, who could hardly be described as a shy young Irishman,
> answered, "You're right, Admiral, and that's why I went down there
> every day." (**82**:156)

However one judges points in this repartee, the reporters' version of
the battle, rather than the Admiral's, won the battle for credibility.

It would be wearying to continue the recital of Government claims and

press denials through the two disorderly years following Diem's down-
fall, through the three years of American escalation and North Vietnamese response which began in 1965, and up to the time of writing. In
1968, the Government is still claiming victory, still claiming that a
"corner has been turned," still claiming that the Viet-Cong are hurting,
that we have stopped losing the war, that there is no stalemate — and
the generals are still demanding more troops.

Unfortunately, the compulsive official optimism John Mecklin noted
in the early 1960's still prevails; there is some evidence that it has even
come to the attention of the President. In March, 1967, Ray Cromley
of UPI reported:

> President Johnson is not happy, of course, that the civilian side of the
> program to "pacify" the countryside hasn't been making sufficient prog-
> ress. But what has really annoyed the President was not so much these
> bobbles as reports sent to him which had painted such a falsely rosy
> picture. Mistakes, bumbles and failures were hidden or glossed over.
> Successes were amplified. Mr. Johnson has discovered some of his polit-
> ical bookkeepers have fudged the books. Now it is one thing to mislead
> the public. It's quite another to mislead the President. (**42**)

It is not surprising, with the gag rule as strict as it is and with Johnson's
insistence on having only team players aboard, that there was considerable distortion about pacification in the intelligence network. It is surprising that the President apparently did not connect this distortion
with his demand that subordinates support a decision, once it is made,
all the way. It is also surprising that, shortly after learning that he had
been deceived about pacification, the President appointed Robert W.
Komer to head the pacification program. Komer is a professional
optimist. In February, 1967, he stated that Viet-Nam's runaway inflation
had been stopped. At the end of the month, it was revealed that the price
rise in Viet-Nam had been 15 per cent, a record rise for a single month.
When queried about this piece of false intelligence, Mr. Komer told reporters, "It was the Tet truce, which always boosts prices." (**115**) From
such servants, the President learned precious little of the unpopular
truth abroad in the world.

The Government has been consistently wrong about Viet-Nam. A few
individual journalists have matched its ineptitude, but by and large,
the descriptive and predictive accuracy of the press has been superior.
But in 1968 is it not possible that we *are* finally winning the war, that

the news releases from Pentagon and White House finally *are* telling the truth? Does a shaky accuracy record really warrant disparagement of Government testimony in the future? Until the rules change, until the directives which govern the collection and transmission of intelligence change, we believe that it is not safe to believe Government intelligence about Viet-Nam. The boy who perennially cries, "Wolf!" may indeed eventually be right; but one has only the record to guide him, and when independently gathered evidence contradicts Government statements, the choice is clear.

Then there is the Dominican crisis of 1965. Since, by definition, this was a crisis, one would expect North's crisis principle (page 75) to apply, and one would expect to find Government intelligence inferior to that of the press and private sources. The evidence is conclusive that this is what one does find. Not only is Government intelligence contradicted by European and Latin American reporters, who do not share the same conservative biases as most Americans, but it is contradicted by those bastions of capitalist rectitude, *The New York Times, The Wall Street Journal,* and *The Christian Science Monitor.* Intelligence about the Dominican crisis has been dissected and analyzed by Theodore Draper, who has written definitive works about Castro's brand of Communism and about the history of the American Communist party, a man who should know a Communist if he saw one.

Draper's indictment of Government credibility on the Dominican crisis begins at the beginning; our intelligence was so poor that the Government was caught napping when the revolt broke out:

> Ambassador Bennett, en route to Washington, had stopped off in Georgia to visit his sick mother. Of the thirteen members of the Military Assistance Advisory Group, eleven had gone off to Panama for a routine conference. The director of the U. S. Economic Mission to the Dominican Republic was attending another conference in Washington. And in Washington, the Assistant Secretary of State for Inter-American affairs, Jack Hood Vaughn, was listening in on a conference of Western Hemisphere intellectuals in Cuernavaca, Mexico. The point is not that these men were particularly remiss in their duties; it is simply that they cannot have any particular claim on our confidence so far as their knowledge or judgment of the immediate, local situation goes. Many of their later assessments were obviously based on informers, who, however, seem to have been singularly uninformative in the pre-revolt period. (**48**:37–38)

What the CIA mission was doing deponent sayeth not.

So, once again, our expensive (approximately $4,000,000,000 a year) intelligence system was caught napping. When it became clear that a real revolution was in progress, not just a palace coup, everybody scurried back to Santo Domingo. Ambassador Bennett, possibly in an attempt to make up for lost time, held an eye-opening press conference on April 29.

> The Ambassador devoted most of the meeting to the "Communist take-over" and rebel atrocities. The first list of 53 Dominican Communists was passed out. The ambassador horrified the assembled correspondents with some of the reports that he had received: the rebels were shooting people against walls to the accompaniment of the Castroite cry, *"Paredón!"* (To the wall!); they had severed heads and paraded them on spikes; Colonel Caamano had machine-gunned [and personally killed] Colonel Calderon .... (**48**:91)

The Ambassador made up in vivid detail for his absence from the country when the revolt broke out. Unfortunately, no evidence was ever produced that people had been shot against walls, nor was the cry "Paredón!" heard in Santo Domingo. There were no witnesses to the severed heads on spikes. Colonel Calderon received a slight neck wound from a street skirmish and within days was drinking beer with the correspondents.

There was a point to the Ambassador's fables, however; they reinforced the diabolical enemy-image the United States desired to create about the rebels. The revolution was at various times described as having been threatened with Communist domination, as having been Communist-inspired from the start, and as having been taken over by the Communists. Naturally, nothing that could be said about Communists could be too horrible.

But at the same time the American Government was attempting to build a picture of Communist domination, it was vociferously insisting that we were strictly neutral, supporting neither side. If it strains one's credulity too much to believe that the United States was really neutral in a dispute between Communists and a conservative military government, then credulity must be strained. This was in fact what the Government claimed. Here it is useful to let a Canadian correspondent tell the story, as Martin Goodman did for the *Columbia Journalism Review:*

> If the debate over Communist involvement had been the only issue between the government and the press, perhaps it would not have reached

the bitter proportions it did. However, there were other questions of fact. Time and again the government spokesman denied things that the reporters had seen. Most of these outside incidents can be lumped together under the question of whether or not the U.S. was neutral in its intervention. The official spokesmen, both political and military, said it was. Against this were the personal observations of scores of reporters, and much evidence dramatically captured by television cameras.

¶ Officials denied that rebel prisoners were being turned over to the junta. Reporters saw it happen. Officials later agreed some had been turned over, but said this would stop. Reporters saw more turned over.

¶ Officials denied that they were allowing armed Dominicans from either side through the U.S. lines. Reporters saw truckloads of armed junta troops go through, notably when the junta embarked on a campaign on May 15 to wipe out rebels in the area north of the corridor.

¶ Officials denied that there was any joint command with the junta. Reporters saw joint commands at San Isidro airport.

¶ Officials denied that there were jointly manned checkpoints searching for weapons. Reporters saw these checkpoints. (**75**:18)

Reporters were not alone in observing a discrepancy between what was happening and what Government spokesmen said was happening. Jose Moreno, Cuban-born, Cornell-trained sociologist who lived through the entire revolution and was probably the most skillful observer present, states that "From the start the U. S. troops sided and fraternized with the loyalists and actually helped them displace the rebels from their positions." (**159**:41)

Then there were the lists of Communists said to have held leadership positions in the revolution — said by the President to have taken it over. Inspecting the lists of fifty-three, fifty-four, and fifty-eight Communists passed out by the State Department, James Nelson Goodsell of *The Christian Science Monitor* found two of them in prison, six out of the country, four jailed shortly after the firing began, and from four to six not in Santo Domingo. (**76**) An error of 20 per cent even before any verification that those participating in the revolution were actually controlling it does not increase Government credibility.

But what of the remaining thirty-five or so? Did they gain control of the revolution? By far the majority were attached to the rebel "commando posts," units of platoon size distributed through the rebel zone. Assuming that many of these were in command of such posts, they would have held a military rank, had there been such, no higher than that of lieutenant.* No member of the "cabinet" of Caamano, the rebel leader, was a Communist. One Communist did sit in on a rebel conference called to discuss whether Garcia Godoy could be accepted as provisional President. Communists did try to start guerrilla warfare in the province of San Francisco de Macoris but failed miserably. Communists were in the thick of the fighting; but to generalize from this involvement to the assertion that the revolution was controlled by Communists is like asserting that Chiang Kai-shek controls China since he rules Taiwan.

Once again, on every important dimension, Government intelligence about the Dominican crisis was fraudulent. Statistics about the number of marines who participated, the number of American nationals evacuated, and the number of negotiators who visited Santo Domingo are probably quite accurate. But on the vital matters, the controversial matters, the matters where American integrity and good will were at stake, Government intelligence was at best false, at worst mendacious.

The 1967 war between Israel and the Arabs hardly established a better record of Government credibility. Of the entire American foreign apparatus, only UN Ambassador Arthur Goldberg and Cairo chargé d'affaires David G. Nes are credited with having anticipated the outbreak of war. Both House Republican leader Gerald Ford and Senate Democratic leader Mike Mansfield said the Government "got caught napping." (65)

In other eras and on other subjects the credibility of the United States Government may be normal for large bureaucratic organizations in the Western World. In the 1960's the credibility of the Government is decidedly below normal. There have been crises in other ages, in inaccessible areas, about matters in which American ideology and the career interests of American officials were involved; but there has never been a credibility gap as wide as the present one.

Newsmen, during Johnson's tenure, attributed most of the blame to the personality of the President. He lied not just about the reasons for the Dominican intervention, about the conduct of the war in Viet-Nam, about the reasons for release of aluminum stockpiles in 1966, about Hanoi's willingness to negotiate in 1964. Reporters believe him to have lied about small things, about the speed at which he drives, about whether he had decided to fill a vacant Government post, about an ancestor claimed to have died at the Alamo of whom no one can find a

* For a description of the rebel command structure see **159**.

record, about the place he claims he was born. These lies may have been minor, but for reporters following the President, they contributed to a belief that the man had little respect for the truth. As Charles Roberts of *Newsweek* put it,

> If the President doubts this, then I invite his attention to a few jottings from my notebooks. In them is a compendium of deceptions that makes Dwight Eisenhower with his occasional lapses (the U-2 incident) and John F. Kennedy with his artful dodges (the Bay of Pigs) look like congenital, undeviating truthtellers. (183)

This is not an isolated judgment. The very sober Freedom of Information and Press-Bar Committee of the American Society of Newspaper Editors observed, in 1968:

> All administrations manipulate the news to a greater or less extent, all have been known to conceal . . . and even lie about important information when it served their interests to do so. Coping with this is the task of every Washington reporter and the ability to cope with it is what separates the men from the boys. But under LBJ the coping is immeasurably more difficult because official deceit is practiced both when there is reason for it and when there is not. (53)

One hopes, with a change in presidents, for a lightening of the gag rule, a lessened ideology and consequent decreased distortion, and a different attitude toward candid reporting of agents. This would improve but not rehabilitate Government intelligence about foreign crises; there will continue to be a modified gag rule, expertise of agents will improve slowly if at all, ideology and career involvement will not disappear. The pathological results Boulding refers to (page 91) are built into the system.

For those disheartened by realizing that the approximately $4,000,-000,000 spent in 1967 by the United States Government for intelligence yielded less than impeccable results, the existence of *worse* intelligence systems may be some comfort. Wise and Ross, astute journalistic observers of intelligence, say of the Chinese system:

> The ultimate test of any intelligence system is how well it describes and analyzes the world scene for its national leadership. Peking's conception of the forces at work outside China — particularly in the United States and the Soviet Union — was so warped that it could only reflect a radical failure of the intelligence process. Much of this could be attributed to Mao's dogmatism and his decision to rule by terror. All intelligence

systems are susceptible to the temptation of telling their leaders what they want to hear. China's system is the most susceptible of all. (**238**:201)

SUMMARY

An overwhelming amount of public intelligence originates with and is dispensed by the Federal Government. The Federal judges speak with authority on legal problems and seem to be relatively free agents. We find their credibility high on topics within the range of their profession. Members of Congress make statements on all conceivable topics; some of these are ghostwritten and of dubious value. But many Congressmen and Senators have made themselves expert on limited fields, and within these fields they are in a position to know the truth. There are many pressures on Congressmen, however, which tend to produce bias, and it is impossible to generalize about Congressional credibility. Individual legislators must be judged on their records. Hearings of Congressional committees also vary a great deal; some of them are mere spectacles, others produce solid evidence. Both the transcripts of Congressional hearings and the *Congressional Record* contain such a wide variety of materials that they defy generalization. Before using testimony from a Congressional hearing or from the *Record*, the student should evaluate the specific witness and never assume that association with Congress necessarily lends credibility to the testimony.

Most of the Federal intelligence output comes from the Executive Branch, which, because it is a bureaucracy with considerable ideological commitments, operates under a gag rule enforcing uniformity of testimony. Thus, on many aspects of Government testimony one can draw generalizations about credibility. When one confines discussion to the crises in foreign relations of the recent past, one finds that as in any period of high tension, Government agents report what they think their superiors want to hear, thus poisoning the network. The gag rule under the Johnson administration was particularly rigid, further blocking candid reporting. The perceptual capacity of Government agents is not always of the first order, and ideology and career involvement seriously distort the intelligence product. The United States government generally refuses to credit intelligence from non-American agents, which tends to increase the effect of the hostility barrier to information.

Finally, on the crises at the Bay of Pigs, in Viet-Nam, and in the Dominican Republic, the Government intelligence record was deplorable.

If, as we believe, accuracy record is the most important index of credibility, Government intelligence on foreign crises in the 1960's can be said to be almost worthless. This may have been due partly to the personality of President Johnson, who was believed by many reporters to place a low value on truth; but no Government can be expected to achieve high credibility, particularly on foreign affairs.

Suggested Readings

Chris Argyris, *Some Causes of Organizational Ineffectiveness Within the Department of State.* Washington: Government Printing Office, 1967.

Max Ascoli, Charles Wertenbaker, and Philip Horton, "The China Lobby," *The Reporter* (April 15 and 29, 1952). Reprinted in *Our Times: The Best from The Reporter,* ed. Max Ascoli. New York: Farrar, Straus & Cudahy, 1960.

Theodore Draper, *The Dominican Revolt.* New York: Commentary, 1968.

David Halberstam, *The Making of a Quagmire.* New York: Random House, 1965.

Roger Hilsman, *Strategic Intelligence and National Decisions.* Glencoe: The Free Press of Glencoe, 1956.

Ole R. Holsti, "Cognitive Dynamics and Images of the Enemy," *Journal of International Affairs,* No. 1 (1967), 16–39.

Ralph K. Huitt, "The Congressional Committee: A Case Study," *American Political Science Review,* XLVIII (June, 1954), 340–365.

Haynes Johnson, *The Bay of Pigs.* New York: Dell, 1964.

Kuno Knoebl, *Victor Charlie.* New York: Frederick A. Praeger, 1967.

Bruce Ladd, *Crisis in Credibility.* New York: New American Library, 1968.

John Mecklin, *Mission in Torment.* New York: Doubleday, 1965.

Herbert L. Packer, *Ex-Communist Witnesses.* Stanford: Stanford University Press, 1962.

Charles Roberts, "LBJ's Credibility Gap," *Newsweek* (December 19, 1966), 24–25.

Smith Simpson, *Anatomy of the State Department.* Boston: Houghton Mifflin, 1967.

Walter W. Stevens, "Inaccuracies in the Texts of Congressional Speeches," *Central States Speech Journal,* IV (August, 1964), 183–188.

David Wise and Thomas B. Ross, *The Invisible Government.* New York: Random House, 1964.

Charles Wolf, Jr., "Indonesian Assignment," in *Public Administration and Policy Development,* ed. Harold Stein. New York: Harcourt, Brace, 1952, 55–60.

7

The Press

It is not often that journalists can be said to have saved the honor of their country. This was, I believe, one of those very rare occasions. Tad Szulc, Barnard L. Collier, Dan Kurzman, James Nelson Goodsell, Philip Geyelin, Bert Quint of CBS, and others, made one feel proud of and grateful for a free press without which the moral and political disaster would have been infinitely greater. When they were struggling against the greatest odds to get the truth and make it known, no public figure was able or willing to speak out against the inconsistencies, contradictions, and outright misrepresentations. In this Dominican crisis, the best and worst of American journalism were manifested — but the worst is far less a stranger than the best.

THEODORE DRAPER (**48**:146)

Newspapers

Most of the intelligence which reaches the American public comes through the mass media. Since this book is intended for students who use evidence in printed form, we do not consider radio and television, important media though they are; the problems in documenting what one hears on the airwaves are so great that radio and television broadcasts are simply unavailable as sources to support a speech or an essay. Consequently, we shall deal primarily with newspapers, news magazines, and general periodicals.

Since many of the concerns which agitate students of the press do not reflect directly on its credibility, we shall not discuss them here: for example, the increasing number of one-ownership towns, the disposition of government to withhold information from the press, the propriety of press coverage of criminal trials, and so forth. While there are many, including the late A. J. Liebling, who hold that monopoly decreases the credibility of the press, we do not believe the evidence supports this contention, and hence we do not deal with the monopoly aspect of newspapers. (See **39**.)

The situational tests of evidence have considerable relevance for newspapers. To begin with the problem of accessibility, reporters face not just the hostility barrier present in foreign operations, but they are denied access to many kinds of data without which their reports are at best incomplete and at worst misleading.

One area where news dispatches suffer from lack of accessibility is in reporting on decision making at high levels of government. Part of what happens in crisis areas is due to government policies made in Washington, and a complete understanding of events in Cuba, the Dominican Republic, and Viet-Nam demands an understanding of what is being decided in Washington. Of course, the press can find out only as much as Government chooses to tell. Arthur M. Schlesinger, Jr., tells what happens when newspapers try to make up for scanty information:

> As for newspaper or magazine accounts, they are sometimes worse than useless when they purport to give the inside history of decisions; their relation to reality is often considerably less than the shadows in Plato's cave. I have too often seen the most conscientious reporters attribute to government officials views the exact opposite of which the officials are advocating within the government to make it possible for me to take the testimony of journalism in such matters seriously again. (**192**:493)

Schlesinger is hardly more sanguine about other sources of information on Government decision making, such as diaries, memoirs, and the like, all of which he acknowledges to be highly tendentious. On this dimension of reality, the public intelligence is presumably to be left eternally in the dark.

For physical access to troubled areas, journalists are again at the mercy of the Government. In the early days of the Dominican crisis, civilian transportation was shut down and the only access was by military vehicles. Reporters who wanted to cover the fracas had to await Government approval. Similarly, the only way a reporter can get to a battle-field in Viet-Nam is by military transport; if the authorities classify an area as too dangerous, reporters can only wait until things cool down and then interview survivors, hardly a satisfactory way to gather intelligence.

These difficulties, however, do not always mean that journalistic sources are incompetent in reporting on classified operations. During the Bay of Pigs operation, the secrecy cover was so ineffective that Tad Szulc of *The New York Times* filed a long report from Miami detailing all the vital data. The Szulc dispatch was so complete that it is possible he knew more about what was really going on than President Kennedy.

As with Government intelligence, newspaper reports are generally more credible when they deal with accessible areas; dispatches from England are less subject to distortion than dispatches from a battlefield, and reports of domestic events are the most credible of all.

When it comes to freedom to report, however, journalists are infinitely better off than Government agents. There are news organizations with gag rules, and they occasionally frustrate a reporter in his attempts to reach the public with a hard-hitting dispatch; but compared with the Government monolith, the press is anarchic and unfettered. Whereas it makes no sense at all to reinforce a statement of Secretary Rusk with the testimony of President Johnson, it makes very good sense to reinforce the testimony of an AP dispatch with the report of a *New York Times* staffer. In Communist countries, by contrast, newspapers are part of the machinery of the state, and a gag rule every bit as strict as that which pervades the American Government inhibits Russian journalists.

Gag rules have been in force at various times on American papers. When Colonel McCormick presided over the *Chicago Tribune*, writers and editors enjoyed little freedom to produce items contradicting the McCormick line. Hearst, the one newspaper chain which still maintains a relatively rigid editorial slant, does not allow its workers complete freedom to report as they see fit, and individual Hearst papers are pretty much in the same mold. Scripps-Howard, which at one time enforced some degree of conformity among its member papers, has relaxed considerably. In 1967, readers of Scripps-Howard papers were treated to the spectacle of a series of articles on American stature and prestige in East Asia by R. H. Shackford, Scripps-Howard Asian specialist, which substantially contradicted dispatches being sent back from Asia by the chain's editor-in-chief, Walker Stone. (Stone was getting the "business," as had his predecessor, Roy Howard, who was also given to whirlwind visits to Asia.) While most American papers do have a basic ideological position — they are naturally for Christian capitalism and against atheistic Communism — they do not impose heavy-handed rules on what their reporters can turn in or on what their editors can pass, at least on most foreign news.

Pressures from advertisers which restrict freedom to report unsavory or uncomplimentary events on the domestic scene are another matter. Newspapers are profit-making concerns, and the good will of substantial advertisers is something no newspaper can do without. A thorough investigation of the censorship exercised over newspapers by business and financial interests would probably reveal as tight a control on local news reporting as the Government exercises over reports of its agents in crisis areas abroad. Were this book oriented toward domestic reporting, where the Federal Government is relatively able to stand up to business pressures, the evaluations of press and Government would no doubt be reversed, with the press bearing the onus of consistently misleading intelligence.

The results of advertiser pressures on newspapers, however, are somewhat different from the results of a Government gag rule. The events about which the Government is sensitive are too visible to suppress intelligence completely, hence the necessity for cover stories or systematic prevarication. But newspapers need not resort to publishing false information; they can simply refuse to publish anything, which protects their clients as well as would the publication of falsehoods. This phenomenon, self-censorship of items hostile to one's clients, is extremely difficult to prove. Evidence that it exists is mostly negative. Paul Dixon, chief counsel for the Kefauver drug hearings in 1959–1960, was startled, when the drug hearings began, at the wide and prominent coverage they received; previous investigations of administered prices had been largely ignored by the newspapers. Why the difference?

Then I realized that at some times the press is more free than at others. The crucial point in this case was that ethical drug companies don't advertise prescription products directly to the layman through newspapers. That meant that since there was no pressure from advertisers, the papers could report whatever they wanted to. (**85**:67)

Reporters, then, although relatively free from gag rules, can report as they see fit *only on such areas as foreign affairs or ethical drug prices where advertisers have no immediate financial interest.*

An outstanding job of rating press freedom has been done by the Freedom of Information Center at the University of Missouri. Using a sophisticated "press independence and critical ability" index and multiple raters familiar with press conditions in at least one of the ninety-four major countries of the world, the Center discovered that the American press ranks sixth in the world. With a rating of plus four representing complete freedom, the top ten countries and their ratings were as follows:

Netherlands	3.25	United States	2.71
Switzerland	3.14	Denmark	2.68
Finland	3.05	Belgium	2.58
Norway	2.98	England	2.37
Sweden	2.77	West Germany	2.36

The factors affecting the American press which detracted from a perfect score were favoritism in the release of news, concentration of network and chain ownership, and the large number of marginal press units. On twenty other factors, the American press scored high. (**138**) We think this is an accurate measure of press freedom in this country. All Communist countries except Yugoslavia scored in the minus column inasmuch as they are basically controlled by the government.

Considering tension, or the crisis principle, newspapers have an advantage over government. Newspapers and the agents working for them do internalize national interests, as we shall see when discussing the objectivity of the press, and to some degree a crisis for the government is a crisis for the reporter also. But reporters are not agents in the strict sense. Because they are not reporting to the government responsible for the crisis, the crisis principle affects their perceptions less directly. They stand aside from the action, they are more observers than participants, and they do not get swept so completely into the march of events. On local matters, this advantage might well be reversed. One can imagine, for instance, that a scandal at DuPont might have crisis implications for a reporter in Wilmington, Delaware.

In general, then, on the situational tests of evidence, one would expect newspapers to achieve somewhat higher credibility in foreign affairs reporting than the Government. Journalists will suffer a bit more because of the inaccessibility of some events, but this will be offset by much greater freedom to report and considerably less crisis involvement.

When one applies the documentary tests of evidence to the press, the major problems of credibility lie in the area of authenticity. In an enterprise so vast and diversified as the American press, practically every known variety of nonauthentic document makes its appearance.

There is, to begin with, substantial plagiarizing. It occurs most often in the form of "black-sheeting," an invidious practice which the better reporters avoid but which continues nonetheless. A reporter writes a story, makes carbons (black sheets) of it, and passes them out to friends, who file the story with their papers as if it were their own. Later on, the recipients of this favor will return it. This practice obviously saves much shoe leather; in unattractive posts it happens frequently. Reporters draw lots or take turns to see who will go out for the story; all then file identical dispatches. This practice serves to compound error: a misquotation, a blurred vision, a garbled translation can become gospel truth to millions of readers. This practice, says Felix Greene, accounts for much of the fictional American picture of Asia: "a single news story can quickly be disseminated and may soon become 'hard fact' because of nothing but sheer repetition." (**81**:xvii)

Even more common, and perhaps more invidious, is misrepresentation of the source of stories. Public relations agents have developed ingenious techniques for cloaking their releases in the guise of legitimate and nonsponsored news. Many foreign governments seeking to tap the American aid program or secure concessions in the American market hire public relations firms to see that they get a favorable press in the United States. Naturally they do not want their releases to appear as paid efforts of the sponsoring government; even the most naïve reader will tend to discount an article paid for by South Africa which touts South Africa's virtues. The most prestigious American public relations firms take contracts with foreign governments to disseminate favorable news: Hamilton Wright, Hill & Knowlton, Harold L. Oram, Max Rogel, and many others have had foreign governments as clients. This practice has led to notable abuses. Carlos Castillo Armas, former dictator of Guatemala, paid $8,000 a month to John A. Clements Associates during the 1950's; Clements happened to be editor of *American Mercury* during this period, and quite naturally his public relations activities affected the coverage of Guatemala in the pages of his magazine. The North American Newspaper Alliance carried in 1959 a number of flattering stories about Formosa written by one Don Frifield; but NANA never informed its outlets (and hence its readers) that Frifield was on the payroll of Nationalist China's public relations firm, and that he had received $19,700 during a two-year period for editorial services. Douglass Cater and Walter Pincus claim that a veteran P. R. man told them that he placed between one hundred and two hundred stories a week in newspapers, sometimes with a prominent reporter's byline falsely added. (**30**) Current investigations of the drug industry show that many of the stories reporting successful testing of drugs which appear in medical periodicals are written and paid for by agents of the manufacturers.

It is not only the minor services that are thus corrupted by propaganda appearing as news; UPI, Newspaper Enterprise Association, Central Press Association (a division of King Features Syndicate) and the former *New York Herald Tribune* News Service all have used stories from Hamilton Wright without identification as propaganda for foreign clients. (**219**:791) The Foreign Agents Registration Act does not clearly prohibit this practice, though the practice seems to be contrary to the spirit of the act. But such disguised sources seriously pervert the public intelligence.

Another problem of authenticity arises when Government agencies attempt to make an end run around the independent and presumably critical news agencies. Especially since the recent widening of the Government's credibility gap, there has been a premium on getting non-Governmental sources to echo the Government line. Theodore Draper, despite his belief that several rugged individualists reporting the Dominican invasion "saved the honor of their country" by telling the truth when the Government was telling lies, notes that other reporters made themselves the willing tools of Government:

Government officials and the press play a game of politics and propaganda which has become as stylized as an 18th-century dance. First the officials hand out privileged information to favored journalists ("U.S. intelligence flatly reported that . . ."). Then the journalists pass on the same information, with or without attribution, to their readers. Finally, pro-administration Congressmen fill pages of the Congressional Record with the same articles to prove that the officials were right. (48:89)

Such articles are, of course, nonauthentic.

Finally, the danger of nonauthenticity is built into the press network by the "gatekeeping" function described by Kurt Lewin. (129) Dispatches from a reporter's typewriter do not go directly into the composing machine on the daily papers. They must pass through the hands of wire-service and local editors, each one of whom can delete, substitute a word to change the flavor, condense to affect the meaning, or discard the whole thing. Wise editing can increase the credibility of dispatches, but unwise editing can do just the opposite. There is no way to determine, for most dispatches, what editing has been done; the only signals of possible interference are to be found in inspecting the bias and accuracy records of the individual wire services, reporters, and newspapers.

Other documentary tests of evidence which can be applied to the press pertain primarily to the columnists, those super-reporters who specialize in opinion rather than on-the-scene coverage. Columnists exercise considerable influence on Government policy makers, and some influence on the newspaper-reading public in general. By convention, field reporters write about only what they see and hear; the latitude for generalizing, the necessity for consistency, and the possibilities of reluctant testimony generally do not apply to them.

Columnists are a different breed. They do frequently generalize, and students who would use these generalizations as sources of evidence must evaluate their adequacy. Columnists have ideological positions which leave them open to credibility-destroying inconsistencies. They also sometimes acknowledge that things are happening which place in doubt their pet theories about the world, and such admissions can be cited as reluctant testimony. We shall discuss specific columnists later on; they are almost important enough to deserve a whole section to themselves.

We come now to those individual tests of credibility — expertise, objectivity, and accuracy record — which loom so large in the evaluation of any witness. The expertise or perceptual capacity of journalists varies widely. Unfortunately it is not what it could be, primarily because of the journalistic tradition that a reporter acquires his education by covering first the court house or police station beat, then working up to more important news, with his career culminating in foreign affairs coverage. The relatively low level of journalists' formal education has been deplored by many observers. The important thing, to newsmen, is experience in observing and reporting, and it is assumed that experience in observing what goes on at the police precinct station equips one for observing what goes on at the United Nations. The necessity for knowing foreign languages, history, sociology, anthropology, political science, business, science, theater, or whatever else a reporter might be assigned to is not, perhaps, *denied*, it is merely ignored. Irving Kristol calls the journalistic attitude "a naïve and blithe non-intellectualism." (**119**:44)

Clearly the greatest and most credible of American newspapers is *The New York Times*. It is not only the newspaper of record; it is the best-financed, the most able to stand up to political and advertiser pressures (when it wants to), the most prestigious, most complete, and most conscientious in getting an important story that may cost it money. One would, therefore, expect the *Times* staff to be superior, not just in relation to other papers but in an absolute sense: to be nearly as knowledgeable about the affairs of the nation as academic authorities.

This is not what Kristol (and many before him) finds. Putting the *Times* staff through a rigorous comparison with other groups of experts, Kristol comes to a gloomy conclusion:

> Clearly, any young man of genuine intellectual distinction and/or literary ability would be out of his mind to go to work for the *Times*, or to contemplate a journalistic career in general. He'd be better advised to go on to graduate school and a university or government career. And the *Times* doesn't really want such young men, for they are bound to be "troublesome" — they will wish to write about subjects they are interested in and know something about, they will resist being assigned here and there, for this and that. The *Times* wants potential "newsmen," who can cover either one-alarm fires or twelve-alarm revolutions, at a moment's notice. And what the *Times* wants, it gets. This explains a phenomenon that could never have come about by mere chance: the extraordinary mediocrity of the *Times*' vast staff. (**119**:43)

Kristol does not deny that there are some stars, some quasi experts, some reporters who have specialized and built up commendable expertise on the areas they generally cover; but they are few and far between.

And if they are few and far between on the *Times,* they are even fewer and farther between on the rest of the country's newspapers. (*The Los Angeles Times* and *The Washington Post* are papers for which we have respect approaching that for the *Times;* they are giving superior coverage of international events and are encouraging their reporters to stay long enough in one place to develop expertise. But they also are exceptions.)

The phenomenon of amateurism, of expecting a good reporter to be able to understand a revolution or a counterrevolution anywhere, is simply too strong to be ignored. And a safe rule-of-thumb for evaluating foreign affairs reporting is this: *the longer the reporter has been covering the same beat, the more likely he is to know something about it.* Case in point, as noted by Malcolm W. Browne, Associated Press correspondent in Saigon since 1961: "I think it is significant that the late President Diem, who so deeply disliked and distrusted the Western press, frequently received visiting newsmen and women, but never granted interviews to resident correspondents. He knew that they knew too much." (**21**:9)

The institutional pressures against getting too close to the locals which afflict Government agents do not generally impinge on reporters, though some do get drawn into the embassy orbit. Reporters are in all ways freer to observe and report than their Government counterparts. But expertise is another matter; the skilled are rare, the amateurs many.

On the dimension of perceptual distortion, however, the press displays a marked improvement over Government intelligence. Reporters do, of course, identify with national purpose and ideology; as John Lofton puts it, they become "cheerleaders for the West" in cold-war conflicts. (**136**) Because of the "beat system," they have a "stake in the fortunes" of their sources, particularly in Washington. (**118**) But they are neither commanded by their sources nor obliged by a gag rule to suppress unfavorable news in order to put the best face on developments. Establishmentarian as it is, the *Times* will still maintain a Halberstam in Viet-Nam against the request of President Kennedy and send a Salisbury to Hanoi to the horror of the State Department. As already noted, not only the *Times,* but *The Wall Street Journal* and *The Christian Science Monitor* carried much irreverent news during the Dominican crisis. Whatever one could say about the extent to which the righteousness of the Christian-capitalist cause is upheld by the press, many of the journalists in Santo Domingo simply did not buy the stories put out by the

American Embassy. The Associated Press even carries occasional dispatches by the Australian Communist reporter, Wilfred Burchett.

The press, as an institution, imposes quite different attitudinal sets on its agents than does a government. Journalistic attitudes in favor of truth and objectivity may be naïve, and most reporters would benefit from a course in social psychology; but team play, with its deadening effect on perception, is simply not one of the journalistic rules. Individual reporters may be highly biased and individual papers may impose distorting ideologies, but there is always the chance that a Homer Bigart or a Herbert Matthews will reject the stereotyped answers and explore things for himself.

Even in reporting on domestic events, where newspapers are under the influence of advertiser pressures, there is room for deviance. While owners and managing editors may identify closely with the business community which supports the paper, many reporters do not. Press objectivity on domestic matters leaves much to be desired, and the press is consistently conservative and Republican. But it is not bound, gagged, and monolithic.

Then there is the vital matter of accuracy record. Since the press is *not* monolithic, one would expect the record to be spotty: some papers and wire services are good, some are bad, and many are in between. Even within the columns of one newspaper there will be writers of both high and low credibility, there will be dispatches which will prove true in the light of history and others which will prove false, all side by side. And since there are no omniscient writers, there will be some stories by a particular correspondent which will be accurate and others which will be quite misleading.

The most influential critique of the press ever done in this country was the study by Walter Lippmann and Charles Merz of *The New York Times* coverage of the Russian revolution and the U. S. intervention in Russia which followed it. This study was published as a special supplement to *The New Republic* on August 4, 1920. It is a chilling document, and if one were to take it at face value, as many liberal writers have during the four and a half decades since it came out, one's history of press accuracy in this century would get off to a most dismal start. We must discuss this study briefly, not only because of its substance but because it has influenced so many subsequent writers on journalistic credibility.

Lippmann and Merz selected certain bench marks which were vital in

American decision making on relations with Russia and investigated how well the *Times* had reported them. In the summer of 1917, for instance, it was vital for us to know if the Russian army, whether under the Tsar, Kerensky, or the Bolsheviks, would continue to fight against Germany. Lippmann and Merz examined headlines, leads of stories, and placement of stories, and concluded that the *Times* misled its readers into expecting that Russia would continue to fight, when in fact she did not. (**133**:4–9) This claim is based not on the absence of pessimistic news from the *Times*, but on the contention that the optimistic stories were given the "right of way" so that the reader's overall impression was wrong. We fail to find this skewed emphasis in the *Times* during this period. There were misleading stories, true, but there were also accurate ones; and a great many of the inaccuracies came from State Department releases. One can say that the *Times* should have known better than to carry Government-released stories; but *what* the Government says was then, as now, news, whether fraudulent or not. In our judgment, the *Times* did about as well as could have been expected during that turbulent period.

Lippmann and Merz also claim that the *Times* played up the various campaigns of the White Russian generals, Kolchak, Denikin, and Yudenitch, portraying these reactionary forces as sweeping to victory when they were not. Here again, we find *Times* coverage to be well balanced; a careful reader would have learned of both strengths and weaknesses in the anti-Bolshevik movements. Lippmann and Merz further picture the *Times* as representing United States recognition of the Kolchak government as a *fait accompli*. This is not an accurate portrayal. Nor did the *Times* mislead its readers into believing that Russia had invaded Poland in 1920; Poland had invaded Russia, and careful attention to the *Times* stories about this event could not have produced the contrary impression.

The monumental Lippmann-Merz study of the *Times* was, so far as we know, the first major critical study of public intelligence in this country. It is unfortunate that it is so faulty. There are indeed many instances where newspapers have misrepresented events, and there were of course mistaken stories in the *Times* during the period studied. Lippmann and Merz were no doubt outraged that so much fraudulent material found its way into that paper's columns. One can share that outrage and strike whatever blows are possible for more accurate news reporting, but one cannot conclude that the *Times* was uniformly bad.

The *Times* was of course anti-Bolshevik and has continued to be hostile to Russia and Communism, but an effort to preserve balance was made. In fact, the *Times* even hired the pro-Russian Walter Duranty as Moscow correspondent.

With the ending of World War II, there was a second Communist revolution of even greater trauma for the United States, and it was more misrepresented in the American press than the Russian revolution. The United States had never been "close" to Russia as she had to China. Our churches had no vested interest in Russia; by contrast, the Christianization of China was a source of peculiar pride for the American religious community, since the Generalissimo, Chiang Kai-shek, had converted to Christianity and married a Wellesley-educated Christian wife. Furthermore, we flattered ourselves that our relations with China had been benevolent compared with the rapine of the European powers; hence, when China went Communist, we had "lost" her in a sense in which we could never have felt that we lost Russia. Chiang Kai-shek and his Madame were portrayed as the Savior of the Orient and Joan of Arc; no one would have used such extravagant language about Tsar Nicholas.

The press generally reflected the prevailing hallucinatory view of the Chinese revolution. In retrospect, it is scarcely believable that, following the lead of C. L. Sulzberger and the grey eminence of the *Times*, the American public at one time believed that Russia was taking over China, detaching the northern provinces, occupying Inner Mongolia, Manchuria, and Sinkiang, obtaining control of China's seven major ports, and demanding 500,000 Chinese laborers for Russian use. (See Felix Greene, in **81**:Ch. 5.) But to a press and a public which could not believe that the depth of Chinese hatred of foreign exploiters, much less American exploiters, could lead to voluntary revolution, Russian control of China was the only plausible explanation of what was happening. Any other belief would have challenged the core of our righteous self-image.

Press reports about the Chinese Communist government have continued to be frequently false. Famine did not ravage the China of Mao Tse-tung in 1960 as it had the China of bygone years — we know this now. The Chinese family was not quite destroyed in 1951, nor was it destroyed with establishment of the communes in 1958; this began to penetrate our intelligence system in 1967. Most pathetic of all, and most disastrous for American policy deliberation, was the impression created by many papers and Hong Kong-based China reporters that Chiang Kai-shek was about to regain control of China. The press as a whole erred in even presenting the constant threats of the Nationalist leader to return to the mainland under his own steam, and the *Times* was in the forefront of the deluders. Commenting on a *Times* story announcing Chiang's invasion plans of October 14, 1962, Greene says,

> Do the *Times'* writers really take all this seriously? Don't they know that often Chiang's pronouncements about which they write so ponderously have been printed in mainland Chinese newspapers for comic relief? The meaning of these solemn absurdities is plain enough. By giving prominence and credence to empty pronouncements *issued for its own purposes by the Chiang regime*, the press wittingly or unwittingly allows itself to become the agent for misleading the public. (**81**:260)

Part of the reason for the miserable press performance on China is her inaccessibility to American reporters. British, French, Australian, Swiss, German, Swedish coverage on China has been markedly superior, partly because these countries have no great national "thing" about China, partly because their reporters have been there. China watchers argue about the extent to which reporters in China can really learn what is going on despite restrictions on their movement, but any of them would give his left arm to be able to see for himself.

As we move into the current decade, American press coverage of the world's trouble spots seems to improve. The *Times* knew the score well on the Bay of Pigs invasion; only third-rate papers seriously bungled that story. The *Miami News*, for example, put the invasion force at five to eight thousand men, instead of fourteen hundred, and said that the invaders had captured Santiago de Cuba and were fighting in four of the six Cuban provinces, when in reality they had gone no farther than thirty miles from the beach. (**102**:142)

Press coverage on Viet-Nam has been largely according to editorial bias. Papers which make a strenuous effort to be fair, such as the *Times*, *The Washington Post*, *The Christian Science Monitor*, and *The Los Angeles Times* have recorded the war in all its ambiguity and confusion and have not spared the sacred cows of the Establishment. Copy filed by David Halberstam, Malcolm Browne, Homer Bigart, Neil Sheehan, Peter Kalischer, and many others has been proved substantially accurate by the passage of time. The misleading coverage, for the most part, has been from the quick-trippers and the anti-Communist crusaders such as Hearst and (initially) Scripps-Howard.

Newspaper coverage of the Dominican crisis was at least good and possibly outstanding. A number of reporters with considerable Latin American experience were available, and the crisis erupted so suddenly that no hard and fast editorial positions had developed to cramp their style. Future scholarly accounts of the Dominican intervention will depend more, perhaps, on raw material from journalists than has previously been the case. When one considers that the newspaper was neither accepted as worthy of scholarly notice nor used as raw material by writers of history until the early part of this century (**189**), the performance of journalists in the Dominican crisis was admirable. (See page 131.)

Accuracy record is a criterion on which it is possible to make some distinction between the two major American wire services. Associated Press, the senior service, seems to maintain higher standards of accuracy than United Press International, an amalgamation of two much smaller bodies, the independent United Press and Hearst's International News Service.

UPI, for instance, was solely responsible for the myth commonly accepted in the United States that Castro was a Communist from his college days and that he brought his revolution to power with full intent of taking Cuba into the Communist bloc. A careful comparison of AP and UPI stories about Castro's lengthy speech of December 2, 1961, shows that the initial AP dispatch was substantially accurate: "Castro said last night that until a few years ago he was 'biased against communism because of imperialist propaganda.' He said the change in his political thinking began after he seized power." (**16**:6) UPI, on the other hand, due to a mistranslation, claimed Castro said "he really has been a dedicated Communist since his college days but he concealed his views so it would be easier to seize power." (**16**:5) UPI was simply wrong, and worse, left the error uncorrected and later even attempted to defend its original story. Mervin Block, in a *Columbia Journalism Review* article from which the above citations were taken, gives the history of the error, the way UPI's version gained maximum display probably because of its shock value, and the attempt by UPI officials to cover up.

UPI similarly misrepresented a speech of David Schoenbrun in which a Hanoi peace feeler of May, 1965, was described. AP had a stringer at the speech, but even so, phoned Schoenbrun to verify his exact words. UPI had no representative at the talks and carried a story without verification which misrepresented the substance of Schoenbrun's statement. (**196**) AP and UPI frequently carry almost identical dispatches. When they vary, our money is on AP.

Moving to the individual writers whose bylines are carried with their stories and whose accuracy records ought to be carefully inspected by some agency concerned with the calibre of American intelligence, one finds again a few stars, a few villains, and a large number who have not distinguished themselves one way or another.

One of the stars with whose work we are familiar is Robert S. Elegant, for many years *Newsweek* correspondent in Southeast Asia, now with *The Los Angeles Times*, and an accomplished student of China. Elegant has scored many times with his perceptive analyses of what goes on behind the bamboo curtain. The most significant coup, primarily because it correctly flew in the face of the Establishment and the vast majority of other China watchers, including many in academic posts, was his confident prediction, in an article in *The New Leader* of December 12, 1960, of the forthcoming Sino-Soviet split. (**55**) There were at that time rumors of Sino-Soviet disaffection. They were not taken seriously by most China watchers, since both countries had so much to lose by a split: Russia, a strong ally in Asia; China, Russian supplies and technological aid; both, a common front against the capitalist powers. Elegant, on the basis of a series of dispatches on Leninism appearing in the Peking press, forecast not only the intensity of the Chinese belief in the superiority of their own path to socialism, but the extent to which this was alienating them from Russia and the inevitable consequences of the alienation. Years later, events proved him correct. Elegant has scored other hits in reporting on China, but the Sino-Soviet split assessment alone is enough to earn him entrance into a reporter's hall of fame.

At the other end of the spectrum is Joseph Alsop. On some subjects, Alsop has a reputation, not wholly undeserved, for probity; on foreign affairs his testimony deserves attention mostly as an example of poor journalism. Felix Greene devotes a whole chapter of *A Curtain of Ignorance* to "Mr. Alsop's China." In it Greene cites a series of Alsop's predictions about China beginning in 1953 and continuing to 1962, all of them wrong. War was imminent; it never came. Invasion of Southeast Asia was imminent; it never came. Chen Yi was out; but Chen Yi was very much in. The rebellion in Tibet would produce a general explosion; there was no general explosion. The Chinese were starving; but the Chinese were not starving. Time and again, the regime was about to collapse; the regime had not, in late 1968, yet collapsed. Even if the Peking regime were to collapse in 1970 Alsop was wrong; a prediction of imminent collapse in 1960 is not fulfilled by a collapse ten years later.

If intelligence about the human world were as important to the community of scholars as the neurological functioning of rats, we would have available a solid series of studies on the accuracy of the various pundits who contribute to what we read. Unfortunately, no such series of studies exists. We are aware of only one full-blown investigation of the predictive accuracy of journalists, an article by Ben Bagdikian, again in the *Columbia Journalism Review*. Bagdikian set as his task a study of the accuracy of predictions made by major columnists during October, 1964. He found, as one would expect, that men describe and predict in accordance with their biases. This was the month preceding the 1964 presidential election; conservative journalists wanted Goldwater to win, liberals wanted Johnson.

> Twenty-two major columnists made an aggregate of 133 explicit and measurable predictions during the study month, of which fifty-five were substantially correct and seventy-eight substantially wrong. Of those who made five or more measurable predictions, the least accurate were seven conservatives whose records ran from 0 to 20 per cent accuracy (examples: de Toledano, 0–8; Allen & Scott, 2–10). Among all conservatives who made five or more measurable predictions, the highest rate of accuracy was Holmes Alexander's, 20 per cent. Seven moderate and liberal columnists made five or more measurable forecasts, of whom five had better than 50 per cent accuracy (Evans & Novak, 15 and 6 for 71 per cent; Drummond and Bartlett, 75 per cent; Childs, 58 per cent; and White, 55 per cent). Richard Wilson scored 58 per cent; Pearson, 28 per cent. (**8**:35)

One would like to have many more such studies to be able to determine whether liberal columnists were as inaccurate during the Eisenhower campaigns as conservatives were in 1964; whether accuracy records change during nonelection periods; whether some columnists are more accurate on foreign affairs, less accurate on domestic, and so forth. Such data are simply not available. A student who wants to know whether one writer is more accurate than another must do the digging himself.

One journalistic practice which has attracted much unfavorable comment, since it allegedly results in low-credibility stories, is "backgrounding." This is when a government official talks to the press with the requirement that he not be identified in their stories; the stories are not to be attributed to the official. These are the stories that begin with "Usually reliable sources said . . . ," "Persons in a position to know claimed . . . ," and other devious phrases. Such anonymity can easily be abused. Government officials have been known to use not-for-attribution conferences to send up trial balloons, to hint at policies which have not yet actually been adopted but are under consideration. If public reaction is unfavorable, the same official will deny vigorously that the Government has ever contemplated such a policy. Since his name has never been publicly associated with the policy, he can get away with the duplicity. Anonymity can also be used to cloak outright lies which the Government intends to stick with as part of a cover story.

Newsmen offer much resistance to the not-for-attribution approach. *The New York Times* and *The Washington Post* have recently exerted pressure to restrict or eliminate backgrounders and have sometimes refused to attend background briefings or to publish stories when they are classified as not for attribution. Both former White House aide McGeorge Bundy and former Presidential Press Secretary Bill Moyers have spoken out against the backgrounder. All Washington correspondents have collections of background horror stories in which not-for-attribution news has seriously misinformed the public. The newsmen have a natural distaste for this practice; Dan Nimmo notes, "It too often means that the reporter, not the official, gets left holding the bag when a controversy develops over what was said at a backgrounder." (**166**:165)

The important question for the student of evidence, however, is not "Do backgrounders produce unreliable intelligence?" but "Are backgrounders generally less reliable than attributed stories?" We have no reason to believe that backgrounders are inferior. Both types of story are of course fallible. But on the basis of comparing the accuracy of backgrounders and attributed stories during the month of May, 1966, in the *Pittsburgh Post-Gazette* (an independent paper taking AP and *New York Times* services) and the *Pittsburgh Press* (Scripps-Howard, UPI) there does not appear to be any significant difference between them.*

* For a seminar paper on backgrounders we are indebted to Peter Longini.

Much as we dislike the anonymity of any source, there may well be factors in the backgrounder situation which counterbalance a Government official's tendency (presuming he has one) to prevaricate. *What* actually appears in the papers is selected, written, and edited by newsmen, not by Government officials. Since it is the newsman rather than the official who takes the rap for a misleading story, the reporters may be more careful about what they print, and more skeptical of the source of it. A backgrounder is not necessarily newsworthy, as is a public statement of a Senator; had McCarthy issued his fraudulent claims about Communists in the State Department anonymously, the newspapers might not have carried them at all.

As comforting as it would be, we cannot subscribe to a general rule that backgrounders are basically less credible than attributed stories. Much more research should be done on this, as on innumerable other aspects of public intelligence. There are at present no data causing us to condemn backgrounders as more inaccurate than other stories.

One of the tests of primary authorities on which the press should be above reproach is eyewitness status. Presumably the dispatches from all over the world which constitute the raw material of newspaper stories are written by eyewitnesses to the events described. But this does not always hold. The daily press suffers from having to work under closely spaced and inflexible deadlines. This limitation strikes the afternoon papers, which are the majority, the hardest. These papers go to press as early as 10:00 A.M., long before the developments of the day are clear. This means that reporters must often anticipate the news. Sometimes this anticipation takes the form of an "overnight," which, according to one wire-service reporter, is a "basically phony operation . . . a story composed the previous evening, but giving the impression when it appears the next afternoon that it covers that day's events." (**29**:108)

If observing and recording what actually happened is difficult, presenting what might happen as if it already had is suicidal. An overnight carried by most American papers had Dag Hammarskjold meeting with Moise Tshombe at Ndola, Northern Rhodesia, on the morning of September 18, 1961. These stories described the scene at Ndola in some detail; but the meeting never took place. Hammarskjold was dead at the time the stories appeared. Many overnights during the course of a year contain items of similar falsity. When the falsehoods are about events of considerable consequence and follow-up stories correct the errors, little damage may be done. But relatively few stories are corrected, and the falsehoods remain in newspaper files to mislead future students and historians.

Overnights represent a structural defect of the press which decreases its eyewitness stature, but there are human and individual failures to achieve eyewitness purity, as well. How can one tell, from a news story, whether the reporter was actually present at the event described? Sometimes the secondhand nature of a report is obvious; Harrison Salisbury produces an unfortunate example. During his December, 1966, sojourn in North Viet-Nam, he went beyond reporting what he himself saw and heard to include statements about a previous bombing of Nam Dinh and about the leveling of the countryside in the vicinity of the seventeenth parallel, neither of which he could have observed. Had he qualified these reports as originating with the Hanoi government, there would not have been the implicit claim to firsthand knowledge. When these irregularities were condemned, Salisbury noted acerbically that it was obvious the information came from the North Vietnamese and no one should have been misled. But this is an inadequate explanation. It is simply against the rules for a reporter to mix personal observation with other sources unless he clearly specifies which is which. Lee Lockwood succinctly analyzes the effect of these incidents on Salisbury's credibility:

> The point Salisbury misses is that though the figures may well be authentic, he needlessly left himself open to attack by neglecting to identify his sources. The Administration had been lying about what it was doing in Vietnam, and Salisbury was in a position to demolish that lie singlehandedly. Instead, through carelessness, he gratuitously created a little credibility gap of his own, which inevitably dulled the impact of his on-the-scene observations. (**134**:23)

One of the great assets of the press as a source of intelligence is that it produces eyewitness reports to many of the world's significant events. This asset is not to be taken lightly. When it is dissipated by overnights or individual transgressions, the press suffers a great loss of credibility.

The Newsweeklies

Given the affluence and freedom from daily deadlines of the weekly news magazines, one would expect them to turn out a superior product. The weekly news summaries carried in the Sunday *New York Times* do take good advantage of the additional time for checking and more leisurely perspective which weekly publication provides, and errors carried in the daily edition are frequently corrected in "News of the Week in Review." But the newsweeklies have an entirely new set of liabilities which, taken as a whole, make their coverage something less than perfect.

There is, first, especially for *Time*, a kind of gag rule which seriously inhibits free reporting. On a typical newspaper, aside from writing editorials, an editor usually confines himself to polishing and refining copy coming from the field; the story published is basically a product of the man at the scene of the story. With *Time*, the reverse is true. Copy filed from reporters in the field is primarily stimulus to editorial imagination. Testimony on this point from defectors from the magazine is unanimous.

One of the first serious studies of *Time* magazine was that of Ben Bagdikian. His conclusion on the purity of *Time* technique:

> The key to *Time* reportage is not the hard news reported to it by the *New York Times*, the *New York Herald Tribune*, the Associated Press, United Press International and its own staff in the field. The key is how it is written in the high reaches of the offices in Rockefeller Center, New York. Noel Busch, cousin of the late Briton Hadden, the man who co-founded *Time* magazine in 1923 with Henry R. Luce, says of his experience on the magazine that *Time* regards as ideal that: "Writers should not witness the events they write about." It is the writer away from the scene, passing the story back and forth among the editors, who gives to the *Time* story the impact it will have on the reader. (7:157)

The implications of this editorial dominance for accuracy are obvious. The eyewitness source of an account will take second place to editorial preference. If enough editors work over a story, no one can be pinned down when a reader protests, blame can be assigned to no one person. The system, as Douglass Cater notes, is "basically irresponsible." (29: 103) The product cannot rise above the system. Ezra Goodman, *Time* Hollywood correspondent for five years, describes how the system affected his cover story on Marilyn Monroe:

> When I worked on a cover story, I devoted my full time to it. In the case of Marilyn Monroe, this ran over a two-month period of intensive, almost detective-style research, during which I immersed myself in the miasmic, emotional swamp world in which most movie actresses exist. I interviewed more than a hundred of Monroe's friends and enemies, spent a good deal of time with her and then transmitted my thoroughly documented findings — running to almost book length — to New York via the

magazine's private teletype system. This material was then put into the editorial meat grinder and came out the other end, as it invariably did, couched in *Time*'s portentous and stentorian gobbledegook and without much resemblance to what had been fed in. As one of the writers at the magazine once pointed out, *"Time"* is "emit" spelled backward, and much that was fed into *Time*'s editorial, word-grinding maw came out facts-backward. Once the editors had made up their minds about something, they did not like to have their opinions dislodged by mere facts. (**74**:217–218)

If such changes (and Goodman details them for many pages) are made in stories where the ideological impact would be minor, one can only imagine what happens when the magazine's biases are touched. There is abundant testimony on this front also. The *summa theologica* under which *Time* operated for many years was simple and derived from Henry Luce's lineage as a son of Christian missionaries in China: his friend Chiang Kai-shek could do no wrong, and all the troubles of the Orient could be blamed on Peking. When Chiang's star began to wane, *Time* turned to the war in Viet-Nam as the vehicle for ultimate salvation.

Six pages of David Halberstam's *The Making of a Quagmire* chronicle one incident in Viet-Nam coverage which illustrates the intensity of editorial dominance.

> Periodically, Charley Mohr, *Time*'s chief correspondent in Southeast Asia, would return to New York for conferences during which he would argue for tougher coverage on Vietnam. Instead his editors, who had lunched with Secretary McNamara and other Pentagon officials, and had seen the most secret of charts and the most secret of arrows and been given what the Pentagon called "the big picture," would explain patiently to Mohr that he understood only a portion of the big picture. And *Time*'s coverage — paralleling the official version — would continue.
>
> Part of the reason for this, I think, was because of the way in which *Time*'s executives view the magazine; to a large degree they see it not just as a magazine of reporting, but as an instrument of policy making. Thus, what *Time*'s editors *want* to happen is as important as what is happening. In Vietnam, where U.S. prestige was staked against a Communist enemy, and the government was Christian and anti-Communist, *Time* had a strong commitment to Diem. (**82**:269)

Thus when Mohr filed a cover story on Madame Nhu, *Time* doctored it just as it had the one on Marilyn Monroe. Mohr and the editors exchanged "uncomplimentary letters." Mohr was asked to do a piece on the Saigon press corps; it never appeared in print. In September, 1963, Mohr was asked to do an exhaustive roundup on the state of the war; he filed twenty-five pages of copy documenting what everybody in Viet-Nam knew: namely, the United States was losing the war. Instead of Mohr's report, *Time* ran a piece written in New York and Washington which backed McNamara and claimed we were winning. In addition, it damned the entire Saigon press corps, including Mohr. He resigned, and went to work for *The New York Times*. In late 1965, Secretary McNamara and *Time* finally acknowledged that we had "stopped losing" the war.

It remains to be seen what effect the death of Henry Luce will have on *Time*'s policy of editorial dominance. Very likely the raging biases Luce brought to his favorite creation will moderate somewhat; whether the practice of requiring field dispatches to be subordinated to editorial opinion will change substantially is anybody's guess. Operational changes are sometimes resisted more strongly than ideological changes.

Neither *U.S. News*, which has strong biases, nor *Newsweek*, the most objective of the three weeklies, has a strong gag rule. This kind of thought control is the exclusive possession of *Time*.

A second dimension on which *Time* is open to serious criticism is consistency. Following Emerson, we have hesitated to invoke this criterion; things do change, and attitudes may legitimately change with them. Consequently, we long regarded as inconclusive the charge leveled by Bagdikian that *Time* is inconsistent:

> The elusiveness of Truth must have worried the editors of *Time* occasionally. But if so, they have spared the reader this human doubt. Each week the world is created absolute and dogmatic, the good guys on one side, the bad guys on the other, with *Time* holding the only scorecard. Only when the reader checks back does he discover that the good guy of October may be the bad guy of January, that Truth and *Time* change. (7:154)

So truth and *Time* change. The generalization here, without specifics, is not impressive. Even when one contemplates *Time*'s inconsistencies, as noted by Bagdikian, there seems some room for excusing them as less than conclusive. *Time*'s June 16, 1952, description of Eisenhower's campaign appearance in Abilene was "a crashing conquest"; on November 3, the same appearance had "not quite 'come across.'" Before Stevenson was a presidential candidate, *Time* described him as a "good governor"; after he became a presidential candidate, *Time* charged him with being easy on Cook County corruption. The income tax, under Truman, was a crushing measure; under Eisenhower, it became something magnificent. Bagdikian gives other examples. They clearly indicate a fatuous partisanship, but, as we see them, do not quite convict *Time* of mendacity.

John Lofton's careful analysis of *Time*'s treatment of the nuclear fall-out danger during 1956 and 1957, however, is persuasive. His case against *Time* is ironclad. During the election of 1956, when *Time*'s favorite Eisenhower chose to minimize the danger of fallout, the magazine went along with him, misrepresenting Stevenson's position, misrepresenting the position of a majority of nuclear physicists, misrepresenting the then-known facts about radioactivity. Once Eisenhower was safely back in the White House, *Time* rejoined the ranks of the sane, carrying a series of articles proclaiming what other publications had been noting all along. *Time* could not have it both ways. The truth did not change in late 1956; only *Time* changed. (**137**) The change was politically motivated, and the inconsistency clearly damaged credibility.

On the test of careful generalization, all the newsweeklies score low. The daily press is in too much of a hurry to generalize at all, except in the editorial columns; news is played straight and kept relatively specific. Weekly editors have three or four days after a deadline has been met to think about the state of the world. Sometimes they produce careful generalizations, sometimes they produce rubbish. Generally the product reflects the degree of perceptual distortion to which the respective weeklies are subject. We will deal with this distortion below.

In expertise, the newsweeklies suffer from the same liabilities as the daily press, except that because of higher salaries and prestige they can generally secure the services of above-average reporters and writers. *Time*, especially, pays well. A very large number of America's most skilled journalists have served with *Time*. But the accent here is on the past tense; the tenure of field men with *Time* is extraordinarily low, since their work is so little used by the editors.

On the dimension of objectivity *Time* and *U.S. News* incur perhaps their most serious liabilities. Both have strong editorial biases, and these spill over into the "news" columns regularly. But the problem is not just with ideologies; it begins with the operational assumptions of the magazines. What the newsweeklies set out to do is explained well by Otto Friedrich:

There is an essential difference between a news story, as understood by a newspaperman or a wire-service writer, and the newsmagazine story. The chief purpose of the conventional news story is to tell what happened. It starts with the most important information and continues into increasingly inconsequential details, not only because the reader may not read beyond the first paragraph, but because an editor working on galley proofs a few minutes before press time likes to be able to cut freely from the end of the story. A newsmagazine is very different. It is written and edited to be read consecutively from beginning to end, and each of its stories is designed, following the critical theories of Edgar Allan Poe, to create one emotional effect. The news, what happened that week, may be told in the beginning, the middle, or the end; for the purpose is not to throw information at the reader but to seduce him into reading the whole story, and into accepting the dramatic (and often political) point being made. (**64**:61)

When facts are thus subservient to "the story," objectivity has to suffer. Facts are often dull, even though they may be of the greatest importance. A newsweekly cannot afford to confine itself to dull facts; as Ralph Ingersoll, former publisher of *Time*, puts it, "Only by the fiction writer's art could the secondhand news that *Time* proposed to package and sell be made inviting enough to attract the readers Luce and Hadden hoped to get." (**98**:3-4) *Time* got its readers, and so did *Newsweek* and *U.S. News*, its siblings. But it got them at the expense of objectivity.

The fiction in two of the weeklies contains substantial ideological content. Only *Newsweek* has managed to retain even a minimal objectivity. David Lawrence, proprietor of *U.S. News*, is not only the archconservative of publishers, he is one of the strongest segregationists in journalism. Lofton describes him as "The South's lawyer in the court of Northern opinion." (**135**) The bias of *U.S. News* is extraordinarily well documented and need not be cited here; Lofton and Bagdikian (**7**) offer the best descriptions of Lawrence's bias, and we refer readers to them.

Time also has a world view. It is more complex and variegated than that of its smaller sister, but Luce's Republicanism was only slightly less dominant than Lawrence's, and his gospel on the Far East probably more interventionist. Much has also been written about the perspective with which *Time* views the world; we commend especially the autobiography of T. S. Matthews, who worked on *Time* for twenty-four years. (**147**)

Finally, we come to accuracy record. So poor is *Time* and *U.S. News* coverage of the trouble spots of the world that it is almost axiomatic for post-mortems of significant crises to comment on falsehoods carried in these magazines. On Cuba, for instance, the facts are clear. On December 8, 1961, *Time* repeated the false translation of Castro's "I Am a Communist" speech, when the accurate Associated Press dispatch was available to it. *U.S. News* followed suit on December 18. **(16**:8**)** Haynes Johnson, foremost authority on the Bay of Pigs, states in his concluding "Bibliographical Notes":

> The magazine which published the most about the Bay of Pigs is also the most misleading. *U.S. News & World Report*, in a number of articles, some of them appearing to be deliberately written to stir controversy without regard to facts, virtually laid the entire blame on President Kennedy. If read with care the articles help to explain why the invasion continued to be so controversial an issue in the United States. **(102**:342**)**

Few episodes in the history of the American press exceed in prevarication the comedy of errors on which Ambassador Bennett and two of the newsweeklies collaborated in 1965. When American newsmen were first allowed to go to Santo Domingo, the Ambassador held an immediate briefing for them. The gravamen of his discourse consisted of a string of atrocity stories. This was a rather unusual order of intelligence for a "neutral" American ambassador to be passing out, and the more cautious reporters took it with a grain of salt, preferring to do some digging on their own before filing dispatches. Not so the agents of *Time* and *U.S. News*. In its issue of May 7, *Time* carried the following:

> No one had an accurate account of the casualties as frenzied knots of soldiers and civilians roamed the streets, shooting, looting, and herding people to their execution with cries of "Paredon! Paredon!" (To the wall! To the wall!) . . . The rebels executed at least 110 opponents, hacked the head off a police officer and carried it about as a trophy.

U.S. News described the same events in its issue of May 10:

> Victims were dragged from their homes and shot down while angry mobs shouted, "To the wall!" — the same cry that marked the mass executions in Cuba in the early days of Fidel Castro. The assassinated Dominicans were dumped into crude graves right at the execution spots.

We know now that this was so much poppycock. And while the leaders of the daily press were checking for themselves and putting out a high order of intelligence, the two gullible weeklies never hinted at a retraction. Draper is right in his assessment:

> As the versions in *Time* and *U.S. News & World Report* show, the worst offenders were precisely the "news" organs that most crudely took their lead from the ambassador: not only did they themselves assume responsibility for some of his stories but they never did inform their readers that the stories had started out as unverified rumors and had ended up as verified myths. There must be thousands of readers who depend on *Time* or *U.S. News & World Report* for their news, and still think that "Paredon! Paredon!" was the theme song of the Dominican revolt. (**48**:94–95)

Time's Viet-Nam coverage has already been discussed under the heading of editorial dominance. It was, at least through the early part of 1967, still highly chauvinistic; *Time* has been very much a part of the Government team. In some instances, *Time* has even gone beyond Government propaganda, as when, in its issue of February 17, 1967, it made claims about Communist disregard of the Tet truce which not even the Pentagon had made. Since then, *Time* has shown signs of wavering. Whether it will in future become an independent news organ with normal journalistic respect for truth or whether it will continue its sycophantic ways cannot be predicted. The machinery is magnificent; what is lacking is integrity.

The best-balanced overall judgment of the newsweeklies is the assessment Sorensen attributes to Kennedy, with which we are in complete agreement:

> [Kennedy] almost never read *U.S. News & World Report*, for example, on the grounds that it had little news and less to report. Yet he read *Time* and *Newsweek* faithfully, and felt their condensed hindsight often influenced their readers more than daily newspaper stories. He had his disagreements with *Newsweek*, particularly on the inaccuracies in its political gossip column in the front, but *Time* was a source of special despair. For, unlike *U.S. News & World Report*, it was well written. Unlike the Chicago *Tribune*, it gave an impression of objectivity. And unlike its White House correspondent, Hugh Sidey, unlike its sister publication *Life*, and unlike what he regarded to be its general pre-1961 attitude toward his efforts, it was in John Kennedy's opinion consistently

slanted, unfair and inaccurate in its treatment of his Presidency, highly readable but highly misleading. (**207**:316)

General Periodicals

If we are woefully short on thorough analyses of press credibility, we are even shorter on analyses of the periodicals. Only *Reader's Digest* has come under systematic scrutiny; for the rest, though some have reputations of sorts, there is a distinct shortage of hard data.

Most nonpolemical periodicals attempt to secure accurate articles by responsible journalists and scholars. They are, in our opinion, generally successful. But even more important than the reputation of the periodical is the credibility of the specific author. As we have noted, Government agents and foreign propagandists masquerade as independent writers and penetrate even such prestigious journals as *Foreign Affairs*. The general-interest periodicals are basically vehicles through which specific writers market their wares; individual credibility rather than institutional credibility is controlling. This principle does little to ease the way of a student wanting to quote X's article in *Harper's;* he must know something about X, and he can only get it by doing his own research.

The strongly ideological magazines are quite a different matter. One could trust neither the (Communist) *Worker* nor the John Birch Society's *American Opinion* magazine. Each may, of course, print a good deal of truth; but by most of the tests of evidence, they would be unlikely vehicles for it.

Reader's Digest is a special case. Like the *Congressional Record*, it may contain anything. Much of its content is just plain trash, but, like the *Record*, it does sometimes carry the works of outstanding writers; one cannot simply write it off as useless. Here the credibility of the individual writer is all-important, that of the vehicle insignificant. A recent, well balanced analysis of the *Digest* was carried in the Winter, 1965, *Columbia Journalism Review*, but it does not pretend to help in assessing those whom a user of evidence needs most to assess, the individual writers. (**34**)

Checking out individual journalists is difficult and time consuming. With perseverance, however, one can learn enough about most writers to judge their general credibility.

One journalist whom we have investigated is I. F. Stone, crusading proprietor of a bi-weekly newsletter which specializes in reluctant testimony, *i.e.*, in proving Government agencies and Establishment journal-ists to be knaves and fools out of their own mouths.* Stone has a circulation of over 40,000, and his is the most widely read of the political newsletters. (**141**) We were obligated to evaluate Stone since his biases so closely coincide with ours, and since we often use the materials he quotes in his newsletter. Our findings were not altogether encourag-ing. Stone may be on the side of the angels (that is, our side), but he is careless. The crucial tests in his case are carefulness of generalization and, since his most valuable material is comment on other writers, accuracy of citation.

Stone does not entirely pass the first test, carefulness of generalization. Of fourteen random items investigated carefully, he drew unwarranted generalizations twice, once about *The New York Times* reporting on a bombed steel plant in North Viet-Nam, once about the intent of an article on the CIA carried in the *Saturday Evening Post*. In both cases, Stone drew conclusions which the original sources did not support. And in four of the fourteen items Stone misrepresented a source — by partial selection, by substituting "is" for "might," by deleting a strategic adverb, and again by partial selection. This is not a good record.

Stone's predictive record is generally fair, and he is certainly his own boss. But his carelessness in generalizing and quoting others means that his articles cannot be taken at face value. One must go back to the original sources.

A second journalist whom we have checked out is the iconoclast Felix Greene, a freelancer whose work on China has gained wide circu-lation, and whose book castigating American intelligence on China *(A Curtain of Ignorance)* we cite frequently.† Green does not seem to be an ideologue; his concern is with truth, and he finds precious little of it in press treatment of China. There is only one criterion on which Greene can be faulted: selection of primary sources. He confines himself to the writers (such as Joe Alsop) and the articles (many from *Time*, but some also from *The New York Times*) misrepresenting events in Asia. He is scrupulously accurate in his citation of them; but the selection presents one side of the picture only.

We regard Greene's credibility as generally high. He does what he

* For a seminar paper on the credibility of Mr. Stone we are indebted to William Barnett.

† For collecting basic documents used by Mr. Greene we are indebted to William McCarthy.

purports to do, as stated in his foreword: "This book proposes to challenge the accuracy of some of the reports about Communist China conveyed to the American people by the press, the experts, and by public officials." **(81**:xiii**)** The emphasis here must be on *some*. We would even agree were he to contend that the accuracy of *most* reports about China could be challenged, especially during the period he covers. But, in reading his text, the qualification "some" drops away. The accurate accounts of events on the Chinese mainland — and there were many (see **161**) — are never acknowledged, so that one ultimately gets the impression that nothing written about China in this country was correct from 1945 to 1963. And this is certainly not true.

Further, Greene assumes a basic rationality which the American public, unfortunately, does not really demonstrate. The villain in his scenario is strictly the intelligence which informs us:

> Mr. William Lederer has called this country "A Nation of Sheep." I reject this title as a slander. I know of no other country with as high a proportion of intelligent and concerned citizens as the United States. The American people are basically generous, genuinely wanting to find their way through the hazards that beset them in the world in as decent a way as possible. The people of America have responded to world events in a perfectly rational and predictable way *given the information with which they have been provided.* Certainly in regard to China we are not a nation of sheep, but a nation that has been profoundly misinformed. **(81**:xv**)**

To some extent, Lederer and Greene are both wrong. We are not a nation of sheep, as Lederer says, in one sense: we are the most crusading, ideologically driven, imperialistic nation extant, with the possible exceptions of China and Cuba. What nation besides America feels justified in exporting its religion and way of life to other nations nine thousand miles away? Even the Russians have learned that this is counterproductive, and our bet is that the Chinese will learn before we do. Greene is wrong in claiming that we have responded to world events in a perfectly rational and predictable way. Even if one has nothing more accurate to read than Scripps-Howard intelligence, our response to it is not rational. It is, as the social psychologists explain so well, distorted on the Hollywood good guy/bad guy model until our fulminations approximate those of our Marxist enemy. **(235**:48**)** Acceptance of a concatenation of Pentagon dispatches so immediately contradicted by events that no one could possibly be deceived can never be described as rational.

Attention to the better sources of evidence about China, available to every American (but which Greene does *not* cite) would produce quite a different conclusion. One is forced back to Greene's original claim: the accuracy of *some* of the reports about China which have appeared in this country does leave much to be desired. What is missing is not accurate intelligence, but the will to attend to it and perhaps the skill to separate the wheat from the chaff. As with the signals we received before Pearl Harbor, truth was there. We simply failed to identify it.

SUMMARY

The daily press is the vehicle through which we receive most of our intelligence. On one of the situational tests of evidence, newspapers are vastly superior to Government; there is no universal gag rule stifling independent reporters. Even newspaper chains with well developed ideological positions carry deviant dispatches. This advantage applies primarily to foreign news; domestic issues, where advertiser pressures are strong, offer less freedom for the press to call a spade a spade. Newsmen do not have direct access to Government decision making, and they are sometimes unable to penetrate crisis areas which Government wants to keep secret; the problem of accessibility does impinge on reporters. And some of them identify so closely with the ideology and policy of the nation to which they belong that they actually serve as Government spokesmen; fortunately these are a minority. Most reporters are relatively free, inquiring, and conscientious.

The daily press contains many stories which are not authentic. Blacksheeting or cooperative plagiarism, articles written by paid propagandists but appearing without such agent identification, and stories taken verbatim from Government officials all result in unauthentic copy. Amateurism and a low level of expertise characterize many reporters, though some have specialized in a subject and know it well. The biases of the press are well known and result in much perceptual distortion; but correspondents are less biased than Government agents, at least on foreign affairs, and even the papers with strong editorial policies carry the dispatches of nonconforming reporters. On the dimension of accuracy, the press performs demonstrably better than Government spokesmen; about the Bay of Pigs, the Dominican crisis, and Viet-Nam the press has performed creditably and sometimes with distinction. A com-

parison of the two major wire services indicates that the Associated Press
is superior to United Press International.

The weekly newsmagazines are an important source of public intelligence, and there are clear differences among them. *Newsweek* is easily
the most credible; *Time* and *U.S. News* run competition for the rating
of "most inaccurate American periodical." *Time* is compromised by editorial dominance: copy written in the field is treated cavalierly in the
editorial offices and is made to conform to rigid editorial positions.
These positions are sometimes so fundamentally inconsistent that they
damage credibility. *U.S. News* has no firm gag rule, but David Lawrence's biases are rampant and debilitating for objective coverage. All
three suffer from fictionalizing news; selling stale intelligence is possible
only if it can be spiced up in a fashion which compromises credibility.
The accuracy record of both *Time* and *U.S. News* is poor; *Newsweek*
is not recorded as having made as many gross errors.

General periodicals, except for strongly ideological ones, defy generalization, except for *Reader's Digest*, which has more than its share of
propaganda. Articles found in the general periodicals must be analyzed
on the basis of the credibility of the specific author.

SUGGESTED READINGS

Ben H. Bagdikian, "Bias in the Weekly Newsmagazines," in *Voice of the
People*, ed. Reo M. Christenson and Robert O. McWilliams. New York:
McGraw Hill, 1962. (Not carried in revised edition.)

Ben H. Bagdikian, "The Columnist as Prophet," *Columbia Journalism Review* (Summer, 1966), 35–39.

Mervin Block, "The Night Castro 'Unmasked'," *Columbia Journalism Review*
(Summer, 1962), 5–10.

Douglass Cater, *The Fourth Branch of Government*. New York: Random
House (Vintage Books), 1965.

Douglass Cater and Walter Pincus, "The Foreign Legion of U. S. Public
Relations," *The Reporter* (December 22, 1960), 15–22.

Joseph Epstein, "Henry Luce and His Time," *Commentary* (November,
1967), 35–47.

Otto Friedrich, "There are 00 Trees in Russia: The Function of Facts
in Newsmagazines," *Harper's* (October, 1964), 59–65.

Felix Greene, *A Curtain of Ignorance*. Garden City: Doubleday, 1964.

Irving Kristol, "The Underdeveloped Profession," *The Public Interest*, VI
(Winter, 1967), 36–52.

Walter Lippmann and Charles Merz, "A Test of the News," supplement to *The New Republic* (August 4, 1920).

John Lofton, "David Lawrence: The South's 'Lawyer' in the Court of Northern Opinion," *The Progressive* (September, 1958), 31–34.

John Lofton, "The Press Manages the News," *The Progressive* (June, 1963), 16–20.

T. S. Matthews, *Name & Address*. London: Anthony Blond, 1961.

8

Pressure Groups

The trouble with the A.M.A. is that there are too many doctors in it. A doctor is, by definition, a man who doesn't have time. One of the things the average doctor doesn't have time to do is catch up with the things he didn't learn in school, and one of the things he didn't learn in school is the nature of human society, its purpose, its history, and its needs. There are hundreds — many hundreds — of exceptions among them. But there are thousands — one hundred forty thousands — of doctors in the A.M.A.

MILTON MAYER (**148**:26)

General Characteristics

Pressure groups are normally thought of as organizations whose purpose is to propagandize the public for their point of view, or lobby a legislative body into passing favorable laws. Some scholars prefer the term "interest groups" since it is more neutral and does not imply propagandistic intent. In this chapter, however, we are concerned only with those groups which do issue propaganda (or allegedly factual statements) with the intent of selling a point of view; hence we feel no need to adopt the clinically antiseptic label "interest group."

Which are the pressure groups? In 1959, Floyd Hunter compiled a list of the top ten "potentially influential" organizations:

1. Chamber of Commerce
2. American Federation of Labor
3. American Legion
4. American Medical Association
5. Congress of Industrial Organizations
6. National Association of Manufacturers
7. American Farm Bureau Federation
8. National Council of Churches of Christ
9. National Education Association
10. National Grange (**97**:8)

This list is dated; the two labor groups are now combined, for instance, and others have changed title. And there is controversy about its accuracy. The American Bankers Association and the National Security Industrial Association (the military-industrial complex) are not listed, while the National Education Association is. But the list is illustrative if not definitive: each of these organizations consists of people who have interests in common, and each one attempts to influence public opinion and legislation. Statements made by these organizations, their officers and employees, frequently appear in student essays and speeches.

These pressure groups play a vital role in society. Particularly in a democracy, where most government action is utilitarian and seeks to remedy injury or injustice, the presence of alert spokesmen for groups which may be benefited or injured by a proposal helps to secure consideration of all possible consequences of an action. (See **19**:235.) Our sole concerns here are with the credibility of such groups and the use of their testimony as evidence.

When one measures pressure groups as a whole against the tests of evidence, they earn a consistent rating: high credibility on five of the criteria, low on seven. There are fewer differences between individual groups than between individual journalists.

The positive indices are as follows:

Accessibility: Because pressure groups get involved with those aspects of society which interest them and with which many of their members are vocationally concerned, they usually have access to the facts.

Consistency: Naturally they have a coherent point of view which is not likely to change, and all perceptions are conditioned by this point of view. Only the ideological groups suffer any significant credibility-destroying inconsistencies.

Expertise: Most of the pressure groups are highly knowledgeable about the subjects which concern them. Their personal involvement results in continued close contact with a subject.

Eyewitness status: The leaders and spokesmen of pressure groups generally have their information firsthand, though this does not apply to less active members.

Contemporaneity of reporting: A continuing, pressing concern usually results in immediate recording of vital incidents.

On the other hand, pressure groups suffer many perceptual disabilities.

Tension: The concerns of a pressure group are perceived as real and vital. The people in the group come together because a subject affects them; hence tension is built into their relationship to it. Developments in medicine, for instance, have a high crisis quotient for doctors.

Freedom to report: Few pressure groups permit deviance. Those who are not with them are against them. Can one imagine a member of the National Grange being allowed to contradict the position that what is good for agriculture is good for the country?

Authenticity: Spurious polls, research reports, and credentials are common in the literature of pressure groups.

Carefulness of generalization: One swallow does make a summer *if* you want badly enough to believe that it is summer. Most pressure groups want so badly to believe that right is on their side that they virtually ignore the other side.

Objectivity: By definition pressure groups are not objective. The cement which holds them together is personal commitment.

Accuracy record: One of the few criteria which can be used to distinguish between generally truthful and generally untruthful pressure groups is accuracy record. Some of them have been caught lying red-handed; others seem to have preserved some degree of integrity despite the biases of their commitment.

Accuracy of citation: Many pressure groups use testimony of their opponents because of its *prima facie* reluctant nature; there is much fiddling with such testimony.

Though there is always commitment, there is not always significant distortion in pressure groups. For one thing, the range of commitment is extreme, from the fanatical devotion of some card-carrying Communists and Birchers to the reluctant affiliation of some members of the American Association of University Professors. One cannot simply write off the evidence provided by pressure groups, despite the fact that most of them carry a heavy burden of bias.

It is no more possible to offer an exhaustive critique of the credibility of pressure groups than it is to analyze all practicing journalists. Furthermore, an analysis done one year would be outdated the next. Even the two most recent books about pressure groups (**243, 244**) leave substantial areas untouched and are out of date in some respects. Our discussion here can at best be suggestive; students of any particular topic will need to do their own investigations. We shall offer examples from two general categories of pressure groups: (1) those exhibiting a proven and disqualifying bias, and (2) those of an indeterminate bias.

Groups with a Disqualifying Bias

There are many pressure groups whose degree of commitment to the cause is so strong that it is almost inconceivable that a sophisticated student would use statements obtained from them as evidence in a speech or essay. Many of these groups, but not all, are bound together by economic interests.

The economically oriented groups are the easiest to understand and deal with. Few will cavil with the judgment that a man's perception is colored by his financial interest. It is obvious, for example, that O. R. Strackbein and his National Committee on Import-Export Policy are going to exhibit a high degree of bias. The import-sensitive industries cannot be expected to cut their own throats for the sake of the "general welfare"; when it is my profits (or job) versus your profits (or job), I am going to see to my profits first. One is hardly going to find a neutral presentation of the facts about international trade from spokesmen for protected industries, nor even a reasonably accurate account of the status of their own operations.

Similarly, the tobacco industry, sorely disturbed (though by no means financially crippled) by medical findings about cigarettes, hires its "research" team to disprove the U.S. Surgeon General's report. We think it unfortunate that scientists would sell their services to an organization which can give them no freedom to report anything except a highly unlikely medical conclusion. Yet in August, 1964, Dr. Clarence C. Little, scientific director of the Tobacco Research Council, told UPI:

> After 10 years the fact remains that knowledge is insufficient either to provide adequate proof of any hypothesis or to define the basic mechanisms of health and disease with which we are concerned. (**217**)

The impartial scientific groups which contradict Dr. Little are legion.

Not all economic groups compromise with truth in an attempt to improve profits, but drug manufacturers have shown themselves remarkably devoid of scruples. Pfizer listed names and addresses of nonexistent doctors who had allegedly used Sigmamycin in an ad promoting that drug (**85**:19) and lied about negative reactions to Diabinese (**156**:18). Merck claimed advantages for Decadron which had been falsified in their own prerelease tests. (**85**:19) Merrell filed fraudulent results on tests of MER/29 (since withdrawn from the market and one of the most dangerous drugs ever produced) with the FDA in order to secure marketing approval. (**85**:218) Parke, Davis lied about the safety of Chloromycetin. (**156**:12) McNeil, presently a subsidiary of Johnson & Johnson, lied about the occurrence of jaundice in patients using Flexin. (**156**:19) Wallace & Tiernan falsely denied that Dornwal was toxic. (**156**:28) The profit motive is indeed a powerful lubricant of the economic machine, but it can be an equally powerful corrupter of the truth.

Further data would only belabor the point. The Chamber of Commerce is never going to be objective about the retail profit margin, the AFL-CIO about wages, the American Legion about Veterans' benefits, the Farm Bureau about agricultural prices, or the NEA about teachers' salaries. Some will be more biased and less scrupulous than others; but it is nonsensical to use testimony from these economic groups to prove a controversial point dealing with their own welfare if any nonpartisan source is available.

Similarly, the propaganda about foreign countries coming from their own agents is too clearly tainted with self-interest to be credible. The source of this propaganda, as we noted in the chapter on the press, is not always identified. Public relations firms have ways of securing distribution of their materials which evade the intent of the Foreign Agents Registration Act. It was disturbing, in 1965, to note that the lead story in the Cater-Pincus article on "The Foreign Legion of U.S. Public Relations" concerned the purchase by former Dominican boss Rafael Trujillo of a "monthly minimum of 425 minutes of news and commentary regarding the Dominican Republic" from Mutual Broadcasting, with Trujillo alone determining whether any broadcast served his country's best interests. (**30**:15) It is small wonder that Americans are misinformed about the Dominican Republic and the forces seething under its United States-dominated surface.

Since the major focus of this book is foreign intelligence, it is appropriate to note briefly two pressure groups whose success in influencing the American public has been phenomenal. Both the Formosan government of Chiang Kai-shek and the Vietnamese government of the late Ngo Dinh Diem had well oiled machines for infiltrating the public intelligence network with propaganda. Chiang was the more astute operator; good analyses of his operations are found in *The Reporter*, by Max Ascoli, Charles Wertenbaker, and Philip Horton (**5**), and in Chapter 4 of Felix Greene's *A Curtain of Ignorance*. The Vietnamese pressure group sold Diem to the United States with almost as much success. Unfortunately for their efforts, Diem was not astute enough to weather the storm of criticism coming out of Saigon in the early 1960's. The story of the propaganda effort on his behalf is told by Robert Scheer and Warren Hinckle in *Ramparts*. (**191**)

Even though pressure groups in general rate well on the criterion of accessibility to information, the accessibility principle still operates to diminish the credibility of propaganda put out by foreign agents. The agents themselves may be in a good position to get the facts; but the rest of us are not. When we read a laudatory description of life in Rhodesia, the Dominican Republic, or Portugal, we have no built-in opportunity to check it out. Neither we nor any of our neighbors are likely to have been there recently, and certainly not for long enough to have gotten the feel of the place. By contrast, propaganda about Westinghouse refrigerators, Corvairs, or Mr. Kleen is not so uncheckable, and the advertising about such products is kept in bounds by an appreciation on the part of copy writers that if they stray too far from the truth, they will be found out. The ease with which one can successfully misrepresent the political freedoms of Formosans is greater than the ease with which one can misrepresent automobiles.

Pressure groups with a direct financial interest in the subjects about which they speak and write often provide the most easily available evidence on a subject. But they are rarely the *only* available source; students should exert every effort to secure disinterested evidence and cite pressure group testimony only with good reason.

Ideological extremists are scarcely more credible. At the opposite ends of the political spectrum, both Communists and Birchers tend to gauge truth not by any objective standards but by ideological purity. What serves the cause is true. Few students would be gullible enough to accept extremist testimony of an eyewitness nature, but we have observed a tendency to believe that when an extremist writer quotes somebody else, he would not dare distort his source; hence extremist writings often serve as a mine from which evidence ultimately attributed to others is extracted. Such a practice is consonant with the opinion of Richard Hofstadter:

> The typical procedure of the higher paranoid scholarship is to start with such defensible assumptions and with a careful accumulation of facts, or at least of what appear to be facts, and to marshal these facts toward an overwhelming "proof" of the particular conspiracy that is to be established. It is nothing if not coherent — in fact, the paranoid mentality is far more coherent than the real world, since it leaves no room for mistakes, failures, or ambiguities. . . . It is nothing if not "scholarly" in technique. McCarthy's 96-page pamphlet *McCarthyism* contains no less than 313 footnote references, and Mr. Welch's fantastic assault on Eisenhower, *The Politician*, is weighed down by a hundred pages of bibliography and notes. The entire right-wing movement of our time is a parade of experts, study groups, monographs, footnotes, and bibliographies. . . . What distinguishes the paranoid style is not, then, the absence of verifiable facts (though it is occasionally true that in his extravagant passion for facts the paranoid occasionally manufactures them), but rather the curious leap in imagination that is always made at some critical point in the recital of events. (**90**:36–37).

We are forced to disagree with this analysis. Extremists of the left and the right do, of course, make careless generalizations, the curious leaps in imagination of which Hofstadter complains, and this practice does impeach their credibility. But they also frequently invent, distort, and misrepresent allegedly factual materials. In short, the accuracy record of extremists is not good.

Consider, for example, the most widely circulated piece of extremist literature, Stormer's *None Dare Call it Treason*, with more than seven million copies presumably in circulation. (**213**) This book cannot withstand the scrutiny of even a half-hearted student of evidence. Inaccurate citations abound and represent every conceivable technique for telling a lie. The book is not even a useful object of study by undergraduates interested in evidence; one finds enough false statements on the first two pages to take the fun out of analysis. In comparison with Stormer, even the State Department ranks higher in credibility (see **223**).

Even if it were true that no other extremist writer were as corrupt as Stormer, it would still be difficult to accept the belief that extremists manufacture evidence only occasionally. Everything we know about individual and social psychology supports the belief that the stronger an ideology, the greater the perceptual distortion of its devotees, even to seeing things that are not there. Manufacturing evidence need not be a conscious process. The psychiatric doctrine from which Mr. Hofstadter borrows acknowledges clearly that paranoids create images out of whole cloth. The persecutors of a paranoid are, to him, infinitely real though no less manufactured.

We know of no specific, detailed studies of the use of facts by such extremists as Dan Smoot, Billy James Hargis, Carl McIntire, and Edgar C. Bundy. It would be wholly illusory, however, to expect that they maintain a standard of integrity higher than that of Stormer. Certainly the Overstreets, in *The Strange Tactics of Extremism*, found these writers using the techniques of distortion we have characterized as indicating low credibility. (**170**) On the basis of accuracy record, we have yet to find the extremist who checks out as credible.

Groups of Indeterminate Bias

Some pressure groups play a dual role: part professional association and part self-serving propagandists. The American Medical Association is such a group. Certainly on medical matters none should know better than the doctors what is true and what is fraudulent. In its capacity as a group of medics, the AMA has performed a great service for American health. Medical education has been strengthened, pure food and drug laws have sometimes been promoted, quackery has been prosecuted, and ethical practices have been established (though some loose ends such as fee-splitting and physician ownership of drug stores remain to be cleaned up).

But as a pressure group, and as would-be authorities on medical economics, the doctors have covered themselves with infamy. (See **44**.) It is not just that the AMA's "Maginot Line mentality" has caused them to bless today (Blue Cross, for instance) what they once decried as Communistic (1932); the burden of our charge against the AMA and its spokesmen is that in the area of medical economics they have dealt in untruths.

There are, for instance, several documented charges against Morris Fishbein, longtime editor of the *Journal of the American Medical Association* and the most powerful figure in the Association. Industrialist Henry Kaiser, American Federation of Labor researcher Nelson Cruikshank, and Federal Security Administrator Oscar Ewing all had the pleasure of exposing Fishbein's inaccuracies on national radio programs. (**149**:83) The *Journal*, under his editorship, was filled with a great deal of fantasy about the British Health Service.

Fishbein's ouster in 1949 did little to improve the integrity of the AMA. False data about foreign medical facilities and about the extent of unmet medical needs in the United States continue to appear in the *Journal*. In 1960, a storm of public protest arose when an AMA-endorsed "survey" of the medical needs of the aged was presented to the Fifth Congress of the International Institute of Gerontologists in San Francisco. The AMA press release concerning the survey claimed that it "emphatically proves that the great majority of Americans over 65 are capably financing their own health care and prefer to do it on their own, without government intervention." (**2**:604) This was a ridiculous assertion, for the survey proved no such thing.

But the AMA learns slowly. Its 1964–1965 campaign against medicare for the elderly was hardly more reputable than previous similar efforts. Even its dealings with Congress showed continuing disregard for the truth:

> The American Medical Association has so tarnished its image in the savage battle against medicare that it may find no one willing to listen to another outcry against federal encroachment. The AMA may have screeched wolf too often. At the end of the battle in the House, the AMA was even isolated from all Republicans but one on the Ways and Means Committee. In fact, the AMA performance at the final committee hearings was so childish as to defy belief. Dr. Donovan Ward, AMA President, marched in waving a clipping from the *St. Louis Globe Democrat* about a "still secret study" which showed that the medicare fund would be depleted by 1976. Later the committee discovered that this "still secret study" — based on lower taxes than the bill provided — had been prepared by the Social Security Administration and handed to an AMA

representative who had asked for it. The AMA then evidently planted it
with the *Globe Democrat.* (**151**)

It is interesting to note that even intercollegiate debaters, whose devotion to credible evidence is not always the highest, have learned to eschew
the AMA as a source of testimony. In two published recent academic
debates on medicare, only one speaker had the temerity to quote an
AMA official. (**139**:374) Apparently the untrustworthiness of the AMA
as a source of evidence is reasonably well known. In the two debates,
however, there are several citations of an organization called the Health
Insurance Institute. The title sounds innocuous enough, rather like the
Pasteur Institute or the Institute for Advanced Study. But when one
learns that this institute is the creature of the nation's insurance companies and provides them with "editorial and public relations services,"
(**56**:139) some question arises about its objectivity.

When testimony of this insurance company lobby is coupled with the
testimony of an insurance company president in a nationally televised
debate, we get the following result:

> E. J. Faulkner, president of the Woodman Accident and Life Company,
> says that the cost of administering the medical care provision of the old-
> age assistance program has been running at 12%. Let's compare that to
> voluntary health insurance. A Health Insurance Institute publication
> dated January 1961 estimated that the group health insurance plans cover-
> ing 95 million workers and their dependents operated at an overhead cost
> of 2.3% — almost 10% less, ladies and gentlemen, than the medical care
> provision of the Social Security program. (**140**:95)

We have checked out these citations and will deal with the second at
some length in Chapter 10. But assuming that the citations are given
accurately, the "evidence" offered still has little credibility. (1) Faulk-
ner, an insurance man, is not a good source for an accurate appraisal
of the costs of a government health program. (2) The Health Insurance
Institute, probably biased in favor of the companies it represents, is not
a good source for data about the overhead costs of private insurance
plans. (3) One of the fundamental rules of statistical comparisons is
that you cannot couple data compiled by one source using its own base
periods, accounting categories, and statistical techniques with data compiled by another source using an entirely different set of assumptions,
methods, and dates. (See **94**:Ch. 9.) If one unbiased authority, such

as the Brookings Institution, had calculated the overhead of both government and private medical programs, using the same assumptions, methods, and periods, the comparison would be meaningful. As used here, it is farcical.

There is no public body of data impeaching the accuracy of the Health Insurance Institute as there is for the AMA. Like the hundreds of similar captive research organizations supported by interests of all sorts, the chance that it will produce reliable results depends on the professional competence of its staff, the freedom with which they are allowed to work, and the editorial control exercised over their publications. When the issues are as clearly drawn and the stakes as high as in the tobacco industry case, a captive research organization has the credibility of Joseph Goebbels. At the other extreme, where no self-interest is involved, a laboratory such as Consumers Union is highly reliable. The rest lie in between. The principle of *caveat emptor* applies to the use of sponsored research results as well as to the purchase of Florida real estate.

One interest group which has played a major role in American political life is the ex-Communists, particularly those "professionals" who have made a career of testifying about their former associations. They do not constitute a pressure group in the usual sense since they are not organized formally. But as refugees from the most highly organized and authoritarian pressure group, and as vocal witnesses to what that party was and is, they share common assets and liabilities.

On the face of it, when a Communist has left the party and is no longer subject to party discipline he is "free" to tell the truth. But in actuality he trades the stringent demands of ideological conformity for a host of new pressures. We referred in Chapter 4 to *Ex-Communist Witnesses* by Herbert Packer of Stanford University. The situations in which these people were asked to testify provided a stimulus to any exhibitionistic tendencies they possessed, producing the reverse of confidentiality of testimony; several of them obviously enjoyed making the headlines and counting as somebody important. Having been conditioned to one set of authoritarian beliefs, they found it difficult to adopt a moderate view of the world in which there are no absolute blacks and whites, merely different shades of gray.

Of the four witnesses Packer dissects, John Lautner and Whittaker Chambers seem to emerge as relatively credible, while Elizabeth Bentley and Louis Budenz are substantially suspect. Thus no generalization seems possible about ex-Communists; there are both plus and minus factors affecting their integrity, and individual differences are all-important. It is quite clear, however, that they do not rate as reluctant witnesses, with the high credibility that implies.

The credibility of the many amateur, casual-interest groups on the American scene is also difficult to assess. When the fishermen, the bird lovers, or the spelunkers get together in an interest group, little of prime economic interest or political objective is involved. Some sportsmen's groups do find themselves embroiled in bitter political fights over such things as clean-streams legislation, where the fishermen, surprisingly well organized, are pitted against the massive mining interests. The cost of and necessity for acid-neutralizing treatment for mine drainage are highly controversial. In this situation the main asset of the mining companies is their probable greater expertise; from our perspective, this is more than offset by the absence of direct financial interest on the part of the fishermen. We would expect distortion from both groups; the distortion of the miners should be greater.

but when one inspects the performance of the gun lobby during recent efforts to restrict purchases of mail-order guns, one is not so sure that "amateur" associations really are distortion-free. Or perhaps the fact is that the gun lobby is dominated by arms manufacturers and is really an economic bloc rather than a sportsmen's association. Legislative proposals for gun registration and limitations on purchase brought forth typical interest-group deception. An official of the National Rifle Association allegedly admitted putting out false statements about opposition to gun control laws on the part of the Boy Scouts and the American Legion, misrepresenting Supreme Court decisions upholding the right of Congress to delegate power to regulatory agencies, and denying the existence of cases in which data required by gun control laws were used to solve felonies. (**165**) Since it does not seem reasonable that mere sportsmen whose only interest is in being able to continue hunting would need to misrepresent evidence, the National Rifle Association performance would seem to indicate that control was in the hands of people whose livelihoods would be affected by gun control legislation. Hence, on balance, low credibility attaches to NRA.

The groups which concern themselves with specific social reforms are somewhat different. There are pressure groups devoted to abolishing the death penalty, preventing vivisection, controlling cruelty to animals, legalizing euthanasia, establishing planned parenthood, furthering separation of church and state, and so on. They are a mixed lot. When one asks, "Can the literature of this group be trusted as evidence?" it is difficult to avoid an emotional reaction in line with one's sympathies. But there are two crucial questions which can help in evaluating the literature of such groups: (1) Is anybody making a living at this? (2) What is the accuracy record of group propaganda?

Looking briefly at a typical social reform group, the American League to Abolish Capital Punishment, there do not appear to be any economic interests involved. None of the officers or board members of ALACP make a living at it. Donal E. J. MacNamara, the president, is Dean of the New York Institute of Criminology. Other officers on the letterhead are prominent citizens whose relationship to the League is quite different from the relationship of Marvin Liebman to the China lobby or O. R. Strackbein to the tariff lobby. ALACP officers may benefit from devotion to the cause in psychological and other ways; but there is no evidence that they benefit financially. This datum, of course, is not conclusive; we have seen the stultifying effects of ideologies in Government and elsewhere, and opposition to capital punishment is a kind of ideology.

More crucial is the moderation and accuracy of the propaganda put out by ALACP. Compared with the fulminations of the American Medical Association, it is restrained and sometimes even understated. Thorsten Sellin, for instance, author of a work quoted in Chapter 2 and Vice-President of ALACP, concludes his major study of homicide rates in capital punishment and noncapital punishment jurisdictions by stating that the evidence does not prove anything one way or another. (197:63) A less cautious witness could with considerable justification claim that the figures proved conclusively that capital punishment did not deter homicide. It does not appear that the abolitionists want to secure their objective badly enough to fiddle with the facts.

The propaganda activities of the League consist mainly of distributing scholarly studies which show scrupulous documentation. The studies are not commissioned or paid for by ALACP, the authors of them are not employees of ALACP, and in many cases they are not actively associated with it. This approach contrasts strikingly with the often fraudulent documentation of the extremists and the self-serving testimony of most pressure groups.

We believe, therefore, that there is a fundamental difference in credibility between the ALACP and the Tobacco Research Council, or any other group where self-interest is involved or a rabid partisanship exists. We would not hesitate to cite ALACP literature in support of an argument on capital punishment, where we would flatly refuse to cite the Committee of One Million on the democratic accomplishments of Chiang's Formosa or the American Medical Association on the effect of medicare on the doctor-patient relationship.

One very unusual pressure group came into being in the spring of 1965, as a result of the commitment of American fighting units to the war in Viet-Nam. This was the Inter-University Committee for a Public Hearing on Viet-Nam; the exchange we cite in our frontispiece between McGeorge Bundy and Anatol Rapoport is part of the "literature" of this group. Rapoport and his colleagues clearly had propagandistic intent: they were interested in reversing the decision to prosecute the war with American troops. But the program of the Committee was not typical of such pressure groups. Instead of issuing propaganda, they organized debates or "teach-ins." A debate is a poor way of furthering a cause or of exerting maximum pressure; and to the extent that this committee welcomed speakers who were hostile to its point of view, it had little in common with the methods of partisans of the extremist or commercial lobby sort. (Teach-ins on individual campuses may have been one-sided; the national effort was, as Bundy said, "fair to a fault.")

The output of this group was equally unorthodox. It did, of course, issue appeals for support. After appeals for support from such veteran propagandists as Conde McGinley ("Leader in the nation's fight against Communism"), Herbert A. Philbrick of *I Led Three Lives* and an organization called "Constructive Action, Inc.," Billy James Hargis of Christian Crusade, Young Americans for Freedom, Major Arch Roberts of "Victory Denied," Liberty Lobby, the John Birch Society, and dozens of other purple-passioned solicitations, the shock of finding a pressure group appeal reading like this was considerable:

> Sponsorship implies only a deep concern with the present situation in Southeast Asia and a conviction that questions related to peace and war should be open to responsible debate. Sponsorship does not entail the endorsement of any particular scheme for settling the situation in Viet Nam. This is precisely what we are searching for. (**152**:152)

One is tempted to observe, with apologies to the railroad people, "This is a hell of a way to run a pressure group."

The major public effort of the Inter-University Committee was a marathon session of speeches in Washington. Twenty-five of the fifty-one participants represented the Government point of view. They were no patsies. McGeorge Bundy did not appear as scheduled, but he was replaced by Arthur M. Schlesinger, Jr., then a Government representative; other major pro-Viet-Nam war speakers were Brzezinski, Fishel, Scalapino, Walt Rostow. It is hard to see how anyone could claim the lists were stacked in favor of the anti-war groups.

Thus we have a pressure group whose plea for support fails to endorse any particular policy and whose major production was a debate. Despite this restrained approach, there were vigorous attacks on the credibility of the Inter-University Committee.

One was by Charles Bartlett, Scripps-Howard columnist:

> Of the 82 professors from all over the country who have arranged a confrontation in Washington on May 15 as "a mobilization of public protest," only eight are political scientists, six are historians, and one is a specialist in government. The specialties of the rest reflect no expertise in the issue at hand. (11)

This is, unfortunately, not an accurate analysis of the purpose or composition of the committee. The committee did not view its effort as "a mobilization of public protest," and Bartlett has misrepresented the committee's statement. (152:152) Furthermore, he implies that only political scientists, historians, and teachers of government have any expertise relevant to the war. This betrays *his* ignorance rather than that of the committee; some of the foremost authorities on Asia in general and Viet-Nam in particular are anthropologists, economists, sociologists, psychologists, geographers, and other area specialists. Our own count of committee members with some expertise on Viet-Nam is thirty, rather than fifteen.

But counting the number of experts on the committee reveals nothing whatsoever about the credibility of the committee's output, an extended debate. The committee arranging this could have consisted of art and English teachers with no derogation whatsoever of the testimony of those appearing as speakers. No matters of fact about the war in Viet-Nam were asserted on the authority of the nonexpert members of the committee. We are very much in favor of critiques of pressure groups and other contributors to public intelligence, but no critique as shoddy as Bartlett's makes a contribution. Groups with propagandistic intent must be watched carefully and analyzed unmercifully; but the analyst must know what he is doing.

Of pressure groups there will be no end. The student must, of course, attend to what they say, since the concerns they voice are often real and rarely irrelevant. But to use pressure group materials as evidence of the truth of a matter of fact is highly risky. Pressure group perceptions are almost necessarily distorted, and even those groups which we have classified as of indeterminate bias are not likely to be the best sources of evidence.

SUMMARY

Pressure groups have some advantages as sources of testimony, rating high on the dimensions of accessibility to the facts, consistency of output, expertise, eyewitness status, and contemporaneity of reporting. But they suffer a much more serious set of liabilities because of the crisis nature of the subjects they deal with, gag rules, low authenticity of much of their product, carelessness of generalization, lack of objectivity, poor accuracy records, and inaccurate citations of other authorities. Some groups exhibit such pronounced biases and amass such poor accuracy records that they can be written off as unbelievable under most circumstances; many of these groups are economically motivated. Among them we put the National Committee on Import-Export Policy, the Tobacco Industry Research Council, the drug companies, agents of foreign governments, and the ideological extremists of both Communist and anti-Communist persuasion.

Other pressure groups cannot be summarily dismissed as sources of evidence, though they must be regarded with great suspicion. The American Medical Association, for instance, while it may tell the truth on purely medical matters, has peddled much falsehood on medical economics. The group of ex-Communist witnesses appears to be of uneven credibility; some of them now prevaricate as easily for their new patrons as they did for their former comrades. The gun lobby would not appear to be primarily economically motivated, but there are nonetheless serious doubts about its accuracy. Social action groups such as the American League to Abolish Capital Punishment are a somewhat different class, and seem less addicted to misrepresentation. Even the anti-Viet-Nam pressure group known in 1965 as the Inter-University Committee for a Public Hearing on Viet-Nam cannot be seriously faulted, at least in its early efforts.

In general, pressure groups are a most unlikely source of credible testimony and should be avoided.

SUGGESTED READINGS

Max Ascoli, Charles Wertenbaker, and Philip Horton, "The China Lobby," *The Reporter* (April 15 and April 29, 1952). Reprinted in *Our Times: The Best From The Reporter*, ed. Max Ascoli. New York: Farrar, Straus & Cudahy, 1960.

Douglass Cater and Walter Pincus, "The Foreign Legion of U.S. Public Relations," *The Reporter* (December 22, 1960), 15–22.

Richard Harris, *The Real Voice*. New York: Macmillan, 1964.

Richard Hofstadter, *The Paranoid Style in American Politics and Other Essays*. New York: Random House (Vintage Books), 1967.

Milton Mayer, "The Dogged Retreat of the Doctors," *Harper's* (December, 1949), 25–37.

Milton Mayer, "The Rise and Fall of Dr. Fishbein," *Harper's* (November, 1949), 76–85.

Louis Menashe and Ronald Radosh, eds., *Teach-ins: U.S.A.* New York: Frederick A. Praeger, 1967.

Morton Mintz, *The Therapeutic Nightmare*. Boston: Houghton Mifflin, 1965.

Harry Overstreet and Bonaro Overstreet, *The Strange Tactics of Extremism*. New York: W. W. Norton, 1964.

Herbert L. Packer, *Ex-Communist Witnesses*. Stanford: Stanford University Press, 1962.

Robert Scheer and Warren Hinckle, "The 'Vietnam Lobby'," *Ramparts* (July, 1965), 16–24.

Harmon Zeigler, *Interest Groups in American Society*. Englewood Cliffs: Prentice-Hall, 1964.

Edward Ziegler, *The Vested Interests*. New York: Macmillan, 1964.

9

Professional Scholars

*The "great society" must and wants to understand itself —
partly as a matter of sheer curiosity, partly because human
beings are in a muddle and cannot get out unless they
know more than they know now. Towards fundamental
knowing the newspaper cannot help much; men of action
— politicians and business men — help but slightly. They
themselves know too little; they are not disinterestedly
concerned with finding out; they have usually their own
axes to grind. Almost the only available agency is the
university. The university must shelter and develop think-
ers, experimenters, teachers, and students, who, without
responsibility for action, will explore the phenomena of
social life and endeavour to understand them.*

ABRAHAM FLEXNER (**63**:10)

*Three overriding political ideals seem to me to be inherent
in the traditions of social science, and certainly involved
in its intellectual promise. The first of these is simply
the value of truth, of fact. . . . All social scientists, by the
fact of their existence, are involved in the struggle between
enlightenment and obscurantism. In such a world as ours,
to practice social science is, first of all, to practice the
politics of truth.*

C. WRIGHT MILLS (**155**:178)

181

Independent Scholars

Professional scholars man the knowledge industry: they are the employees of universities, research institutes, and educational foundations whose business it is to know an academic discipline. We use the term "professional scholars" rather than the partially synonymous term "intellectuals" because the latter is broader and includes many who have no expertise on subjects of public deliberation. The poets, artists, fiction writers, musicians, and other similar intellectuals do often testify on controversial policy matters and we frequently value their testimony highly, but we shall not discuss them here.

Most members of the professoriate would, by our definition, be classed as professional scholars. Exceptions are those employed by institutions with strong ideological or theological biases, such as Harding College, seat of one of the extremist groups, which have commitments other than the disinterested pursuit of knowledge. Also, many "institutes" and "foundations" allegedly established for research purposes are captives of interest groups, and their employees are not professional scholars in our sense; instances are the Tobacco Research Council, the Health Insurance Institute, the Foundation for Economic Education. About RAND employees we are ambivalent. Most of them possess the formal qualifications of professional scholars, including advanced degrees. RAND has in the past demonstrated its independence of its primary benefactor, the Air Force. But as we shall see later, there is some question about the immunity of scholars to the ideological positions of their employers, and while RAND employees may occasionally make dissonant noises, they are not likely to bite the hand that feeds them.

On many important controversial policy matters, professional scholars are almost the sole plausible source of information. The choice for evidence on the functions of the Supreme Court is between a dozen competent scholars who have studied and dissected that body, and, say, Senator Sam Ervin. (For an analysis of Ervin's credibility on the Court see 114.) Those who know about the viability of a multinational economic community, the adequacy of contemporary mechanisms for detection of nuclear explosions, or the deterrent effect of capital punishment are the professional scholars.

Since the primary focus of this book is on foreign intelligence, most of the scholars whose credibility we shall discuss are social scientists. It is not clear whether historians come under this classification or not.

Most historians, including Arthur M. Schlesinger, Jr., regard their professional expertise as divorced from the process of deliberation: "I have always been among those who believe that history should be studied for its own sake, not as a guide to the present or a blueprint for the future." (192:496) But when it comes to advocating a "way out" of Viet-Nam, Schlesinger, no less than other authorities, makes abundant use of historical data, including testimony provided by professional historians. We know of nothing other than historical data to use for evaluating the present and predicting the future. Therefore, however historians wish to classify themselves, we regard them as social scientists and as prime sources of usable public intelligence.

In fast-breaking situations, such as the American invasion of the Dominican Republic or the Russian invasion of Czechoslovakia, one must depend on journalists for up-to-the-minute information; academicians cannot provide the latest developments. But for background information we usually turn to the professional scholars.

Our reflections on professional scholars have led us to consider their credibility as a function of the role they play vis-à-vis the power structure of society. Those who have no overt or covert connections with the power structure, the independent scholars, we discuss first. Those who serve the power structure by representing it or contracting with it to produce research we consider next. Those who join the power structure, who hold line or staff positions in government (or industry, though we do not focus on industry) we discuss last.

Until recently, independent scholars were looked on as the best source of testimony about almost any subject. Partly, no doubt, this was self-serving on the part of academics. Any product of the educational system who has it drummed into him by every instructor that the best authority is an academic authority is bound to emerge with considerable bias in that direction. The hypothesis of scholarly superiority does have much to commend it. On most of the dimensions of credibility, independent scholars — those whose sole responsibility is to scholarly institutions — earn very high ratings. Independent scholars, for instance, probably suffer less from distortions due to tension than do other witnesses; foreign crises are less a crisis for them than for responsible governments or assigned reporters. As scholars, they have generally better access to sources of information, though recent developments may have compromised this advantage. They are, of all groups, with the possible exception of Supreme Court justices, most free to call a spade a spade.

Scholarly rules against any violation of authenticity are very firm. Consistency and carefulness of generalization are as highly valued in the academic community as elsewhere. The perceptual capacity of professional scholars is generally high. Standard criteria for entrance into the scholarly world — academic degrees and publications — do not guarantee knowledge, but they largely rule out total ignorance.

But scholarly independence is the possession most respected both within and without academia: when the rhetorical question "Whom do you serve?" is put to a scholar, the answer expected is "I serve the cause of truth." This is the first dimension on which scholars excel. During the first quarter of this century, when Upton Sinclair and Thorstein Veblen were derogating American higher education, which was controlled along with business by "interlocking directorates" and was administered by "captains of erudition" emphasizing public relations over learning, many professional scholars faced considerable pressure on their work. (See **202** and **227**.) This source of corruption in academia is no longer so powerful. The American Association of University Professors list of censured administrations reminds us of a danger that was, rather than a disease that is. In the old days, the University of Pittsburgh fired Frederick Jackson Turner for espousing unpopular ideas and justifiably incurred long and bitter tenure on the AAUP blacklist. Today it stands up to the legislature, the press, and the local Babbitts to defend an historian who belongs to the Fair Play for Cuba Committee and who fought with the Abraham Lincoln Brigade. Paul F. Lazarsfeld and Wagner Thielens, Jr., who studied the pressures on scholars during the McCarthy era, report that though there was widespread apprehension among social science teachers, it was not paralyzing; their heads were "bloody but unbowed." (**125**:95)

The universities, and most research institutes and foundations, are their own bosses. Promotion and pay increments are determined primarily by the evaluations of other scholars. Neither public opinion nor political pressure, nor in most cases ecclesiastical requirements, impinge significantly on the work of the professional scholars. The contrast with Government, journalism, and pressure groups is fundamental; independent scholars face the least pressure to produce results congruent with some ideology. When, therefore, errors creep into their work, one expects them to be random errors.

A second dimension on which professional scholars achieve relative freedom from perceptual distortion is in their emancipation from socially and culturally determined perspectives. This is the concern of Mannheim and the sociology of knowledge; both the events that one perceives and one's evaluation of perceived events are socio-culturally determined, says Mannheim. This was not really a new discovery by the sociologists; historians have long known that we tend to see what we want to see. Mannheim's contribution was in pointing out the systematic bias of observers: the influence of class and culture in determining our perceptions.

Academic scholars (Mannheim uses the term "intellectuals") are peculiarly able to appraise the perspectives with which they grew up and correct or counteract them. They will thus look for a broader range of data, and the ways in which they process what they find will be less culturally determined. This is true both because of the nature of their calling as scholars, and because of the fact that they tend to cut their socio-cultural ties when they enter the scholarly world. They are "socially emancipated": neither proletarian, bourgeois, nor aristocratic.

Recruitment of scholars from various classes of society presumably aids in this process, though Mannheim overestimates the extent to which professional scholars come from a cross-section of society:

> One of the most impressive facts about modern life is that in it, unlike preceding cultures, intellectual activity is not carried on by a socially rigidly defined class, such as a priesthood, but rather by a social stratum which is to a large degree unattached to any social class and which is recruited from an increasingly inclusive area of social life. (**144**:156)

Lazarsfeld and Thielens indicate that more than 50 per cent of the scholars in their study came from professional and managerial backgrounds (**125**:7), and it is common knowledge that the chances for children of a laboring or blue-collar family to enter academia are much smaller than for children of their higher-income neighbors. Mannheim's cultural cross-section is not yet a reality. But his claim that scholars shed their class orientation once they are in the scholarly world is largely borne out; despite their origin, most of them are liberal in politics and more tolerant of deviation in political belief than the class into which they were born. (**125**:17) Professional scholars, because of their membership in a "classless" community, are relatively free of constricting ideologies and guiding presuppositions.

The third characteristic of professional scholars which sets them apart from other witnesses is their professional code: devotion to truth.

Neither profits nor power is acknowledged as a proper goal. We are not talking about a timeless, unitary set of laws or beliefs, about Truth with a capital "T". We are talking about the devotion to empirical methods which has come with the growth of the natural sciences. It is perhaps best stated by the mathematician Jacob Bronowski:

> The activity of science is directed to one overriding end, which is to find the material truth. In our scientific society, this end is accepted as the supreme value. (**20**:62)

Bronowski is talking about the whole of Western society, and were the ideal of truth as supreme as he claims, we would have little occasion to write this book. But in the society of scholars this ideal does prevail more than elsewhere. A student searching for credible evidence is more likely to get it from the writings of professional scholars than from those of journalists, Government spokesmen, or representatives of pressure groups.

But no blanket approval can be awarded to professional scholars. They are human. As strong as their code of integrity may be, there is no effective mechanism for expelling deviants or disciplining the careless. Even the professional code protecting confidentiality of informants, common to doctors, lawyers, and clergymen, cannot be enforced in academia. Sanctions of willful university administrations there may be; sanctions of unprofessional professors there are not. As sociologist Robert Nisbet puts it, "It is possible, indeed, to be promoted and to draw excellent royalties in the behavioral sciences for actions that would lead to suspension from the legal or medical professions." (**167**:67)

Therefore one must watch for error and prevarication even on the part of professional scholars. The substantial plagiarism of Anthony Bouscaren has already been mentioned (Chapter 4); Bouscaren is a political scientist at a presumably respectable college. Deane W. Malott, in his inaugural address as president of Cornell University, plagiarized several passages from an address by another university administrator. (**68**) Scholarship is often ridiculed as "cooperative plagiarism," and for every incident of individual plagiarism brought to light and proved, there must be many dozens which are covered up or are merely marginal.

Bouscaren is guilty not only of plagiarism but of plain inaccuracy. He at one time asserted that North Viet-Nam refused to hold free elections in accordance with the Geneva agreements, which simply is not true. (**232**:1) Noam Chomsky, prominent professor of linguistics, tampered with a quotation from a book about Malaya, and when called on it, misrepresented the intent of the original author. (**33**:24) Colin Clark, prominent agricultural economist, has asserted that "anxieties about exhausting the resources of the world may be deferred for several centuries, however fast population increases." (**35**:138) This is careless generalization, whether from a professorial pen or not.

On the dimension of predictive accuracy, also, professional scholars sometimes seem no more reliable than less prestigious groups. Perhaps the prime examplar of mindless prediction is James Burnham, best-selling author of *The Managerial Revolution* and until recently Professor of Philosophy at New York University. Peter Drucker (**49**), Malcolm Cowley (**40**), Arthur Schlesinger, Jr. (**193**), and William Barrett (**10**), among others, have all dissected Burnham's inaccurate predictions, which include the following:

> 1941: Russia will split apart, with the western half gravitating toward Europe and the eastern toward Asia. (**26**:180)
>
> 1941: The presidential election of 1940 may well have been the last regular presidential election in the history of the country. (**26**:261)
>
> 1945: Russia is in sight of conquering the whole of Eurasia. (**25**)
>
> 1950: Communism is going to be defeated within a very few years, especially if the United States follows the Burnham plan. (**23**)
>
> 1959: The United States Congress is on its way out as an institution. (**24**)

One could merely laugh at these if they had not come from the pen of a teacher at New York University, and had Burnham's writings not been used with such stridency to challenge so many anti-depression measures of the Federal government.

Periodicals claiming to be scholarly sometimes carry articles of no more value than an astrologer's chart. *Orbis*, a journal published at the University of Pennsylvania and a prominent outlet for right-wing ideologues, in 1960 carried an article by Suzanne Labin and Christopher Emmet which claimed that all the talk about a Sino-Soviet split was wrong: "In what concerns the essential activities of a modern state, China will be chained to Russia for decades." (**120**:29) "In the Afro-Asian world, Soviet and Chinese penetration has proceeded harmoniously and in perfect coordination." (**120**:31) "For all these reasons, the national interests of an aggressive China and Russia seem indissolubly linked even from General de Gaulle's purely nationalist point of view."

(**120**:35)   These things were not true in 1960, no matter with what scholarly panoply *Orbis* presented them.

Even the overwhelming *Encyclopaedia Britannica* cannot always be trusted. Harvey Einbinder, a sober scientist with no discernible axe to grind, has documented dozens of errors in that massive work (**54**); as a final authority it leaves something to be desired. The 1962 edition, still found on the shelves of many libraries, offers the following amazing statement about guerrilla warfare, for instance:

> In conclusion, we may say that guerrilla warfare can be a valuable adjunct to the operation of a regular army, but too much should never be expected from it. Because guerrilla bands are loosely knit, poorly disciplined, and must remain so, they can never overthrow an enemy or win a war. (Volume X, p. 952)

Many *Britannica* articles are undated, as is this one; but since its bibliography cites literature written in 1956, somebody connected with the encyclopedia could have revised this article to account for Tito, Mao Tse-tung, and General Giap, at least, even if no more basic correction were made. Einbinder's discussion of the *Britannica* is not mere nit-picking, and however many generations have been brought up to worship its accuracy, we do not recommend blind acceptance of *Britannica* evidence.

Deviations from scholarly accuracy are not so common as to vitiate the generalization that independent scholars are the most credible source of testimony. The exceptions do not destroy the rule, but they are frequent enough for a conscientious student to worry about. As we consider scholars who are servants of power, that worry may well intensify.

Scholars as Servants of Power

Among social scientists, new realms of achievement have risen to prominence, challenging the ancient indices of teaching and publication as measures for renown and promotion. In many instances, these new avenues of achievement discourage and prevent publication. The touchstone of success in contemporary academia is coming to be neither the length of one's list of publications nor their quality, nor yet one's skill in inspiring and enlightening youth; rather it is the size of one's Federal research grant or contract. And where research is conducted on politically sensitive topics, publication is the last thing a harried Government desires. Some academicians must, therefore, prove their worth by public display not of what they know but of how much the Government pays them to keep quiet.

Not all Government-sponsored research is classified, and after the furious struggles at the University of Pennsylvania and elsewhere (see 117) to bar secret research from the campus, many formerly restricted projects are being declassified. But whether secret or not, an increasing proportion of the time of social scientists is being devoted to Government-sponsored research. Estimates of the percentage of total research funds available to social scientists which come from Government vary, and we hesitate to accept any one of them as reliable; yet the percentage is assuredly large and growing larger. "Project titanship" is replacing endowed chairs and departmental chairmanships in prestige. Robert Nisbet describes the change this way:

> The relevant model of behavioral science research is fast ceasing to be the scholar — he of "furrowed brow in bookish corner" — and fast becoming the brisk executive, at home, equally, in institute, business, and government. We still use the beguiling image of the scholar and his natural right to freedom of inquiry. It is to today's large-scale, corporate research what the image of the small individual businessman and his natural right to profit is to corporate industry: a compound of honest nostalgia, guilty conscience and camouflage. The structure, the incentives, and even the language of contemporary large scale research have more in common with business than with the academy. (167:68)

We grant immediately that involvement of academicians with practical affairs has some advantages besides moving professors into the $20,000 income bracket. Their knowledge is often useful in policy making, and they learn how responsibility can alter perspectives. We do not question the fact that professional scholars can help to solve the problems of the modern state. What we do question is how the servants of power can maintain their objectivity, how the testimony of men on government payrolls shapes up as evidence on controversial issues.

On the face of it, it is unreasonable to expect any human being to look a gift horse in the mouth. A government which demands that its employees support current policy all the way is not going to tolerate dissonant opinions from casual associates. Nor can one forget the alacrity with which the German academic community sold out to or acquiesced in the lies of Hitler's National Socialists. (See **131**.) If many of the professional scholars in Soviet Russia are less than critical seekers after truth, we can expect some degree of ideological commitment to rub off on American scholars working for an increasingly mission-oriented government.

There is abundant testimony that the corrupting process has already seriously affected academia. As Senator Fulbright observed on December 13, 1967:

> The universities might have formed an effective counterweight to the military-industrial complex by strengthening their emphasis on the traditional values of our democracy, but many of our leading universities have instead joined the monolith, adding greatly to its power and influence. Disappointing though it is, the adherence of the professors is not greatly surprising. No less than businessmen, workers and politicians, professors like money and influence. Having traditionally been deprived of both, they have welcomed the contracts and consultantships offered by the Military Establishment. (**67**)

To the extent that the worship of money and power has compromised the dedication to truth, scholarly testimony is devalued.

Not only outside observers like Fulbright but insiders like anthropologist Marshall Sahlins have diagnosed the problem:

> The cold war researcher is potentially a servant of power, placed in a sycophantic relation to the state unbefitting science or citizenship. The scholar sells his services to a military, intelligence or foreign policy client, who has certain plans for the product. Although formal clearance requirements may be suspended, it is only artless to claim there is no informal selection of academic personnel on the basis of agreement in cold war principle — if not tactic — or no penalty to outspoken public criticism. Academicians who have demonstrated creative support are at least differentially favored for higher appointments in the existing scheme of things; those who cannot agree run some risk of being shut out, unless they shut up. (**188**:76)

Even where increments of power and money are relatively minor, those who go along with the prevailing ideology by seeking clearance to use classified materials are compromised. William R. Polk, a political scientist, claims:

Obviously, to some extent, the scholar loses his freedom when he becomes, even indirectly, an employee of the government. At the very least, he acquires access to confidential information. In the government work, as in private business, this gives him a privileged position and imposes restraints on his pen. (174:257)

Those in whom the myth of academic purity dies hard, who find it impossible to believe that sponsorship could really deflect the opinions of professors, need but to visit a campus where secret research has become an issue. We have ourselves been through this battle. The University of Pittsburgh Senate struggled through two long meetings in the fall of 1967 at which various statements on secret research were debated. There had been no scandal on the Pitt campus as there was at the University of Pennsylvania (where research on the effectiveness of chemical warfare in Viet-Nam was conducted), but there were various classified contracts which some faculty members wished to have cancelled.

The opponents of secret research were a mixed lot. Some of them were in nonsensitive areas where Federal funds were not involved. But a number of the most outspoken were in political science, anthropology, and psychology, where the University stood to lose lucrative contracts if it opposed Government secrecy. The testimony of these men could be classed as reluctant; they were going against their own monetary interest. The advocates of secret research who publicly supported acceptance of classified contracts were without exception those who stood to benefit: the natural scientists, engineers, members of the Graduate School of Public and International Affairs (which is overwhelmingly supported by Federal funds), and knowledge-availability systems specialists. It would be asking too much to believe that their opinions were unrelated to self-interest. Some of them privately confessed that their public stance was conditioned by the source of their salaries. In general, one would expect errors on the part of scholars who are servants of power to correlate with their self-interest and the ideology of their patron.

There is, for instance, the history of Project Camelot, which "may well have been the worst single scientific project since King Canute dealt with the tides: the worst conceived, worst devised, worst designed, and worst executed." (167:45) Camelot was an Army project begun in 1963 to study the social forces which lead to insurgency in developing countries and to find how such forces might be countered. Some thirty-three consultants, including many of the most distinguished social scientists in the United States, served as advisors. Preliminary budget was in the neighborhood of $6,000,000, an unbelievably magnificent sum to fall into academic hands. And, as Robert Nisbet says,

> *Gloria in Excelsis Deo*, it was a project at long last in which Outsiders were Insiders — most of the social scientists involved were, to one degree or another, on the liberal-left of the political spectrum, and it is not likely that there was a single supporter of the Viet Nam war among them. Across the River Styx, the shades of Plato and all his descendants down to C. Wright Mills must have danced in joy at the sight of this final ascent of the pure in heart to the very citadel of modern power. (**167**:47)

But the liberal-leftists in academia were no more capable of sound judgment once the dollar sign was waved in front of them than were the conservative-right columnists studied by Bagdikian. Camelot "surfaced" in Chile, where a sensitive people decided that it was none of the United States Army's business what potential for insurgency their society contained; their protest reached all the way to the Pentagon, and McNamara, "in one of the fastest actions ever recorded in official Washington" (Nisbet's description), summarily cancelled the project in the summer of 1965.

A study of the history of Camelot is probably the most enlightening pursuit a student of evidence could engage in. Fortunately the affair has been explored thoroughly in a volume edited by Irving Louis Horowitz. (**93**) In it one can find the whole spectrum of perceptual distortion and fraudulent testimony, all documented and all coming from the community of scholars.

There was outright misrepresentation on the part of an anthropologist, whose actions are described in a letter from the faculty of the Catholic University, Santiago, Chile, to the president of the International Sociological Association:

> In fact, Dr. Hugo Nutini [Assistant] professor in the Department of Anthropology at the University of Pittsburgh, who came to Chile to establish contact with Chilean sociologists to make them interested in participating in Project CAMELOT, affirmed both in writing and orally that the project was financed by the National Science Foundation when in reality it was financed by the Army of the United States and the Department of Defense of that country. Moreover, in the copy of the Project Design that he gave to Chilean sociologists all references to the Army had been meticulously erased. Finally, efforts were made to make us believe that it pursued purely scientific interests when in reality it was

intended to serve as a basis for the counterinsurgency politics of the United States. (**69**:293)

When Nutini was confronted with documentary evidence of Army sponsorship, he asserted his ignorance of it and claimed he "had been fooled." (**200**:86)

There was also distortion. Alfred de Grazia, political science impresario who edits *The American Behavioral Scientist* and an ambitious bibliography of behavioral science research, wrote off the whole blowup in Chile with the allegation that "A Norwegian pacifist named Johan Galtung egged on a Chilean communist paper to agitate South American antiyanqui jingoism among a few professors . . . ." (**43**:40) The facts were slightly different. There is no evidence that Galtung "egged on" anybody. Conservative as well as Communist papers were horrified. And the antiyanqui sentiments of the professors were, if anything, less strenuous than those of Chilean society as a whole. De Grazia is not only a project titan and a "cheerleader for the West" in the cold war, but also inaccurate when shooting from the hip.

There was, finally, predictive stupidity on the part of the Camelot advisors. They approved a research design which could only have resulted in disaster.

> But what cannot be overlooked is the fact that a group of American social scientists, acting as social scientists, allowed the American military to believe there was nothing *scientifically* wrong in an American social science project, under American Army sponsorship, entering the historically sensitive areas of Latin America for the express purpose of discovering, through every possible penetration of culture and mind, the conditions of social unrest, conflict, and insurgency.
>
> Here is a cross-cultural consideration that one might justifiably assume to be understood by every sophomore in an introductory sociology, or anthropology course, one that might occur to any lay American who has been reading the news over the past decade or two. Was there no one in the administrative organization of SORO [Special Operations Research Office, an affiliate of American University and the contracting agency for Camelot], no one among the social scientists who were appointed as *professional* men, not as simple technicians, to say in effect to Lt. General William Dick, Chief of Research and Development, Army: "Your objective is your business and no doubt admirable from the point of view of the Army; as behavioral scientists we desire to be of such help as we can; *but everything we know as behavioral scientists suggests the monumental, possibly catastrophic, unwisdom of such a project.*" (**167**:53)

The channels of public intelligence are now flooded with information originating in Government-commissioned projects such as Camelot, information which bears the imprimatur of America's most prestigious social scientists. But can it be credible? Can it be objective when the researcher knows to what use his results will be put, knows that he is not to find anything which might suggest that insurgency might actually be a good thing for a country dominated by a feudal aristocracy? Army funding of a research project will probably result in perceptual distortion on the part of the investigator. Fulbright, again, explains it clearly:

> The corrupting process is a subtle one: no one needs to censor, threaten, or give orders to contract scholars; without a word of warning or advice being uttered, it is simply understood that lucrative contracts are awarded not to those who question their Government's policies but to those who provide the Government with the tools and techniques it desires. The effect, in the words of the report to the Advisory Commission on International Education, is "To suggest the possibility to a world — never adverse to prejudice — that academic honesty is no less marketable than a box of detergent on the grocery shelf." (**67**)

Camelot is merely the *locus classicus* of academic perversions. A complete catalog of untrustworthy results produced by those who have taken on the Government mantle via sponsorship, subsidy, or direct employment would be voluminous. Many of those involved are political scientists. This is not surprising, perhaps, since students of the political process would necessarily be thrown into close contact with government. Horowitz, a sociologist, confirms this relationship:

> The men who established the institutional and organizational patterns of social science to social policy were by training and inclination engineers, managers, and planners. When they did link up to a social science, it was invariably to political science — a field which in its successful attempts at rapid professionalization chose alignment with federal interests rather than criticism of such interests as its high road to success. (**93**:371)

But the interests of recovery from the Depression, which drew many political scientists into active collaboration with the Federal Government at a time when its policies were avowedly humanitarian, were fundamentally different from the interests of the 1960's, which are largely ideological. These new interests show through such questionable academic practices as the following.

Richard Louis Walker, political scientist, Chairman of the Department of International Studies at the University of South Carolina, and a regular lecturer on the War College circuit, has produced much writing about Asian affairs whose accuracy leaves something to be desired. In a 1958 publication of the Foreign Policy Association, he seriously misrepresented an article from *The Economist* by the easy device of changing tenses and number. (**229**:60. See also **161**:132.) In the same publication, he asserted that at a SEATO conference of November, 1957, one hundred key leaders of Pakistan, the Philippines, and Thailand supported United States China policy — this at a time when two of those three nations recognized China. (**229**:50) Throughout Walker's numerous writings, scholarship plays second fiddle to the perspectives of his client, the Department of Defense.

Frank N. Trager, former United States Point Four director in Burma, now Professor of International Affairs at New York University, has written a book subsidized by USIA entitled *Why Vietnam?* The book presents 219 pages of polemic with some history thrown in. The "history" consists of gems such as the statement that the Vietnamese Communists went along with the Geneva Agreements since they "were pleased to acquire all of Viet Nam above the 17th parallel because they had been unable to eliminate the French Expeditionary Corps from Hanoi, Haiphong, and key areas in the southern Red River delta area." (**216**:97) This, of course, was precisely the area where the Communists were most effective in eliminating the French, as every other writer on the First Indochina War attests. Since the list of myths in Trager is long, the book is hardly worth scholarly attention. (But see **59**.)

Robert A. Scalapino, political scientist at the University of California at Berkeley, broadcaster on the Voice of America, and chief spokesman for Government policy at the 1965 Washington Teach-In, provides some interesting studies in accuracy of citation, eyewitness status, and internal consistency. His defenses of current policy are sprinkled with misleading generalizations. Consider this statement from an article in *The New York Times Magazine* of December 11, 1966: "It is no exaggeration to assert that at present not a single non-Communist Asian government wishes the United States to withdraw from Southeast Asia or to be defeated in Vietnam." (**190**:133) Of course not. But this is not the issue with which Scalapino is dealing, as the title ("We Cannot Accept a Communist Seizure of Vietnam") and text of his article reveal. His assertion is of the "Would you rather be tarred and feathered or strung from the rafters" type, as if there were no other options. Scalapino made a flying trip to Southeast Asia and presumably interviewed responsible leaders. One would expect them to reply to a question from a supporter of American policy, "Of course we do not want you to be defeated in Viet-Nam." To expect any other reply would be naïve. One might also expect Asian leaders to assure such an ideologue that they did not want the United States to withdraw from Southeast Asia. But both these responses sidestep what Scalapino was trying to prove, namely, that these leaders supported the contemporary American action in Viet-Nam, either in whole or in part. When red herrings of this sort appear in "scholarly" literature, ideology seems to have triumphed over objectivity.

Ithiel de Sola Pool, Professor of Political Science at Massachusetts Institute of Technology, close collaborator with the Pentagon and author of many articles dealing with the contributions of social science research to national security, has produced a generalization which military men will no doubt parade as a slogan whenever skeptical citizens complain about the cruelties of napalm, fragmentation bombs, gas and germ warfare, or nuclear weapons. Time was when military types crudely spoke of "dropping a couple of nukes in the Kremlin men's room," or "bombing North Viet-Nam back to the Stone Age." No more. McNamara, according to Pool, has introduced cost-effectiveness into defense planning. This, says Pool, "has had the effect of taming what would otherwise be a terrifying institution." Cost-effectiveness "compels a measurement of consequences rather than asking whether the better weapon fits the military cliché of always seeking a bigger bang." This and other contributions of social science analysis has remade American defense policy. And the payoff? "The result has been the humanization of the Department of Defense." (176:268–269) If this is social *science*, this millennial contribution to the education of the generals, then God spare us from social science. As the Duke of Wellington is reported to have said to a gentleman who addressed him as "Mr. Smith," "Sir, if you can believe that, you can believe anything."

The writings of scholars with Government connections are sometimes censored, which may well be more damaging to credibility than the subtle effects of perceptual distortion. Scholars who have acquired classified data are inhibited not just by fear of losing future consultantships and grants if they displease their sponsors but by the security laws. Former diplomats, scholars who have used classified papers, ex-employees of many Government branches often cannot admit that they know many relevant facts.

Consider, for instance, our knowledge about the many abortive attempts by the CIA to overthrow hostile governments. An attempted coup in Syria in the fall of 1957 was supported by the CIA; it failed, with disastrous consequences for American operations in the Middle East. Syrian conspirators were subsequently put on public trial, and every literate Arab read the details of this attempted American intervention in his daily newspaper. Independent scholars processing publicly available information acknowledge this event. (See, for instance, **234**:461.) But the insiders who had access to primary (and classified) information about the CIA role and who have written the major works on United States policy in the Middle East are silent about the whole affair. (**41, 111, 175**) Such histories cannot be credible if they neither incorporate known and relevant data nor offer a perspective conducive to understanding the subjects about which they are written.

Users of evidence need to look hard at the testimony of professional scholars and at the sources of their income, power, and prestige. Not only control follows the purse; influence also follows the purse, as it does the symbols of status and power. There are strong forces working within the professional associations to eliminate the causes of distortion and inaccuracy in scholarly efforts. They will never succeed completely, but one hopes that they will succeed enough so that when a second edition of this book goes to press the need to warn readers about the corrupting effects of Government sponsorship of scholars will have diminished. William Marvel, president of Education and World Affairs, told the International Studies Association in 1965:

> Maybe it is a *code of ethics* or a *statement of best practices* that would be a first step. Maybe in the social sciences we need the functional equivalent of the Hippocratic Oath. Whatever form it takes, the major requirement is the elimination of deception, whether *self-deception* or the *deception of others*. . . . making sure that reality and appearance are reasonably in accord for the research scholar . . . making certain that if we must serve two masters — the government agency and also the canons of our own profession — we have our own priorities clear . . . that we are not posing as something which, at the moment, we are not. (**145**:183)

Scholars as Wielders of Power

Three decades ago, when the movement of scholars into government service was catching on, Walter Lippmann sounded a warning:

It is only knowledge freely acquired that is disinterested. It is only on such knowledge that a democracy, seeking guidance, can rely. When, therefore, men whose profession is to teach and to investigate become the makers of policy, become members of an administration in power, become politicians and leaders of causes, they are committed. Nothing they say can be relied upon as disinterested. Nothing they teach can be trusted as scientific. It is impossible to mix the pursuit of knowledge and the exercise of political power and those who have tried it turn out to be very bad politicians or they cease to be scholars. (132:604)

The same warning has been sounded in recent times by Russell Kirk, who is fortified with watching several generations of scholars turn public servants. To Kirk they are no more credible, whether left or right, than they were to Lippmann. (112)

If, as we have contended, scholars who serve power by accepting research grants and contracts are corrupted, it would be carrying coals to Newcastle to offer evidence that scholars who go one step further — who accept political appointments — are also corrupted. Yet there are some lessons to be learned from reflecting on the careers of several such individuals. Some of them are nationally known figures, and their departures from the path of truth are the more striking and damaging. The dog catcher who lies injures but few; the Presidential Assistant who lies injures the whole nation. The principle involved is familiar — Lippmann stated it well. Nothing scholars in Government service say can be relied on as disinterested. Perceptual accuracy is a casualty of their employment. Or if they retain their personal integrity, their accuracy of statement becomes a casualty. The result is the same: their testimony cannot be trusted.

We begin with John Foster Dulles, a lawyer by profession but also an accomplished scholar in foreign affairs. During the 1940's he headed a commission of the National Council of Churches dealing with foreign policy and wrote a remarkable book entitled *War or Peace*, published in 1950. In this book Dulles took a thoroughly pragmatic view of international relations: one of the tenets of this view was that the embryonic United Nations, rather than guarding its purity as an assembly of the "peace-loving" nations, should include all nations:

> I have now come to believe that the United Nations will best serve the cause of peace if its Assembly is representative of what the world actually is, and not merely representative of the parts which we like. Therefore, we ought to be willing that all the nations should be members without

attempting to appraise closely those which are "good" and those which are "bad." Already that distinction is obliterated by the present membership of the United Nations.

. . . .

If the Communist government of China in fact proves its ability to govern China without serious domestic resistance, then it, too, should be admitted to the United Nations. . . .

If the United Nations membership were made substantially universal, that might end a preponderant voting superiority of the United States and its friends, which, while pleasant, is somewhat fictitious. (**52**:190–191)

Dulles was regarded as the top Republican expert on foreign policy and advised the Truman Administration in nonpartisan endeavors. It was natural that Eisenhower should offer him the Secretaryship of State. When he assumed that high office, there were a number of abrupt changes in his perceptions. One of the most startling was his complete repudiation of the principles argued in the above quotation. He no longer held that the United Nations should represent reality; its roster should be restricted to those peace-loving nations which play by Marquis of Queensberry rules, and the UN should not become a "reformatory for bad governments." (**51**) The "qualitative test for participation in the United Nations" should be strictly enforced, and this means no China. Thus, to one of the vital policy questions of the post-war world, "Should the peace-loving clause of the United Nations Charter be adhered to scrupulously and China excluded because of this clause?" Dulles the scholar answered, "No"; Dulles the politician answered, "Yes."

This was one of the more naked examples of political pressure changing, whether fundamentally or only superficially we shall never know, the opinion of a candidate for high office. C. L. Sulzberger, foreign affairs specialist for *The New York Times*, describes how it happened:

In May 1952 Dulles met Eisenhower for the first time in Paris. Soon afterward, it became probable that he would be chief diplomatic officer of an Eisenhower administration. Nevertheless, his previously published judgments worried some party stalwarts. Before the inauguration, Republican legislators representing the Know-Nothing faction inquired if Dulles still favored Peiping's entry into the UN. They indicated he might have difficulty in obtaining confirmation as Secretary unless he clarified his stand. Dulles gave private assurances that he no longer backed such a concession to Red China. Furthermore, he promised to give favorable consideration to any candidate his questioners might recommend as assistant secretary in charge of Far Eastern Affairs. The choice of Walter Robertson resulted. (214:193)

In evaluating this incident, one need not hold a brief for the rightness or wrongness of any particular China policy. Its significance for a theory of evidence is that disinterested scholarship is usually incompatible with wielding power.

A second case study is from the other side of the party fence. Arthur M. Schlesinger, Jr., son of a distinguished historian, established his own reputation as one of America's leading scholars in 1946 with the publication of *The Age of Jackson,* for which he received a Pulitzer prize. He is a Democrat; his *magnum opus* is a series of largely sympathetic volumes under the title *The Age of Roosevelt.* During the 1950's while at Harvard and under the influence of the redoubtable Reinhold Niebuhr, he published a wide-ranging series of articles commenting on the contemporary scene. They were hard-bitten, skeptical, contemptuous of the lofty dreams and panaceas of old-fashioned "liberals."

In 1961, Schlesinger became Special Assistant to President Kennedy and took up a new set of duties in the White House. But he continued writing. Somehow the product of his pen took on a new flavor, alien to and sometimes in stark contrast with the skepticism and hardheadedness of his previous writings. In 1962, a volume called *The Politics of Hope* came out, incorporating writings of both the old and the new Schlesinger. The essays in this volume are not arranged chronologically, to facilitate comparison of the "old" Schlesinger with the "new"; but the dates of original composition are provided so that the reader who wants to can follow the "progress" of Schlesinger's thought from academic critic to partisan New Frontiersman. Those who doubt the influence of commitment upon so vigorous and incisive a mind as Mr. Schlesinger's are urged to read these essays in chronological order.

The decade of the 1950's, when Schlesinger was the critic, was, according to him, a period of drift, relaxation, and irresponsibility (not to mention the fact that the Department of Defense had not yet been humanized):

> In our decade of inertia, we squandered, for example, a commanding weapons lead until our own officials now frankly concede that by the early '60's the Soviet Union, a nation supposedly far behind our own in

economic and technological sophistication, will have a superiority in the thrust of its missiles and in the penetration of outer space. . . . This period of sterility in our conduct of foreign affairs stands in particular contrast to the astonishing decade of creativity which preceded it, from the Atlantic Charter to NATO and from Lend-Lease to Point Four. (**194**:86–87)

But now contemplate what happened as we entered the decade of the 1960's:

Self-righteousness has ceased to be the main instrument of our diplomacy. . . . The life of the mind enjoys a new freedom and a new status. . . . The word "togetherness" has passed from the language. Few would describe American society any longer in last decade's condescending vocabulary of conformism and homogenization. In short, the older American faith in leadership and diversity and contention and individualism and experiment and irreverence is beginning to reassert itself. We are Sons of Liberty once again; or, at least, we admit this as a legitimate ambition. We have awakened as from a trance; and we have awakened so quickly and sharply that we can hardly remember what it was like when we slumbered. (**194**:xi)

These lines have no doubt added considerably to Mr. Schlesinger's reputation as a humorist, especially in Latin America. Sociologist Lewis Coser, reviewing this purple-passioned oratory in *Commentary*, tartly observes:

All this is a bit hard to take, coming as it does from the pen of a man whose official address is The White House. . . . It is asking a bit much to have us believe that the mere advent of Mr. Schlesinger's employer on the scene has, as with one wave of a magic wand, changed the major characteristics of an era and of a society. (**38**:77)

But this is what happens when scholars become partisans. Such extravagances of description are not all, however. Wielders of power not only lose their scholarly sense of carefulness, they become subject to the gag rule. Perhaps there was only one time when Mr. Schlesinger lied as a member of Kennedy's staff, in passing out the official cover story that the Bay of Pigs invasion was not an invasion at all but just a landing of supplies for guerrillas opposing Castro. Schlesinger, at least, apologized for the lie. (**195**) The crucial point for the student of evidence is that, given a scenario in which lying is possible, one can never know when a witness is telling the truth. And professional scholars who become politicans are no more credible than careerists.

When one has been edified by the transfigurations of John Foster Dulles and Arthur M. Schlesinger, Jr., it is perhaps wearisome to follow also the dramatic conversion of Walt Whitman Rostow. The documents are easily available, however, to one who has the inclination. Rostow wrote *The United States in the World Arena* (**185**) in 1960 when he viewed the world from an academic post at M.I.T. He wrote *View From The Seventh Floor* (**186**) in 1964 as a high official in the State Department. Saul, the scriptures relate, was blinded on the road to Damascus. Modern conversions produce similar perceptual changes, except that the road these days leads to Washington.

Some academics have held power without, apparently, compromising their credibility. Their Government careers generally have not lasted long, and perhaps the difficulty of maintaining integrity has been responsible for their short tenure. But it is hard to separate sheep from goats in this corral. The prudent policy is to measure academics in power by the same standards used for nonacademic officials.

SUMMARY

Independent scholars, employed by academic institutions with no fixed ideological positions, are generally highly credible witnesses on many areas of controversial public policy. By virtue of their training, professional code, emancipation from socio-cultural biases, and the atmosphere in which they work, they should produce results superior to those of nonacademic witnesses. This generally high rating cannot be applied to all scholars; there is no professional control over deviants, and professors are human.

Scholars who are beholden to the Government for grants, contracts, and consultantships are substantially compromised. Those who have had access to classified documents are prevented from telling the whole truth under penalty of prosecution. Those who look forward to future Government plums will not be professionally critical and objective. Even scholars generally hostile to the Government, when they are caught up in the coils of a lucrative and prestigious project like Camelot, fail to exercise the critical detachment of which they are capable. At the extreme, they become apologists and propagandists, and their inaccuracies are easily detected.

Scholars who forsake the academy for positions of power are indistinguishable in credibility from career Government officers. To hold their posts, they must pronounce only such "facts" as are congruent with the policies of their masters, including lying when necessary.

Professional scholars come in several shapes and colors. As with other categories of witnesses, the greater their independence the greater their credibility.

SUGGESTED READINGS

Lewis A. Coser, review of Arthur Schlesinger, Jr., *The Politics of Hope, Commentary* (July, 1963), 76–78.

George B. de Huszar, *The Intellectuals.* Glencoe: The Free Press of Glencoe, 1960.

Harvey Einbinder, *The Myth of the Britannica.* New York: Grove Press, 1964.

Irving Louis Horowitz, ed., *The Rise and Fall of Project Camelot.* Cambridge: The M.I.T. Press, 1967.

Gabriel Kolko, "Universities and the Pentagon," *The Nation* (October 9, 1967), 328–332.

Paul F. Lazarsfeld and Wagner Thielens, Jr., *The Academic Mind.* Glencoe: The Free Press of Glencoe, 1958.

Frederic Lilge, *The Abuse of Learning.* New York: Macmillan, 1948.

Karl Mannheim, *Ideology and Utopia,* tr. Louis Wirth and Edward Shils. New York: Harcourt, Brace (Harvest Books), 1960.

Louis Menashe and Ronald Radosh, eds., *Teach-ins: U.S.A.* New York: Frederick A. Praeger, 1967.

Statistics

PART FOUR

10

Statistical Evidence

> *Any kind of alleged yardstick or "meter" commands initial respect. Yet the low repute of statistical proofs in debate ("You can prove anything by figures") should remind us that it is far easier to go through the motions of measurement, or to cite its supposed results, than it is to understand exactly what a set of figures signifies.*

> HAROLD A. LARRABEE (**123**:272)

Credibility as a Function of Purpose

There are no special indices which will reveal credible statistics. Like testimony about specific historical events or about any nonstatistical generalization, the credibility of statistics depends on the competence and objectivity of the compiler and the reporter.

In that "wilderness of fraud" (Darrell Huff's phrase, in **94**) loosely termed statistics, ways of misrepresenting a situation are even more numerous and ingenious than when one is dealing with eyewitness testimony. Yet the disarming definiteness of figures, the concreteness and apparent precision of percentages, the solidity of charts and graphs lend a specious air of veracity to evidence.

Social scientists have lately developed a fondness for statistics. Many believe that if something exists it can be measured precisely and accurately. This has led to the trivialization of research; scholars investigate not what is important but what can be quantified. C. Wright Mills has said what needs to be said about the nitpicking studies involving orthogonally rotating factor matrices and other such devices:

> Those in the grip of the methodological inhibition often refuse to say anything about modern society unless it has been through the fine little mill of The Statistical Ritual. It is usual to say that what they produce is true even if unimportant. I do not agree with this; more and more I wonder how true it is. I wonder how much exactitude, or even pseudo-precision, is here confused with "truth"; and how much abstracted empiricism is taken as the only "empirical" manner of work. If you have ever seriously studied, for a year or two, some thousand hour-long interviews, carefully coded and punched, you will have begun to see how very malleable the realm of "fact" may really be. (**155**:71–72)

Numerical statements about important issues must be handled by students, however, and we find variants of three of the general tests of evidence described in Chapter 5 to be most useful for this purpose:

(1) *Objectivity:* Who wants to prove what?
(2) *Authenticity:* What do the figures really represent?
(3) *Carefulness of generalization:* What conclusions do the figures support?

The importance of the compiler of statistics is enormous because of the endless ways he can manipulate figures. Base periods can be selected to give a desired result; different formulas can be used to calculate averages; profits can be figured on any of several sets of data about the same business; correlations can be drawn which have no logical connection; questions on a survey can be loaded; samples can be too small and not representative; comparisons may deal with noncomparable units; conclusions may go beyond the supporting data; and, of course, data can simply be invented. Statistics are neither people nor things; they are symbols, like words, and while the symbols can be manipulated with great precision, the realities behind the symbols, if any, frequently get lost.

One of the most famous statistical gaffes was the *Literary Digest* poll of 1936 which predicted that Republican Alfred Landon would defeat

Franklin D. Roosevelt by winning 57 per cent of the popular vote. Landon's actual percentage was 37.5, and the *Digest* was so discredited that it shortly ceased publication.

The *Digest* began taking a poll on Presidential elections in 1916. The technique was to mail out postcard ballots, with subscription blanks attached, to a large number of people. Until 1936, the *Digest* was always correct in picking the winner, and along the way it gathered a healthy following; it was, at the time of its demise, one of the most widely read magazines in the country. The postcard ballots were mailed to people listed as owning automobiles and having telephone service; in the 1936 effort, 2,375,000 ballots were returned. The trouble was that the car and telephone population was generally against Roosevelt; his major support was among poorer classes who did not yet enjoy such luxuries. This atypical nature of the *Digest* sample did not appear in previous polls, but in 1936 it gave this type of opinion polling the *coup de grace*.

More sophisticated and accurate polls were being conducted in the 1930's by George Gallup, Elmo Roper, and Archibald Crossley. These pollsters took great pains to see that their samples of the electorate genuinely represented a cross-section. Gallup tchniques today are highly refined, even to the point of skipping the first corner house in a target area since corner houses tend to be occupied by people slightly above their neighbors in affluence. (62:14) These professionals have consistently been accurate in election predictions; their only major mistake came in 1948, when they stopped polling too long before the election, only to see a crusading Truman pick up enough last-minute strength from undecided voters to beat Dewey. Today Gallup and other major polls keep working right up to the election.

Gallup, as a professional polling organization, is not out to prove anything. The costs are borne entirely by the more than one hundred newspapers who subscribe to the service. Copy sent out by Gallup is carefully worded so that no unwarranted claims are made; the figures represent closely what Gallup says they do: the responses given by a representative sample of the American populace to specific questions. Private polls taken by politicians and pressure groups for their own ends are quite a different matter. They often suffer not just from deliberate bias but from inept design and overdrawn conclusions. However, a Crossley poll financed by Nelson Rockefeller in August, 1968, showed Eugene McCarthy rather than Rockefeller leading in popular preference at that time.

Another objective source of important statistical data is the United
States Census. This, too, is a thoroughly professional effort and given
the magnitude of the task, remarkably efficient. The Census Bureau is
not part of the policy-making machinery, it is not out to prove anything,
and it reports precisely what it finds. Users of census data frequently
draw unwarranted conclusions from it, but the basic statistics are accurate. The Bureau of Labor Statistics has a somewhat more complicated
job, since awkward terms like "employment" have to be defined for it
to carry out its task. But the professionals responsible for BLS operations are protected against political pressures and have a high degree of
objectivity. Employment figures leave themselves open to a greater
possibility of distortion than more simple enumerations, and one must
make sure that employment statistics coming from a secondary source
are not tampered with.

Obviously, however, lack of bias on the part of a compiler of statistics
does not guarantee credibility. There are many instances of inaccurate
statistics due to faulty collection and careless generalization.

One pervasive myth created by the reiteration of statistics which do not
really prove what is claimed of them is that there are 100,000 high school
graduates who fail to go on to college each year primarily because of
financial reasons. This 100,000 figure first appeared in 1955, when
Charles C. Cole, an academician, took a mail survey of those not attending college. Since that time, a solid phalanx of Secretaries of Health,
Education and Welfare and Commissioners of Higher Education has
appeared before Congress to testify to the existence of this substantial
body of disadvantaged would-be students. By 1963, the source of the
100,000 figure had either been forgotten or was so ancient that officials
no longer wished to acknowledge it. Commissioner Keppel's testimony
of that year, which cited this statistic, was generally impressive and well
supported; but in strange contrast to the meticulous documentation of
other (and less important) data in his testimony, the source of this
estimate of nonattendance for financial reasons was simply not given.
(**109**:4) For users of this testimony, Huff's warning about carefully
inspecting the relation of an authority to statistics applies: "When an
O.K. name is cited, make sure the authority stands behind the information, not merely somewhere alongside it." (**94**:125) Keppel was, at best,
alongside the 100,000 estimate.

But what does this 100,000 figure refer to? What do the figures really
represent? The original Cole study was of a *sample* of college non-

attenders. Presumably it was a representative sample, though we cannot be sure. One of the questions asked was like this: "Why did you not go to college?" Extrapolating the proportion of respondents who checked "financial reasons" on the list of prepared responses, Cole came up with the 100,000 figure.

But the motives for checking this response could be quite varied. Since going to college is "the thing" these days, many young people would be reluctant to admit that they had not gone for insubstantial reasons. What could be more self-justificatory than failure to attend because one could not afford to? Cole did not know, the many Government witnesses before Congress did not know, and Secretary Keppel did not know how many of those who responded to this question were genuinely motivated to go to college, had made an effort to find funds, or would go if funds were dropped in their laps. So we had a statistical sample, projected into a body of 100,000 youths, about whom we knew only that they gave a convenient answer to an emotionally charged question. There were no doubt many would-be students who failed to go to college because of financial reasons. But whether the number in 1963 was 5,000, 100,000, or 500,000, Francis Keppel did not know. This statistic may not have suffered from biased intent, but the figures neither represented what was claimed for them nor supported the conclusion drawn from them.

Similar statistical treatment, equally definite but also unwarranted, is given the income differential between high school and college graduates. College graduates earn more. But what does this imply? One thing it is alleged to imply is that we can indefinitely increase the income of citizens by sending an ever larger proportion of them through college. The 1963–1964 college debate topic was that the Federal Government should guarantee an opportunity for higher education to all qualified high school graduates. One of the most prominent bits of testimony used by the collegians on this topic was this statement attributed to Secretary of Labor Willard Wirtz: "The lifetime earnings of workers are clearly associated with their educational attainment. The difference in lifetime earnings between a high school and a college graduate is close to $180,000." (**179**:45) Almost identical statements are available from several other sources.

This alleged difference in earnings is considerable. It may even be accurate. But what does it mean? What do these extra dollars represent? As one reads the literature on education, one is struck with the frequently made assumption that this extra income represents a payoff for what the student learns in college. But does it? Suppose that, some June, we locked up all the college-bound youths and substituted for them the entire group of those not planning to go to college. Suppose we somehow nursed this collection of unexpected collegians through to diplomas. Would this new group of college graduates top the earnings of nongraduates by $180,000 in their lifetime? Assuredly not.

To begin with, we know that the college-attending group comes largely from the upper socio-economic classes. Its members therefore have developed greater expectations of success, have had wider horizons built into them; their self-image is better than that of their noncollege counterparts. Furthermore, they generally get better education at home, which accounts for much of their knowledge and ambition. Some of them will know the right people, have better social skills, adjust better to the business way of doing things. Some of them, a significant enough number to distort the figure if it is an arithmetic mean rather than a median (and this was not indicated in the $180,000 figure), will begin careers with financial help from their relatives. Most of them would be relatively successful even if they never attended college. So what the extra earnings represent we do not know for sure. We simply cannot run any single individual through his life in two different patterns to see what he would make with and without a college degree. Statistical treatments of average incomes simply do not tell us what the independent influence of education is.

One clear payoff of a college degree is that it opens doors. College graduates from lower socio-economic classes who might otherwise have very rough sledding do get a boost and an opportunity to prove themselves simply because they have college degrees. Thomas Sowell notes:

> Before being willing to seriously question the value of American higher education, one may well ask: if that value is so much less than is claimed or commonly believed, why are college degrees so much in demand by employers? Surely practical businessmen do not continue to pay hard cash for something which proves to be of no value to them. Of course not. College graduates are in demand, for one reason, because a degree does indicate something, not necessarily about the education itself but about the person. It is a handy screening device. (**208**:380)

But there are other ways of screening. Sowell goes on to suggest that we could separate the sheep from the goats without the staggering costs involved in buildings, equipment, salaries:

As it is, an elaborate and costly charade is enacted on campuses across the country, with "education" being directed toward people who do not want it, but who go through the motions in order to qualify for jobs which do not need it. (**208**:381)

So while there may indeed be a $180,000 income differential between high school and college graduates, it is not at all clear that the figure represents an *educational* increment in the lifetime income of an individual. And it is not clear that the figure supports the conclusion that we should spend more on higher education in order to increase the income of our citizenry. There may be dozens of more efficient ways to do the same thing.

Thus, even though the calculation of this income differential may be disinterested and flawlessly accomplished, it is something less than credible when it is used with the purpose of promoting large expenditures on higher education for all.

We turn now to statistical operations where the intention of the collector from the beginning has been to prove something.

Tendentious Government Statistics

Governments have various motives for wanting to prove things statistically. One of the motives currently actuating the United States Government is proving that we are winning the war in Viet-Nam. When the testimony of the press is too overpowering for the Government to get away with the claim that we are winning, it tries to prove that we have at least stopped losing. However the release is phrased, the Government has an interest in casualty statistics which look good for us and bad for the enemy.

Casualty statistics are not collected by the Bureau of the Census or the Bureau of Labor Statistics or the Department of the Interior; they are collected by the Department of Defense, which, despite Professor Pool's belief that it has been rationalized and humanized, still manages to produce some statistical ineptitudes.

Casualty statistics usually come out after every major battle and are summarized weekly. What do they represent? According to Pentagon theory, at least for the years 1966 and 1967 they represented Viet-Cong soldiers killed and counted on the battlefield. Counting dead bodies seems to be as solid and substantial a way of getting casualty figures as one could find.

But *somebody has to do the counting;* and when the counter's boss is highly desirous of getting a big count, the human failings of the system come to the fore. For one thing, there is the difficulty of distinguishing, in a populated area, between Viet-Cong soldiers and civilian casualties. Most of the Vietnamese wear black "pajamas" in or out of the military service. Many Viet-Cong soldiers have no weapons or share weapons with comrades. Soldiers are of the same ethnic stock as civilians. When these conditions obtain, how can one be sure that a "body count," even if accurately made, is a count of soldiers?

For another thing, how does one prevent a body from being counted more than once? Platoon A may go through an area and count twenty bodies; half an hour later Platoon B may do the same thing. As Charles Mohr, now of *The New York Times,* says, "After certain battles it is possible to count bodies with some accuracy, although anyone who has watched three platoons of one company move out into the scrub can easily believe that duplications in counting may take place." (**157**)

And given sufficient pressure for congruent results, the figures are bound to represent some guesses and fabrications. It would, of course, be unpatriotic to report that American servicemen fudged the body count. Reporters of other nationalities are not patriotically inhibited, however. Kuno Knoebl, Austrian correspondent who spent many months following the troops, offers several specific observations of rigged casualty counts. (**116**:208–213) And even American reporters sometimes tell of miscounts. *The New York Times* of July 7, 1967, notes that Lt. General Robert E. Cushman asserted that the bodies of 250 North Vietnamese soldiers had been counted after the battle of Con Thien; newsmen who accompanied the first troops into the area reported "probably not more than 20 were seen." (**71**)

In June, 1966, Charles Mohr reflected on the accuracy of some of the counts he had observed:

> One morning late last year, when the nine-day siege of the Special Forces Camp at Pleiku was being lifted, Maj. Charles Beckwith, a grizzled man in a dirty camouflage "tiger suit," was told by his radio operator that the chief of staff in Saigon wanted an immediate body count for a military briefing. "We haven't even been outside the wire yet," snapped the major. "Tell them I'm not going to give any figure until I can count."
>
> In the end Maj. Beckwith and his men counted a little more than 40 bodies on one side of the camp, the only area they could cover that day. But the figure already announced in Saigon was about five times that big.

In a more recent action in the Central Highlands, a company commander who had been under heavy attack in a tight defensive perimeter received a request for a body-count figure. He radioed one of his platoon leaders to ask what the officer could tell him. "I don't know, Captain," said the lieutenant. "Maybe 3 or 5 or 15. Put me down for 15 and I'll try to find them for you in the morning." (**157**)

Of such precision measurements are official casualty statistics constructed. There are additional difficulties. Various Government estimaters disagree with each other and sometimes contradict themselves. While General Westmoreland was claiming a steady 8,000 infiltrators from North Viet-Nam a month, Secretary McNamara estimated some months as low as 1,600. At the end of 1965, Westmoreland said enemy troop strength in the South was 230,000; McNamara claimed 250,000. The General's figures seemed not to agree with each other for 1966. If one takes his claimed enemy strength at the beginning of the year, adds claimed infiltrators and recruits, subtracts estimates of killed, wounded, captured, and defected, the result should be the enemy strength at the end of the year. But, as R. W. Apple of the *Times* notes, this is not what one gets; there is a discrepancy of 53,000. (**3**) What do the figures represent? Plain perceptual distortion.

But there must have been large numbers of enemy casualties in the war. Pentagon totals passed 200,000 by the middle of 1967. What conclusion does this figure support? Since enemy casualties are alleged to be much higher than American casualties, the inference is often drawn that we are winning. After all, we are killing more of them than they are of us. But it is not all that simple. Unless we obliterate the enemy force, which does not seem about to happen, or unless we "punish" the enemy so that he sues for peace, which, despite the Paris talks also seems unlikely at time of writing, high casualties on either side may indicate the success of the insurgents. There is a strong belief on the part of guerrilla war authorities that in a successful counterinsurgency action, casualties do not rise but drop. When you are doing well, the war simply goes away. High casualties may indicate that we are losing control of the war and the population. This possible interpretation has not been popular at the Pentagon.

The major misinterpretation of casualty statistics, however, was made early in the war, at a time when the United States still had hopes of goading the South Vietnamese into doing their own fighting. In the early months of 1965, Arvin casualties were rising and Government supporters rejoiced. Guy Pauker of the RAND Corporation, appearing on the *CBS Reports* Viet-Nam debate on June 21, 1965, pointed with immense pride and confidence to growing casualty lists of Saigon forces. Entirely apart from the question as to whether these statistics were accurate, the question as to what conclusion they would sustain was never really comprehended by Mr. Pauker.

For the statistics were not broken down into casualties sustained by government troops on offensive operations and casualties sustained by static troops merely attempting to hold defensive points against Viet-Cong attack. The former indeed might indicate some success in prodding our reluctant allies; the latter would indicate the reverse. According to Halberstam, 70 per cent of the total Arvin casualties during his period in Viet-Nam (1962–1964) were inflicted at static points, thus representing a phenomenon diametrically opposed to what Pauker was claiming. (**82**:170) War statistics may always have represented a wilderness of fraud; our Vietnamese experience certainly offers no convincing data to the contrary.

Election results are sometimes no more significant than war statistics. Communist elections we believe to be a farce; they are rigged so that the "party list" must come up with a 99 per cent plus vote. But Communists are not the only ones who can rig elections. Just before he was assassinated, Vietnamese President Diem organized elections for the National Assembly (on September 27, 1963); he got 99.9 per cent of the vote.

There was, however, a much-praised "free" election in South Viet-Nam on September 3, 1967. President Johnson sent a high-level observer mission of twenty-two men to cover the seven thousand plus voting places and tell us if the election we sponsored was honest. Richard Scammon, statistician and American expert on elections, proclaimed the Vietnamese affair to be as "reasonably efficient, reasonably free and reasonably honest" as elections in the United States. (**198**) When one asks "Who wants to prove what?" the answer is clear: the American government wanted to prove the elections free and fair.

In the September balloting, the Thieu-Ky ticket, backed by the Americans, was reported to have received slightly more than a third of the ballots cast. Since this was a plurality, "our" ticket was returned to power. But one must still ask the question. "What do the figures represent?" A partial list of what the figures in this election represent would surely include the following:

An election in which a hopeful candidate thought by many to be the most popular in the country was not allowed to run.

An election in which those who were openly opposed to continuing the war or favored accommodation to the Viet-Cong were not allowed to run.

An election in which master lists of registered voters were somehow not available at most polling places, preventing a check on multiple voting. (**242**)

An election in which Saigon government appointees were the sole certifiers of poll results; Michael Novak of the *National Catholic Reporter* describes in detail how these officials could pad the result in their polling place in order to keep their government jobs. (**169**)

An election in which 42.5 per cent of the *winners*, voting on a resolution to validate the election results in the Constituent Assembly, declared the election fraudulent. (**198**)

R. H. Shackford, Scripps-Howard Asian correspondent, in a masterpiece of understatement, described the elections and our involvement in them as "badly tarnished." (**198**) An even more pessimistic evaluation was made by William Lederer. (**127**:35–40)

What conclusions do the figures support? The most certain conclusion is that Thieu and Ky could not obtain a majority in an election which they themselves controlled.

One of the most expensive and elaborate statistical studies ever done in this country, the 1965–1966 Office of Education-commissioned investigation published under the title *The Equality of Educational Opportunity* (**225**), offers fertile ground for questioning some of the results of massive social statistics. The study was conducted by James Coleman of Johns Hopkins University and Ernest Campbell of Vanderbilt University, at a cost approaching $1,500,000. The results are in two huge volumes totalling 1,200 pages. The subjects of the study were some 900,000 students, half white and half nonwhite, ranging from grades one to twelve, and their teachers, principals, and superintendents. Questionnaires and tests were administered to find out various things about home life, attitudes, and achievements of the students; about financial expenditure, class size, programs, teacher qualifications, and access to physical facilities of the schools.

Who was trying to prove what by this study? It appears that the sponsors were not entirely disinterested. The speed with which it was pushed through — it took only ten months to complete after data collection was started — and the use which has been made of it to support programs of school desegregation suggest that the Office of Education was looking for evidence of a certain kind. Ilene Albert and Pamela Sheldon note:

> While some of the findings of this particular study are gratifying for those of us who feel strongly about the evils of segregation, there is a rather somber note that needs to be added. Rather than solely being an objective study of the problem, the U. S. Office of Education's research seems to be a vehicle for the support of political policy, namely, desegregation. (1:287)

What do the millions of figures in this study represent? Supposedly, numerical values for 103 variables reflecting social, cultural, and educational characteristics of a representative sample of American students, schools, and families, white and Negro. But do they? Of the 3,223 elementary schools in the representative sample, about 74 per cent returned both principal and student questionnaires. Of the 1,170 high schools in the representative sample, 59 per cent returned both sets of questionnaires. Since the principal's questionnaire was the only source of percentages of white and Negro students in the school, the missing returns could be significant. Despite much sophisticated maneuvering with subsamples and checking characteristics of the nonparticipating schools independently of the questionnaires, the study directors have not convinced us that "an analysis of the nonparticipating schools indicated that their inclusion would not have significantly altered the results of the survey." (225:8)

Nor is it clear that the 103 variables chosen represented a scientific selection of the possible variables. Are verbal ability scores really the best measures of achievement? Does the presence of an encyclopedia in a home really indicate support for education? Does the size of a family really influence attitudes toward education? The Coleman-Campbell study can come up with many thousands of complicated intercorrelations of these variables; what it cannot do is establish clearly that these are the important variables for which correlations are needed.

And finally, what conclusions do the figures support? We are not at all sure, nor are most of those who have publicly commented on the study. The most striking claimed conclusion, which has great political import and has been used by the United States Civil Rights Commission to support the contention that equal educational opportunity cannot exist in schools which are predominately Negro, is really not so certain:

Because Negroes in predominately white schools did better than Negroes in predominately Negro schools, it was intimated that the school population explains the observed differences. Yet is the comparison completely fair? What kind of Negro student attends a school of a predominately white student body? Perhaps he represents a different population than the Negro in an all-Negro school due to differences in achievement motivation of his parents not assessed only by the encyclopedia variable mentioned above. (1:285–7)

There are other questionable conclusions based on this study. Coleman may be, as one reporter claimed, one of "the new breed of social scientists who dig for facts first and theorize second." (153) He may also be the outstanding methodologist in social science today. The conduct of this study, however, does not support either one of these statements.

The Government is one of the most assiduous and ubiquitous collectors and users of statistics. Many of them are professionally compiled, routine, objective, and cautious; others are not.

Pressure Group Statistics

By definition, pressure groups want to prove something with the evidence they generate. At a very elementary level, politicians want to get people to believe that the crowds which attend their appearances are large and enthusiastic. Crowd figures belong in never-never land, yet the counting of crowds is not an incorrigibly subjective task. Herbert A. Jacobs reports techniques for crowd estimation which can be applied under most conditions, if the witness wants an objective count. Typical of the biased figures about crowds which Jacobs uncovered was the following:

When Vice President Nixon stopped at the Milwaukee airport during the 1960 campaign, a Republican party official estimated the welcoming crowd at 12,000. The police put it at 8,000. A reporter said there were 5,000. *The Milwaukee Journal* enlarged a crowd picture and counted heads; the number turned out to be near 2,300. (100:38)

Unfortunately, most of the biased statistics put out by pressure groups are neither so harmless nor so easily refuted as the crowd myths. Calculation of ratios and percentages is the technique with which liars do most of their figuring. If one selects base periods advantageously and is careful to calculate percentages of the wrong things, one can prove that black is white.

Perhaps the most misleading percentages in the Western world are those representing business profits. Profits, one might think, simply represent what is left over to a business after expenses and taxes have been paid. Surely this can be reckoned as a straightforward and uncomplicated ratio? But it is not that simple. In addition to costs and taxes, allowances may be made for depreciation and reserve funds. How much can legitimately be put aside for these purposes? There is no fixed answer; hence, the calculation of profits is as subjective as the rating of art at the Carnegie International.

But when a reasonable amount for depreciation and reserves has been set aside, what then? Profit can be calculated using either annual sales as a base or using invested capital, and in high-turnover industries such as merchandising, the difference can be astronomical. Atlantic and Pacific food stores, for instance, earn approximately 1 per cent annually on sales. Is this chain heading for bankruptcy? Not in the least. Because of high turnover, the profit ratio expressed as a percentage of invested capital is above 10 per cent — enough, obviously, to obtain the capital needed and keep the share-owners happy. (**94**:81) Even General Motors, whose capital investment exceeds that of A & P by a considerable amount, had in one year a profit of 12.6 per cent on sales, 44.8 per cent on investment — probably figured before depreciation and reserve allowances. (**94**:81)

And when the drug companies put out profit statements, beware. Even Senator Hruska of Nebraska, whose support for the profit motive in American industry is second to none, boggled a bit at the rates of return found by Kefauver in his investigation of the drug industry. The companies justified these high rates by the necessity to provide money for research; yet Smith, Kline and French realized a net profit on investment of 50 per cent in 1955 by marketing chlorpromazine, a drug developed abroad and manufactured here under license, and hence on which they had no expense for research. (**85**:213) One may not agree with Senator Pastore that this rate of return was "immoral," but one must agree that the relevant basis for figuring profits here was return on investment rather than on sales.

Nonetheless the drug companies continue to cry poor, using as their data profits figured as a percentage of sales. On June 29, 1964, Pfizer Laboratories published in major newspapers a letter sent by Charles A. Kapp, Pfizer's general manager, to every medical doctor in the United

States. Pfizer bragged that this letter had also been published in the *Congressional Record:*

Dear Doctor:

We are pleased to advise you that we have again reduced our prices to the pharmacy for Terramycin and Tetracyn Capsules, Syrups and Pediatric Drops, effective May 25th. We would anticipate that this action will be reflected in lower prescription prices for these drugs to your patients. Full information regarding prescription pricing is available from your local pharmacy.

You are no doubt aware of the distribution of so-called generic tetracycline imported into this country from Italy and offered at very low prices. Our announced price reductions do not make us competitive with this imported tetracycline which infringes our United States patent. We can emphatically state that if we are to continue to spend millions of dollars a year on drug research; if we are to pay American wage scales to the people in our plants producing our drugs; if we are to maintain a sales and marketing organization to promote to you the fruits of our research in keen competition with others in our industry in a free enterprise system; if we are to pay very significant sums by way of federal, state and local taxes — if we are to do all these things and at the end of the year's activity turn over a little better than four cents to our stockholders for every dollar of our sales by way of a modest return on their investment, then we will never be in a position to compete with antibiotic pirates who contribute nothing to the development of a drug and find their haven in a country that does not give any recognition to drug patents; who pay wages and offer working conditions which are substandard in comparison to those in this country; and, finally, who contribute nothing in the way of taxes to support our democratic institutions.

No, Doctor, the price reductions we are announcing to you obviously will not match prices of the infringing foreign competition. Rather, they reflect a sincere effort on our part to make available the finest possible drug therapy at the lowest possible cost within the framework of operating as an American institution. As you are aware, there have been substantial price reductions in recent years, not only in broad spectrum antibiotics, but also in penicillin, streptomycin, corticoids, hormones, and dozens of other drugs which are now available at a fraction of their original cost.

We of Pfizer Laboratories assure you of our continuing efforts in this direction.

The letter was signed "Sincerely, Charles A. Kapp."

Before one works up a purple passion at the thieving Italians, however, recall that this is the same Pfizer that invented names, addresses, and telephone numbers of eight fictitious doctors, claimed that these non-existent doctors found Sigmamycin "the antibiotic therapy of choice," and used these "endorsements" in a flier advertising the drug (**85**:19)

So we ask, "Who wants to prove what?" Pfizer, of course, wants to prove that their intentions are good but that making an honest living in the highly competitive United States is tough when the Italians are also competing with you.

What do the figures represent? Strange, the letter is all about a price reduction, but nowhere is it specified. Was it 1 per cent, 5 per cent, 10 per cent? One simply does not know. There is one figure in the letter, though: Pfizer pays stockholders 4 per cent profit on *sales*. This rate is described as a "modest return." But A & P pays 1 per cent on sales, which works out to 10 per cent on investment. Could one conclude that every Pfizer shareholder got 40 per cent return on his invested dollar each year? The rate was assuredly something like this. Mr. Kapp may label this a modest return, but Wall Street would take a different view. In short, the figures in this advertisement (which cost $2,499 for one insertion in the *Pittsburgh Press* alone) represent a good healthy profit, whatever the rhetoric may claim.

What conclusion does this figure support? Simply that Pfizer, behind the smokescreen, is making an unconscionable rate of profit and needs to build up some good will against the day when it will be called to account. In late 1967, a New York Federal Court jury convicted Pfizer and two other firms of conspiring to control the production and distribution of $1,700,000,000 worth of the same antibiotic on which the 1964 letter bragged about a price reduction. Far from fighting for its corporate life, Pfizer was doing very well indeed. Said the Government prosecutor at the trial:

> Pfizer and Cyanimid realized "enormous" profits on an antibiotic called tetracycline. He said the cost of manufacturing 100 capsules of the drug ranged from $1.59 to $3.87 for the two companies, but that each sold to druggists for $30.60 and that the cost to consumers was $51. . . .
> The maximum penalties on the charges are fines of $150,000 against each defendant. The convictions would also open the way for civil suits from major purchasers. The Sherman Act provides for treble damages against violators. (**50**)

Perhaps the inventive Mr. Kapp will discover a way to soften this penalty. An equally gross miscarriage of truth occurred in a national television network debate on compulsory health insurance. A speaker claimed that private group health insurance plans covered ninety-five million workers and their dependents at an overhead cost of 2.3 per cent. (**140**:95) A 2.3 per cent overhead which maintains salesmen, headquarters, and regional offices, pays dividends to the owners, advertises, and meets all the other costs of operating a business is no less than phenomenal. This claim was attributed to the Health Insurance Institute, a propaganda firm previously mentioned.

Our first inclination on reading this startling claim was to wonder if the debater had misplaced the decimal point; 23 per cent should be closer to the truth than 2.3 per cent. On checking with the Health Insurance Institute, however, we discovered that it had indeed issued this figure in a lithographed publication entitled *Fact File for Use in the 1960 National Intercollegiate Debate on the topic "Resolved, That the United States should adopt a program of Compulsory Health Insurance for all citizens."* The exact citation read:

> The most recent government survey of employee benefit plans estimated that combined operating expenses in hospitalization plans covering 95 million workers and their dependents cost less than 2.3 per cent of premium.

To support this claim, reference was made to the *Social Security Bulletin* for March, 1960. In this issue of the *Bulletin* there is an article entitled "Employee-Benefit Plans, 1954–58." (**203**) The author, Alfred M. Skolnik, works for HEW, which is in a sense competing with private health insurance companies. Any testimony by him that his competitor's costs were moderate, therefore, might be classed as reluctant and would have high credibility.

Unfortunately, Mr. Skolnik offers no such testimony. The Health Insurance Institute statement is, in short, false from beginning to end. First, the Skolnik article does not mention operating expenses of private hospitalization plans. The 2.3 per cent figure does not appear in it. The article does give a table showing hospitalization premiums and hospitalization benefits paid in 1958. From these HII miscalculated what they mislabel combined operating expenses.

Second, HII's arithmetic is incorrect. The data in the Skolnik article show that in 1958 estimated hospitalization benefits under employee benefit plans were 97.3 per cent of estimated contributions. The difference, 2.7 per cent, not 2.3 per cent, was the amount of total premiums *retained* by the companies and bore no relation to operating expenses.

Third, insurance companies occasionally have bad years, when they must pay out more than they expect. The worst one on record was 1958, in which the private insurance companies sustained an enormous underwriting loss on group hospitalization plans. Retentions in that year did not begin to cover operating costs; retentions in previous and subsequent years were considerably higher. (**204**)

Fourth, isolating a single type of benefit such as hospitalization is an illegitimate way to calculate the operating costs of insurance carriers. Underwriting losses sustained on one type of coverage may be made up on another type. Even considering hospitalization-medical-surgical benefits together may be too narrow an approach, if one is concerned with the social costs of insurance. For the carriers that provide medical coverage also provide life, disability, and other types of insurance sometimes at generous profits. Their underwriting losses on hospitalization may be more than made up on some other coverage, much as the deficit incurred by a "loss leader" in a food store may be offset by a markup on meat. The consumer is enticed by the low price on one item, but he pays for it on other purchases.

But disregarding social costs and assuming that retentions expressed as a percentage of income constitute a significant index of the cost of private health insurance, the figure for 1958 — for all health plans, not just hospitalization — was 13.8. (**178**:9) Combined operating expenses may have been much more than that. The Health Insurance Institute ventured into cloudcuckooland to serve its clients in this instance.

Who wanted to prove what? HII wanted to prove how efficient its clients were and what a bargain private health insurance was. What did the figures represent? A tremendous underwriting loss, not operating expenses at all. What conclusions did the figures support? That 1958 was an atypical year, at least in the hospitalization insurance business.

Let us look at one more way in which a clever research team can "prove" what is not so. In our previous discussion of the American Medical Association, we mentioned a study commissioned by the AMA and reported to the 1960 Congress of the International Institute of Gerontologists. This was when AMA was fighting a rearguard action against medicare; the doctors wanted to prove in the study that medicare was not needed.

The compilers, sixteen academic sociologists, found some statistics to prove this, but the latitude within which the investigators operated made accuracy impossible. Fifteen hundred persons aged sixty-five or over were interviewed; the AMA summary of the results claimed the survey "emphatically proves that the great majority of Americans over 65 are capably financing their own health care and prefer to do it on their own, without government intervention." (2)

What did the figures represent? They did not represent the opinions of aged persons living in apartments, hospitalized at the time of the survey, living in homes for the aged or in any other institution; the persons interviewed all lived in single homes, they were all white, and none were receiving old-age assistance. Thus the entire population most likely to be having trouble meeting medical expenses was excluded from consideration.

The figures represented answers to a multiple-choice question asking what the aged thought should be done to make medical coverage more easily available to them, even though they were the ones least likely to need it; and the question did not list as a possible answer adding medical coverage to social security. As the Communists have discovered, one way to keep the opposition from racking up a big vote in an election is to keep them off the ballot. The AMA has learned this lesson, too. Professor Wayne Thompson of Cornell described the crucial question asked of those interviewed as "badly designed, poorly conceived and completely misleading." (2)

The basic figures on income, assets, and health status reported by the AMA differed by as much as 100 per cent from those reported by other recent studies and from figures available from such sources as the Bureau of the Census and the National Health Survey. At the Gerontologists' meeting, the survey and the AMA were bitterly attacked; not a single scientist present defended either.

What conclusion did the figures support? That aged persons able to pay their medical bills were not worried about paying medical bills.

Such a brief tour through statistical fantasylands merely reinforces the contention that the most important backing of quantitative evidence is the competence and integrity of its source. If you would not believe a man who testifies that he has seen a flying saucer, do not believe him when he claims to have seen fourteen flying saucers each measuring twenty-two feet in diameter and weighing eleven tons.

SUMMARY

Numerical statements seem to have a solidity which purely verbal evidence lacks, but the solidity is often specious: statistics are just as fallible as nonquantitative evidence. There are no specific tests of credible statistics, but three questions can help guide an evaluation of statistical evidence:

(1) Who wants to prove what?
(2) What do the figures really represent?
(3) What conclusions do the figures support?

Many collectors of statistics have no discernible bias and produce consistently reliable results. The professional poll takers, the Bureau of the Census, and the Bureau of Labor Statistics are in this category. However, absence of bias alone does not guarantee credibility. The defunct *Literary Digest* produced an erroneous result in polling before the Roosevelt-Landon election; an inadequately designed mail questionnaire reported in 1955 that there were 100,000 eligible high school graduates who failed to go to college because of financial reasons; and many authorities erroneously believe that a college degree adds an educational increment of $180,000 to a person's lifetime income.

Governments are major producers of tendentious statistics. Casualty statistics from the Viet-Nam war are often thoroughly corrupt; election statistics from Viet-Nam are not much better. A major study of educational opportunity commissioned by the United States Office of Education has many flaws; it is not clear what the figures really represent, or that they support some of the implied conclusions.

Pressure groups also produce their share of faulty statistics. Drug companies, calculating profits on sales rather than investment, claim near-bankruptcy at times when they are making lush profits. Captive research institutes issue fraudulent statistics about overhead costs of private hospitalization insurance. The American Medical Association commissioned research into the ability of the aged to pay medical bills which was completely misleading.

The credibility of the source of statistical evidence is just as important as the credibility of a witness to specific historical events.

SUGGESTED READINGS

Ilene Albert and Pamela Sheldon, "Equality of Educational Opportunity," *Educational Leadership* (December, 1966), 281–287.

"AMA Attacked for Use of Disputed Survey in 'Medicare' Lobbying," *Science* (September 2, 1960), 604.

Darrell Huff, *How To Lie With Statistics.* New York: W. W. Norton, 1954.

Roger Hufford, "The Logician, The Historian, and Rhetorical Criticism," *Journal of the American Forensic Association*, II (January, 1965), 14.

Harold A. Larrabee, *Reliable Knowledge*, Revised Edition. Boston: Houghton Mifflin, 1964.

Charles Mohr, "Vietnam Victory Linked to Opinion," *The New York Times* (June 27, 1966), 1.

W. J. Reichmann, *Use and Abuse of Statistics.* London: Methuen, 1961.

Thomas Sowell, "The 'Need' for More 'Education,'" *AAUP Bulletin*, LII (December, 1966), 380.

Notes on the Study of Evidence

Only as a branch of jurisprudence is the study of evidence recognized as a discipline in its own right. Despite this, the legal theory of evidence is almost totally irrelevant outside the courtroom; it is concerned with procedural rules rather than substantive evaluation. Aside from the pioneering (and ponderous) works of Jeremy Bentham (**13**) and John Henry Wigmore (**236**), we do not believe the study of legal evidence has much to offer the student of public intelligence.

There is, however, an extensive literature available in various fields. The most useful work on the theory of evidence is that of Nicholas Rescher (**180, 181, 182, 87**). We regret that Rescher has shifted his field of interest to Arabic logic and the philosophy of science. Historians have produced many volumes on method, and much of their material is useful in analyzing contemporary evidence. We particularly recommend the works of Gottschalk (**78**), Allen Johnson (**101**), and Nevins (**160**), all of which are well written and devoid of the prolixities of the more encyclopedic historiographers like Bernheim, Garraghan, and Langlois and Seignobos.

Many textbooks in social psychology are useful to the student of evidence, as is Mannheim's *Ideology and Utopia* (**144**). Excellent recent works incorporating the social-psychological insight are Holsti (**92**) and White (**235**). Since World War II, Government intelligence has concerned a number of writers. Works with application to public evidence are those by Hilsman (**88**), Kent (**108**), McGovern (**143**), Wasserman (**231**), Wilensky (**237**), Wise and Ross (**239**), and Wohlstetter (**240**). De Jouvenel's *Art of Conjecture* (**103**) is stimulating on prediction, though less so than the Helmer-Rescher monograph.

Of contemporary journalistic critiques of public intelligence, the best are Cater (**29**), Halberstam (**82**), Haynes Johnson (**102**), Lederer (**126**), Greene (**81**), McGaffin and Knoll (**142**), and Ladd (**121**).

Useful books on miscellaneous topics are Boller on the art of quoting (**17**), Einbinder on the *Britannica* (**54**), Horowitz on Project Camelot (**93**), Packer on the ex-Communists (**171**), the Overstreets on extremists (**170**), Inkeles and Bauer on refugees (**99**), Menashe and Radosh on the teach-in movement (**152**), and Philip Green on the deterrence theorists (**80**). Each one of these contributes substantially on some dimension relevant to evaluating the vast flood of intelligence assaulting our eyes and ears. Fred Goerner's *The Search for Amelia Earhart* (**73**) is a fascinating detective-like study of evidence, with considerable relevance to Government testimony on foreign policy.

A number of magazine articles are worth separate mention: John Lofton on press management of news (**136**), Irving Kristol on the amateurishness of the press (**119**), Ben Bagdikian on the biases of *Time* and *U.S. News* (**7**), Otto Friedrich on the function of facts in the newsweeklies (**64**), Andrew Kopkind on the press as spokesman for the Government (**118**). The major critique of the press is still the Lippmann-Merz study of 1920 (**133**); it should be read by any student of evidence despite what we believe to be wrong conclusions.

On Government testimony, the most valuable analysis is Theodore Draper's *The Dominican Revolt* (**48**). Noam Chomsky's "The Responsibility of Intellectuals" is equally stimulating, though not as accurate (**33**). Milton Mayer has done a thorough job on the doctors (**148, 149**) and Max Ascoli *et al.* on foreign public relations agents (**5**). On the latter, one should also read the Hamilton Wright hearings (**219**).

Book reviews will always be a major source of critiques useful to students of evidence. Of these, the best by far appear in *The New York Review*. The *Saturday Review* is good, and *The New York Times Book Review* is easily available, though more inclined to represent an Establishment outlook. For consistently outstanding evaluations of the press, the *Columbia Journalism Review* is in a class by itself. It should have been started long before 1960 and should be read by as wide an audience as reads *Time* and *Reader's Digest*. *I. F. Stone's Newsletter* exposes a vast amount of fraudulent intelligence, and is the most thorough general monitor of publicly available evidence. But original sources should be checked before using any of the materials Stone refers to.

The student of evidence should, of course, read whatever newspapers he can get hold of. *The New York Times, Washington Post,* or *Los Angeles Times* should be on the list. It is also useful to be able to compare AP and UPI subscribers, and a Canadian paper serves as a needed counterbalance to Yankee prejudices. Many periodicals carry occasional good pieces about evidence; memoirs, current history, the *Congressional Record* are all grist for the mill. Were they not so fleeting, television "documentaries" and special shows would be more helpful. Some of the better shows, such as *CBS Reports*, publish mimeographed texts.

REFERENCES

1. Albert, Ilene, and Pamela Sheldon, "Equality of Educational Opportunity," *Educational Leadership* (December, 1966), 281–287.

2. "AMA Attacked for Use of Disputed Survey in 'Medicare' Lobbying," *Science* (September 2, 1960), 604–605.

3. Apple, R. W., Jr., "Vietnam Numbers Game," *The New York Times* (February 8, 1967), 2.

4. Argyris, Chris, *Some Causes of Organizational Ineffectiveness Within the Department of State.* Department of State Publication 8180. Washington: Government Printing Office, 1967.

5. Ascoli, Max, Charles Wertenbaker, and Philip Horton, "The China Lobby," *The Reporter* (April 15 and April 29, 1952). Reprinted in *Our Times: The Best From the Reporter*, ed. Max Ascoli. New York: Farrar, Straus & Cudahy, 1960.

6. Associated Press, " 'Unified Support' Expected by LBJ from State Department," *Durham Morning Herald* (August 20, 1965), 2.

7. Bagdikian, Ben H., "Bias in the Weekly Newsmagazines," in *Voice of the People*, ed. Reo M. Christenson and Robert O. McWilliams. New York: McGraw-Hill, 1962, 148–164.

8. Bagdikian, Ben H., "The Columnist as Prophet," *Columbia Journalism Review* (Summer, 1966), 35–39.

9. Bagdikian, Ben H., "News as a Byproduct," *Columbia Journalism Review* (Spring, 1967), 5–10.

10. Barrett, William, "Decline and Fall," *The Atlantic* (May, 1964), 140.

11. Bartlett, Charles, "Students Harass U.S. Team," *Pittsburgh Press* (May 11, 1965), 22.

12. Bell, Daniel, "Twelve Modes of Prediction," *Daedalus*, XCIII (Summer, 1964), 845–880.

13. Bentham, Jeremy, *Works*, ed. J. Bowring. Edinburgh: William Tait, 1843. Vols. VI and VII are on evidence.

14. Bernstein, Victor, and Jesse Gordon, "The Press and the Bay of Pigs," *Columbia University Forum* (Fall, 1967), 5.

15. Blackstock, Paul W., *Agents of Deceit.* Chicago: Quadrangle Books, 1966.

228

16. Block, Mervin, "The Night Castro 'Unmasked'," *Columbia Journalism Review* (Summer, 1962), 5–10.

17. Boller, Paul F., Jr., *Quotemanship*. Dallas: Southern Methodist University Press, 1967.

18. Boulding, Kenneth E., "The Learning and Reality-Testing Process in the International System," *Journal of International Affairs*, No. 1 (1967), 1–15.

19. Braybrooke, David, and Charles E. Lindblom, *A Strategy of Decision*. New York: The Free Press of Glencoe, 1963.

20. Bronowski, Jacob, "The Values of Science," in *New Knowledge in Human Values*, ed. Abraham H. Maslow. New York: Harper & Brothers, 1959, 52–64.

21. Browne, Malcolm W., "Viet Nam Reporting: Three Years of Crisis," *Columbia Journalism Review* (Fall, 1964), 4–9.

22. Burchett, Wilfred, *Vietnam: Inside Story of the Guerilla War*. New York: International Publishers, 1965.

23. Burnham, James, *The Coming Defeat of Communism*. New York: John Day, 1950.

24. Burnham, James, *Congress and the American Tradition*. Chicago: Henry Regnery, 1959.

25. Burnham, James, "Lenin's Heir," *Partisan Review* (Winter, 1945), 61.

26. Burnham, James, *The Managerial Revolution*. New York: John Day, 1941.

27. Butterfield, Herbert, *George III and the Historians*. London: Collins, 1957.

28. Cahill, Robert S., review of Anthony T. Bouscaren, *The Last of the Mandarins: Diem of Vietnam*, in *American Political Science Review*, LIX (December, 1965), 1013–1014.

29. Cater, Douglass, *The Fourth Branch of Government*. New York: Random House (Vintage Books), 1965.

30. Cater, Douglass, and Walter Pincus, "The Foreign Legion of U.S. Public Relations," *The Reporter* (December 22, 1960), 15–22.

31. Chennault, Claire Lee, *Way of a Fighter*. New York: G. P. Putnam's Sons, 1949.

32. Childs, Marquis, "Behind the Errors on Cuban Invasion," *The Washington Post* (April 26, 1961), A18.

33. Chomsky, Noam, "The Responsibility of Intellectuals," *The New York Review* (February 23, 1967), 16–26.

34. Christenson, Reo M., "Report on the Reader's Digest," *Columbia Journalism Review* (Winter, 1965), 30–36.

35. Clark, Colin, "Do Population and Freedom Grow Together?" *Fortune* (December, 1960), 136–139.

36. Coffey, J. I., "The Anti-Ballistic Missile Debate," *Foreign Affairs*, XLV (April, 1967), 403–413.

37. Coffin, Tristram, *Senator Fulbright*. New York: E. P. Dutton, 1966.

38. Coser, Lewis A., review of Arthur Schlesinger, Jr., *The Politics of Hope*, in *Commentary* (July, 1963), 76–78.

39. Cowles, John, "Fewer Papers Means Better Papers," in *Reporting the News*, ed. Louis M. Lyons. Cambridge: Harvard University Press, 1965, 160.

40. Cowley, Malcolm, "The Managerial Revolution," *The New Republic* (April 28, 1941), 607.

41. Cremeans, Charles D., *The Arabs and the World*. New York: Frederick A. Praeger, 1963.

42. Cromley, Ray, "Viet Slip Irks LBJ," *Pittsburgh Press* (March 20, 1967), 24.

43. De Grazia, Alfred, "Government and Science," *The American Behavioral Scientist* (September, 1965), 40.

44. DeMougeot, William R., *Argumentation in the National Health Insurance Movement, 1932–1940*. Unpublished Ph.D. dissertation, Cornell University, 1959. University Microfilms No. 59–1951.

45. Dennen, Leon, "Envoy's Creed: Agree With Boss," *Pittsburgh Press* (February 17, 1967), 22.

46. Dinerstein, Herbert S., *Intervention Against Communism*. Baltimore: Johns Hopkins Press, 1967.

47. "Does the U.S. Really Have the World's Finest Medical Care?" *Consumer Reports* (March, 1965), 146–150.

48. Draper, Theodore, *The Dominican Revolt*. New York: Commentary, 1968.

49. Drucker, Peter, "The Rulers of Tomorrow," *The Saturday Review of Literature* (May 10, 1941), 9.

50. "Drug Firms Convicted of Conspiracy," *Pittsburgh Post-Gazette* (December 30, 1967), 5.

51. Dulles, John Foster, *Our Policies Toward Communism in China*. Address before the International Convention of Lions International, San Francisco, June 28, 1957. Washington: Department of State, Public Services Division, Series S, No. 58.

52. Dulles, John Foster, *War or Peace*. New York: Macmillan, 1950.

53. "Editors Assert Administration Practices Deceit for Its Own Sake," *The New York Times* (April 18, 1968), 30.

54. Einbinder, Harvey, *The Myth of the Britannica*. New York: Grove Press, 1964.

55. Elegant, Robert S., "The View From Peking," *The New Leader* (December 12, 1960), 8–11.

56. *Encyclopedia of Associations*, Fourth Edition, Vol. I. Detroit: Gale Research Co., 1964.

57. Epernay, Mark [John Kenneth Galbraith?], *The McLandress Dimension*. Boston: Houghton Mifflin, 1963.

58. Evans, Rowland, and Robert Novak, "Labor Would Aid HHH to Stop Robert Kennedy," *Pittsburgh Press* (April 16, 1968), 8.

59. Fall, Bernard B., "The One-Eyed Hawk," *New Republic* (December 17, 1966), 24–26.

60. Fall, Bernard B., "The Second Indochina War," *International Affairs* (January, 1965), 59–73.

61. Fall, Bernard B., "South Viet-Nam's Internal Problems," *Pacific Affairs*, XXXI (September, 1958), 241–260.

62. Fenton, John M., *In Your Opinion* . . . . Boston: Little, Brown, 1960.

63. Flexner, Abraham, *Universities: American, English, German*. New York: Oxford University Press, 1930.

64. Friedrich, Otto, "There are 00 Trees in Russia: The Function of Facts in Newsmagazines," *Harper's* (October, 1964), 59–65.

65. Fritchey, Clayton, "Mideast Muddled by U.S.," *Pittsburgh Press* (July 13, 1967), 18.

66. Fritchey, Clayton, "The Politicians *vs.* the Foreign Service," *Harper's* (January, 1967), 90–94.

67. Fulbright, J. William, "The War and Its Effects — III." *Congressional Record*, 90th Congress, 1st Session (December 13, 1967), S18485, 113.

68. "Funny Coincidence Department," *The New Yorker* (November 10, 1951), 102.

69. Galtung, Johan, "After Camelot," in *The Rise and Fall of Project Camelot*, ed. Irving Louis Horowitz. Cambridge: The M.I.T. Press, 1967, 281–312.

70. Garraghan, Gilbert J., *A Guide to Historical Method*. New York: Fordham University Press, 1946.

71. "General Denies a Defeat," *The New York Times* (July 7, 1967), 5.

72. Gerstein, Richard M., "A Prosecutor Looks at Capital Punishment," *Journal of Criminal Law, Criminology, and Police Science,* LI (July–August, 1960), 252–256.

73. Goerner, Fred, *The Search for Amelia Earhart.* Garden City: Doubleday, 1966.

74. Goodman, Ezra, *The Fifty-Year Decline and Fall of Hollywood.* New York: Simon and Schuster, 1961.

75. Goodman, Martin, "Numbers Game," *Columbia Journalism Review* (Summer, 1965), 16–18.

76. Goodsell, James Nelson, "Are Dominican Rebels Reds?" *The Christian Science Monitor* (May 19, 1965), 1 and 4.

77. Goodwin, Richard N., *Triumph or Tragedy — Reflections on Vietnam.* New York: Random House (Vintage Books), 1966.

78. Gottschalk, Louis, *Understanding History.* New York: Alfred A. Knopf, 1951.

79. Gowers, Sir Ernest, *A Life for a Life?* London: Chatto and Windus, 1956.

80. Green, Philip, *Deadly Logic.* Columbus: Ohio State University Press, 1966.

81. Greene, Felix, *A Curtain of Ignorance.* Garden City: Doubleday, 1964.

82. Halberstam, David, *The Making of a Quagmire.* New York: Random House, 1965.

83. Halperin, Ernest, "Dangling Countries," *The New York Review* (July 13, 1967), 36–37.

84. Hare, R. M., *Freedom and Reason.* Oxford: Oxford University Press, 1963.

85. Harris, Richard, *The Real Voice.* New York: Macmillan, 1964.

86. Hart, H. L. A., and A. M. Honoré, *Causation in the Law.* Oxford: Oxford University Press, 1959.

87. Helmer, Olaf, and Nicholas Rescher, *On the Epistemology of the Inexact Sciences.* Santa Monica: RAND Corporation, 1958. Also carried under same title in *Management Science,* VI (1959), 47. Page references in the text are to the RAND monograph.

88. Hilsman, Roger, *Strategic Intelligence and National Decisions.* Glencoe: The Free Press of Glencoe, 1956.

89. Hinton, Harold C., *Communist China in World Politics.* Boston: Houghton Mifflin, 1966.

90. Hofstadter, Richard, *The Paranoid Style in American Politics and Other Essays.* New York: Random House (Vintage Books), 1967.

91. Hohenberg, John, "The Flow of News Between Asia and the West," *Nieman Reports*, XXI (March, 1967), 10–15.

92. Holsti, Ole R., "Cognitive Dynamics and Images of The Enemy," *Journal of International Affairs*, No. 1 (1967), 16–39.

93. Horowitz, Irving Louis, ed., *The Rise and Fall of Project Camelot*. Cambridge: The M.I.T. Press, 1967.

94. Huff, Darrell, *How to Lie with Statistics*. New York: W. W. Norton, 1954.

95. Hufford, Roger, "The Logician, The Historian, and Rhetorical Criticism," *Journal of the American Forensic Association*, II (January, 1965), 14–16.

96. Huitt, Ralph D., "The Congressional Committee: A Case Study," *American Political Science Review*, XLVIII (June, 1954), 340–365.

97. Hunter, Floyd, *Top Leadership, U.S.A.* Chapel Hill: University of North Carolina Press, 1959.

98. Ingersoll, Ralph, "*Time*: The Weekly Fiction Magazine," *Fact*, I (January–February, 1964), 3–4.

99. Inkeles, Alex, and Raymond A. Bauer, *The Soviet Citizen*. Cambridge: Harvard University Press, 1959.

100. Jacobs, Herbert A., "To Count a Crowd," *Columbia Journalism Review*, VI (Spring, 1967), 37–40.

101. Johnson, Allen, *The Historian and Historical Evidence*. New York: Charles Scribner's Sons, 1934.

102. Johnson, Haynes, *The Bay of Pigs*. New York: Dell, 1964.

103. Jouvenel, Bertrand de, *The Art of Conjecture*. New York: Basic Books, 1967.

104. Jouvenel, Bertrand de, *Futuribles I*. Geneva: Droz, 1963.

105. Kennan, George F., "Disengagement Revisited," *Foreign Affairs*, XXXVII (January, 1959), 187–210.

106. Kennan, George F., *Russia, the Atom and the West*. New York: Harper & Brothers, 1958.

107. Kennedy, John F., *Profiles in Courage*. New York: Harper & Brothers, 1956.

108. Kent, Sherman, *Strategic Intelligence*. Princeton: Princeton University Press, 1949.

109. Keppel, Francis, *Statement Before the Subcommittee on Education of the Committee on Labor and Public Welfare*, U.S. Senate, February 20, 1964. Washington: Department of Health, Education and Welfare (mimeographed).

110. Kerr, George H., *Formosa Betrayed*. Boston: Houghton Mifflin, 1965.

111. Kerr, Malcolm, *The Arab Cold War: A Study of Ideology in Politics*. New York: Oxford University Press, 1965.

112. Kirk, Russell, "The Scholar Is Not a Lion or a Fox," in *Teach-ins: U.S.A.*, ed. Louis Menashe and Ronald Radosh. New York: Frederick A. Praeger, 1967, 262–268.

113. Kirkpatrick, Lyman B., *The Real CIA*. New York: Macmillan, 1968.

114. Kleinau, Marvin D., *Senator Ervin's Speaking on Supreme Court Segregation Decisions: A Study in Evidence*. Unpublished Master's thesis, Illinois State University at Normal, 1960.

115. Knap, Ted, "Pacification Escalating in Vietnam," *Pittsburgh Press* (March 30, 1967), 38.

116. Knoebl, Kuno, *Victor Charlie*. New York: Frederick A. Praeger, 1967.

117. Kolko, Gabriel, "Universities and the Pentagon," *The Nation* (October 9, 1967), 328–332.

118. Kopkind, Andrew, "Times' Square — *The Artillery of the Press: Its Influence on American Foreign Policy*, by James Reston," *The New York Review* (May 4, 1967), 12–15.

119. Kristol, Irving, "The Underdeveloped Profession," *The Public Interest*, VI (Winter, 1967), 36–52.

120. Labin, Suzanne, and Christopher Emmet, "Is There a Sino-Soviet Split?" *Orbis*, IV (Spring, 1960), 28–38.

121. Ladd, Bruce, *Crisis in Credibility*. New York: New American Library, 1968.

122. Ladejinsky, Wolf, "Vietnam: The First Five Years," *The Reporter* (December 24, 1959), 20–23.

123. Larrabee, Harold A., *Reliable Knowledge*, Revised Edition. Boston: Houghton Mifflin, 1964.

124. Larson, Don R., and Arthur Larson, "What is Our 'Commitment' in Vietnam?" *The Viet-Nam Reader*, ed. Marcus G. Raskin and Bernard B. Fall. New York: Random House (Vintage Books), 1965, 99–108.

125. Lazarsfeld, Paul F., and Wagner Thielens, Jr., *The Academic Mind*. Glencoe: The Free Press of Glencoe, 1958.

126. Lederer, William, *A Nation of Sheep*. New York: W. W. Norton, 1961.

127. Lederer, William, *Our Own Worst Enemy*. New York: W. W. Norton, 1968.

128. Leites, Nathan, *The Operational Code of the Politburo*. New York: McGraw-Hill, 1951.

129. Lewin, Kurt, "Channels of Group Life," *Human Relations*, I (1941), 145.

130. Liebenow, J. Gus, "Liberia: Growth Without Development," *Africa Report* (May, 1967), 52–53.

131. Lilge, Frederic, *The Abuse of Learning*. New York: Macmillan, 1948.

132. Lippmann, Walter, "The Deepest Issue of our Time," *Vital Speeches of the Day*, II (July 1, 1936), 602–604.

133. Lippmann, Walter, and Charles Merz, "A Test of the News," supplement to *New Republic* (August 4, 1920).

134. Lockwood, Lee, "Salisbury's Stake," *The New York Review* (August 3, 1967), 22–27.

135. Lofton, John, "David Lawrence — The South's 'Lawyer' in the Court of Northern Opinion," *The Progressive* (September, 1958), 31–34.

136. Lofton, John, "The Press Manages the News," *The Progressive* (June, 1963), 16–20.

137. Lofton, John, "Time Catches Up With A Dangerous Campaign Issue; Radioactive Fallout Now Seems Dangerous," *The Independent* (December, 1957), 1.

138. Lowenstein, Ralph D., *World Press Freedom, 1966*. Columbia: University of Missouri School of Journalism, Freedom of Information Center. Report No. 181 (May, 1967).

139. McBath, James H., ed., *Argumentation and Debate*. New York: Holt, Rinehart and Winston, 1963.

140. McBath, James H., ed., *TV Championship Debates*. Portland, Maine: J. Weston Walch, 1964.

141. MacDougall, A. Kent, "The Newsletters: Capsulated Journalism," *Columbia Journalism Review* (Fall, 1963), 21–25.

142. McGaffin, William, and Erwin Knoll, *Anything but the Truth*. New York: G. P. Putnam's Sons, 1968.

143. McGovern, William M., *Strategic Intelligence and the Shape of Tomorrow*. Chicago: Henry Regnery, 1961.

144. Mannheim, Karl, *Ideology and Utopia*, tr. Louis Wirth and Edward Shils. New York: Harcourt, Brace (Harvest Books), 1960.

145. Marvel, William W., "Remarks," *Background*, IX (November, 1965), 177–183.

146. Commonwealth of Massachusetts Special Commission Established for the Purpose of Investigating and Studying the Abolition of the Death Penalty in Capital Cases, *Report and Recommendations*. Boston: Wright and Potter, 1959.

147. Matthews, T. S., *Name & Address*. London: Anthony Blond, 1961.
148. Mayer, Milton, "The Dogged Retreat of the Doctors," *Harper's* (December, 1949), 25–37.
149. Mayer, Milton, "The Rise and Fall of Dr. Fishbein," *Harper's* (November, 1949), 76–85.
150. Mecklin, John, *Mission in Torment*. Garden City: Doubleday, 1965.
151. Meisler, Stanley, "The Impact of Medicare," *The Nation* (May 3, 1965), 481.
152. Menashe, Louis, and Ronald Radosh, eds., *Teach-ins: U.S.A.* New York: Frederick A. Praeger, 1967.
153. Meyer, Philip, "Social Science: A New Beat?" *Nieman Reports* (June, 1967), 3.
154. Mills, C. Wright, *Power, Politics and People*. New York: Ballantine Books, 1963.
155. Mills, C. Wright, *The Sociological Imagination*. New York: Grove Press, 1961.
156. Mintz, Morton, *The Therapeutic Nightmare*. Boston: Houghton Mifflin, 1965.
157. Mohr, Charles, "Vietnam Victory Linked to Opinion," *The New York Times* (June 27, 1966), 1.
158. Montagu, Ewen, *The Man Who Never Was*. Philadelphia: J. B. Lippincott, 1954.
159. Moreno, Jose, *Sociological Aspects of the Dominican Revolution*. Unpublished Ph.D. dissertation, Cornell University, 1967. An enlarged version of this dissertation will be published under the title *Barrios in Arms* by the University of Pittsburgh Press in 1969.
160. Nevins, Allan, *The Gateway to History*. Garden City: Doubleday (Anchor Books), 1962.
161. Newman, Robert P., *Recognition of Communist China? A Study in Argument*. New York: Macmillan, 1961.
162. Newman, Robert P., "The Spectacular Irrelevance of Mr. Bundy," *Today's Speech*, XIII (September, 1965), 30–34.
163. Newman, Robert P., and Keith R. Sanders, "A Study in the Integrity of Evidence," *Journal of the American Forensic Association*, II (January, 1965), 7–13.
164. Nichols, Alan, *Discussion and Debate*. New York: Harcourt, Brace, 1941.
165. Nicodemus, Charles, "Shots of Ridicule Silencing Bullets of Gun Lobbies," *Pittsburgh Press* (June 11, 1965), 13.

166. Nimmo, Dan D., *Newsgathering in Washington*. New York: Atherton Press, 1964.

167. Nisbet, Robert A., "Project Camelot: An Autopsy," *The Public Interest*, V (Fall, 1966), 45–69.

168. North, Robert C., *et al.*, *Content Analysis*. Evanston: Northwestern University Press, 1963.

169. Novak, Michael, "How to Cheat in an Election," *The National Catholic Reporter* (September 6, 1967), 1.

170. Overstreet, Harry, and Bonaro Overstreet, *The Strange Tactics of Extremism*. New York: W. W. Norton, 1964.

171. Packer, Herbert L., *Ex-Communist Witnesses*. Stanford: Stanford University Press, 1962.

172. Pike, Douglas, *The Viet Cong*. Cambridge: The M.I.T. Press, 1966.

173. Plato, *The Republic*, in *Dialogues of Plato*, tr. Benjamin Jowett. New York: Charles Scribner's Sons, 1911, Vol. II.

174. Polk, William R., "Problems of Government Utilization of Scholarly Research in International Affairs," in *The Rise and Fall of Project Camelot*, ed. Irving Louis Horowitz. Cambridge: The M.I.T. Press, 1967, 239–266.

175. Polk, William R., *The United States and the Arab World*. Cambridge: Harvard University Press, 1965.

176. Pool, Ithiel de Sola, "The Necessity for Social Scientists Doing Research for Governments," in *The Rise and Fall of Project Camelot*, ed. Irving Louis Horowitz. Cambridge: The M.I.T. Press, 1967, 267–280.

177. Raskin, Marcus G., and Bernard B. Fall, *The Viet-Nam Reader*. New York: Random House (Vintage Books), 1965.

178. Reed, Louis S., "Private Consumer Expenditures for Medical Care and Voluntary Health Insurance, 1948–63," *Social Security Bulletin* (December, 1964), 1–11.

179. *Report on the Eighteenth National Debate Tournament*. West Point: United States Military Academy, 1964.

180. Rescher, Nicholas, "On the Probability of Nonrecurring Events," in *Current Issues in the Philosophy of Science*, ed. Herbert Feigl and Grover Maxwell. New York: Holt, Rinehart and Winston, 1961, 228–244.

181. Rescher, Nicholas, "A Theory of Evidence," *Philosophy of Science*, XXV (January, 1958), 83–94.

182. Rescher, Nicholas, and Carey B. Joynt, "Evidence in History and in the Law," *The Journal of Philosophy*, LVI (June, 1959), 561–578.

183. Roberts, Charles, "LBJ's Credibility Gap," *Newsweek* (December 19, 1966), 24–25.

184. Rostow, W. W., *Stages of Economic Growth*. New York: Cambridge University Press, 1960.

185. Rostow, W. W., *The United States in the World Arena*. New York: Harper & Brothers, 1960.

186. Rostow, W. W., *View From the Seventh Floor*. New York: Harper & Row, 1964.

187. Rusk, Dean, "Chinese-American Friendship," *Vital Speeches of the Day*, XVII (June 15, 1951), 514–515.

188. Sahlins, Marshall, "The Established Order: Do not Fold, Spindle, or Mutilate," in *The Rise and Fall of Project Camelot*, ed. Irving Louis Horowitz. Cambridge: The M.I.T. Press, 1967, 71–79.

189. Salmon, Lucy Maynard, *The Newspaper and the Historian*. New York: Oxford University Press, 1923.

190. Scalapino, Robert A., "We Cannot Accept a Communist Seizure of Vietnam," *The New York Times Magazine* (December 11, 1966), 46 and 133–140.

191. Scheer, Robert, and Warren Hinckle, "The 'Vietnam Lobby'," *Ramparts* (July, 1965), 16–25.

192. Schlesinger, Arthur M., Jr., "The Historian and History," *Foreign Affairs*, XLI (April, 1963), 491–497.

193. Schlesinger, Arthur M., Jr., "Middle-Aged Man With a Horn," *New Republic* (March 16, 1953), 17.

194. Schlesinger, Arthur M., Jr., *The Politics of Hope*. Boston: Houghton Mifflin, 1963.

195. "Schlesinger Says He Lied to Times," *The New York Times* (November 25, 1965), 8.

196. Schoenbrun, David, "My Peace Feeler," *Columbia Journalism Review* (Winter, 1966), 26–27.

197. Sellin, Thorsten, *The Death Penalty*. Philadelphia: The American Law Institute, 1959.

198. Shackford, R. H., "U.S. Loses Face in Viet Assembly Vote," *Pittsburgh Press* (October 4, 1967), 38.

199. Sheehan, Neil, "Clifford Emerges as the President's Chief Spokesman on Vietnam," *The New York Times* (April 28, 1968), Sec. 1, p. 3.

200. Silvert, Kalman H., "American Academic Ethics and Social Research Abroad: The Lesson of Project Camelot," in *The Rise and Fall of Project Camelot*, ed. Irving Louis Horowitz. Cambridge: The M.I.T. Press, 1967, 80–106.

201. Simpson, Smith, *Anatomy of the State Department.* Boston: Houghton Mifflin, 1967.

202. Sinclair, Upton, *The Goose Step.* Pasadena: The author, 1923.

203. Skolnik, Alfred M., "Employee-Benefit Plans, 1954–58," *Social Security Bulletin* (March, 1960), 3–12.

204. Skolnik, Alfred M., "Empolyee-Benefit Plans: Developments, 1954–63," *Social Security Bulletin* (April, 1965), 3–19.

205. Snyder, Richard C., H. W. Bruck, and Burton Sapin, *Foreign Policy Decision-Making.* New York: The Free Press of Glencoe, 1962.

206. Sorensen, Theodore C., *Decision-Making in the White House.* New York: Columbia University Press, 1963.

207. Sorensen, Theodore C., *Kennedy.* New York: Harper & Row, 1965.

208. Sowell, Thomas, "The 'Need' for More 'Education'," *AAUP Bulletin,* LII (December, 1966), 380–386.

209. Stephen, Sir James Fitzjames, "Capital Punishments," *Fraser's Magazine,* LXIX (June, 1864), 753.

210. Stevens, Walter W., "Inaccuracies in the Texts of Congressional Speeches," *Central States Speech Journal,* XV (August, 1964), 183–188.

211. Stilwell, Joseph W., *The Stilwell Papers.* New York: William Sloane Associates, 1948.

212. Stone, I. F., "How the Government Secretly Subsidizes Books as Foreign Policy Propaganda," *I. F. Stone's Weekly* (October 17, 1966).

213. Stormer, John A., *None Dare Call it Treason.* Florissant, Missouri: Liberty Bell Press, 1964.

214. Sulzberger, C. L., *What's Wrong with U.S. Foreign Policy.* New York: Harcourt, Brace, 1959.

215. Thompson, James C., Jr., "How Could Vietnam Happen?" *The Atlantic* (April, 1968), 47.

216. Trager, Frank N., *Why Viet Nam?* New York: Frederick A. Praeger, 1966.

217. United Press International, "Tobacco Council Denies Cancer Tie," *Pittsburgh Press* (August 17, 1964), 14.

218. U.S. Congress, House of Representatives, Committee on Foreign Affairs, Subcommittee on the Far East and the Pacific, *United States Policy Toward Asia.* 89th Congress, 2nd Session. Washington: Government Printing Office, 1966.

219. U.S. Congress, Senate, Committee On Foreign Relations, *Hearings on Activities of Nondiplomatic Representatives of Foreign Principals*

in the United States. Part 7 (March 25, 1963). 88th Congress, 1st Session. Washington: Government Printing Office, 1959.

220. U.S. Congress, Senate, Committee on Foreign Relations, *Study of United States Foreign Policy: Summary of Views of Retired Foreign Service Officers.* 86th Congress, 1st Session. Washington: Government Printing Office, 1959.

221. U.S. Congress, Senate, Committee on Government Operations, Subcommittee on National Security and International Operations, *The Atlantic Alliance.* 89th Congress, 2nd Session. Washington: Government Printing Office, 1966.

222. U.S. Congress, Senate, Hearings before the Subcommittee on Education of the Committee on Labor and Public Welfare, *Education Legislation — 1963.* 88th Congress, 1st Session. Washington: Government Printing Office, 1963.

223. U.S. Department of State, *Facts and Fallacies Concerning "None Dare Call it Treason."* Washington: Office of Public Services, Bureau of Public Affairs, December, 1964.

224. U.S. Department of State, *Aggression From the North.* Publication 7839, Far Eastern Series 130. Washington: Government Printing Office, 1965.

225. U.S. Office of Education, *Equality of Educational Opportunity.* Washington: Government Printing Office, 1966.

226. U.S. Strategic Bombing Survey, *Overall Report (European War).* Washington: Government Printing Office, 1945.

227. Veblen, Thorstein, *The Higher Learning in America.* New York: B. W. Huebsch, 1918.

228. *The Vietnam Hearings,* with an introduction by J. William Fulbright. New York: Random House (Vintage Books), 1966.

229. Walker, Richard Louis, "The U.S. Should not Change its China Policy," Foreign Policy Association *Headline Series,* No. 129 (May–June, 1958).

230. Wallace, Karl R., "The Substance of Rhetoric," *Quarterly Journal of Speech,* XLIX (October, 1963), 239.

231. Wasserman, Benno, "The Failure of Intelligence Prediction," *Political Studies,* VIII (1960), 156–169.

232. Weinstein, Franklin B., *Vietnam's Unheld Elections.* Ithaca: Cornell University, Southeast Asia Program. Data Paper No. 60 (1966).

233. Wellman, Francis L., *The Art of Cross-Examination.* New York: Macmillan, 1929.

234. Westerfield, H. Bradford, *The Instruments of America's Foreign Policy.* New York: Thomas Y. Crowell, 1963.

235. White, Ralph K., "Misperception and the Vietnam War," *Journal of Social Issues*, XXII (July, 1966), 1–164.

236. Wigmore, John Henry, *A Treatise on the Anglo-American System of Evidence*, Third Edition. Boston: Little, Brown, 1940. Ten volumes.

237. Wilensky, Harold L., *Organizational Intelligence*. New York: Basic Books, 1967.

238. Wise, David, and Thomas B. Ross, *The Espionage Establishment.* New York: Random House, 1967.

239. Wise, David, and Thomas B. Ross, *The Invisible Government.* New York: Random House, 1964.

240. Wohlstetter, Roberta, "Cuba and Pearl Harbor: Hindsight and Foresight," *Foreign Affairs*, XLIII (July, 1965), 691–707.

241. Wolf, Charles, Jr., "Indonesian Assignment," in *Public Administration and Policy Development*, ed. Harold Stein. New York: Harcourt, Brace, 1952, 55–60.

242. Wurfel, David, "Vietnam Election Observer Gives Vote to Novak Stories," *National Catholic Reporter* (October 18, 1967), 4.

243. Zeigler, Harmon, *Interest Groups in American Society.* Englewood Cliffs: Prentice-Hall, 1964.

244. Ziegler, Edward, *The Vested Interests.* New York: Macmillan, 1964.

INDEX

RAND Corporation, 182, 214
Rating of press freedom, 135
"Reaction principle," as bias causing perceptual distortion, 64–66
"Refugee mentality," as bias causing perceptual distortion, 63–64
Reader's Digest, 158
Relevance of evidence: to causal explanations, 22–23; to historical analogies, 11–12, 24, 26, 47–48; to predictions, 43, 47–49
Reluctant testimony, as test of evidence, 79
Rostow, Walt Whitman, 36, 178, 202
Rusk, Dean, 8, 82, 112, 117, 118

Scalapino, Robert A., 178, 195–196
Schlesinger, Arthur M., Jr., 67, 76, 118, 132, 178, 183, 187, 200–202
Scripps-Howard newspapers, 134, 145
Secondary authorities. See Tests of secondary authorities.
Selection of primary sources, as test of evidence, 84–85
Simpson, Smith, 107, 109, 111, 116
Situational tests of evidence: accessibility, 75–76; freedom to report, 76; tension, 74–75
Sources of evidence: government, 91–130; press, 131–163; pressure groups, 164–180; professional scholars, 181–203
Southeast Asia Treaty Organization, 8–10
Statistics as evidence, 205–225
Stone, I. F., 158–159
Strackbein, O. R., 167, 176
Substituting words or phrases, 86, 159
Supporting evidence, 20–24, 37–40
Supreme Court. See Federal Government: judiciary.

Tension test of evidence, 74–75. See also Crisis principle.
Tests of evidence. See Characteristics of the writer; Documentary tests; Negative evidence; Relevance of evidence; Situational tests; Supporting evidence; Tests of primary authorities; Tests of secondary authorities.
Tests of primary authorities: contemporaneity, 84; eyewitness principle, 83–84
Tests of secondary authorities: accuracy of citation, 85–86; selection of primary sources, 84–85
Time, 85, 121; accuracy record of, 156–158; biases of, 155; consistency of, 153–154; editorial dominance of, 151–153; gag rule on, 151–152
Tobacco industry, 167–170, 176
Tobacco Research Institute, 81, 167–168, 182

United Press International, 145–146
U. S. News and World Report, 119; accuracy record of, 156–158; biases of, 153, 154–155; gag rule on, 153
U. S. S. R., 41–43, 58–60, 141–143

Values, as bases for policy goals, 4–6
Viet-Nam, 4–15, 40–41, 57, 108, 110–115, 119–124, 211–215

Walker, Richard Louis, 194–195
Wasserman, Benno, 115–116
White, Ralph K., 9, 39, 60, 81–82, 112, 160, 226
Willful distortion, 66–67
Wire services, 145–146
Wohlstetter, Roberta, 47–48